3rd Edition

THE WRITING CLINIC

Ralph E. Loewe

Cuyahoga Community College

PRENTICE-HALL, INC., ENGLEWOOD CLIFFS, N.J. 07632

Library of Congress Cataloging in Publication Data

LOEWE, RALPH E.
  The writing clinic.

  Includes bibliographical references and index.
  1. English language—Rhetoric.   2. English language—Grammar—1950-   I. Title.
PE1408.L635 1983   808'.042   82-15120
ISBN 0-13-970319-5

Editorial development, design,
and production supervision: Hilda Tauber
Interior design assistance: Jayne Conte
Cover drawing by Ann Jasperson
Manufacturing buyer: Harry P. Baisley

"A Women's Liberation Movement Woman" from *People and Other Aggravations* by Judith Viorst (The World Publishing Company). Copyright © 1970 by Judith Viorst. Reprinted by permission of Harper & Row, Publishers, Inc.
"Ex-Basketball Player" copyright © 1957, 1958 by John Updike. Reprinted from *The Carpentered Hen and Other Tame Creatures,* by John Updike, by permission of Alfred A. Knopf, Inc.

Continued on page iv.

Printed in the United States of America
10 9 8 7 6 5 4 3 2 1

ISBN 0-13-970319-5

PRENTICE-HALL INTERNATIONAL, INC., *London*
PRENTICE-HALL OF AUSTRALIA PTY. LIMITED, *Sydney*
EDITORA PRENTICE-HALL DO BRASIL, LTDA., *Rio de Janeiro*
PRENTICE-HALL CANADA, INC., *Toronto*
PRENTICE-HALL OF INDIA PRIVATE LIMITED, *New Delhi*
PRENTICE-HALL OF JAPAN, INC., *Tokyo*
PRENTICE-HALL OF SOUTHEAST ASIA PTE. LTD., *Singapore*
WHITEHALL BOOKS LIMITED, *Wellington, New Zealand*

to Bess, Ron, Deborah, and Pradip
with all my love
•
to those who work for peace

Contents

Part **I** CHECK INTO THE CLINIC 1

1 The Diagnosis 3

2 Directions, Details, and the Need to Read 27

7 Writing Complex Sentences 103

8 Review of Sentences; Sentence Combining 126

Part III POLISHING SENTENCES 153

9 Handling Punctuation, Capitalization, and Apostrophes 155

Acknowledgments

It takes many skillful hands to build a book.

My sincerest thanks go to my teachers, who helped lay foundations, and to all those who helped construct, test, and improve the text during the past decade.

Special thanks are due to my students, who work hard for a living and an education.

I am grateful to my colleague Normal Prange who has again contributed sound advice and devised many exercises, and who is largely responsible for the new Chapter 11.

Hilda Tauber, development editor at Prentice-Hall, has for the third time managed a tough editing and production assignment with great skill—and with patience.

Ann Jasperson has helped the Clinic come alive with her artful drawings. Thomas W. Ashton of Graphic Production at Cuyahoga Community College took the photographs of college students in Chapter 1. Jayne Conte did the fine part and chapter opening designs.

I also wish to thank the following professors and instructors who reviewed the three editions in manuscript and made constructive suggestions. *First edition:* Michael J. Cardone, Henry Ford Community College; Donald C. Rigg, Broward Junior College; and William F. Smith, Fullerton Junior College. *Second edition:* Beulah H. Gloster, Morehouse College; Betty Gillette, Odessa Junior College; and Larry Tjernell, San Jose State University. *Third edition:* Raul S. Murguia, San Antonio College; Judith

Flynn, Penn Valley Community College; and Gordon L. Figge, Community College of Allegheny County.

I appreciate the extensive critical help of David M. Humphreys and Phyllis Melnick and the many worthwhile suggestions offered by Marjorie Scott.

As with previous editions, wife Bessie has added to content and accuracy with her comments and criticism and to motivation with her magnificent cheese cakes.

A final acknowledgment is to my old friend Bill Fierman, construction manager, who spurred me to complete this revision by claiming that he could write the book faster than I could build his garage. He was right.

To the Student

"Sick" compositions hurt your grades, not only in English classes but in every course where writing is required. Success in school, on the job, and even in your social life often depends on your ability to communicate effectively. THE WRITING CLINIC is designed to do just that—help you communicate effectively.

You are the doctor.
Your compositions are the patients.
Your instructor is the Director of the Clinic.

THE WRITING CLINIC will help you produce good sentences in well-developed paragraphs and themes. It does this in a number of ways:

It provides pictures, cartoons, poems, and brief articles to stimulate your thinking and give you something to write about.

It places most of its emphasis on *performance;* that is, you are required to do a lot of writing. The reason for this is that most students need to learn correct methods of writing and then practice them sufficiently to cure nonstandard writing habits and implant new ones firmly in their minds.

It provides you with the *answers* to many of the questions and problems. With access to answers as well as instructions, examples, and questions, you have all the tools necessary to teach yourself a great deal—if you use the tools responsibly and wisely. Self-teaching is the best kind of teaching.

It moves you gradually from sentence writing to paragraph and theme writing, providing many examples and models for you to follow.

You are rapidly arriving at the stage where you will be responsible for doctoring your own work, no longer relying on someone else to suggest remedies. How long it takes you to reach that stage depends on how seriously and effectively you study.

To the Teacher

What's New in the Third Edition

- To augment the work of the first two editions, the exercises in Part II: "Building Sentences" have been extended and improved. Some are now branching, and new techniques have been developed for others.

- To motivate students to use the answer keys effectively and to take responsibility for *teaching themselves* as much as possible, a new chapter has been added: "Directions, Details, and the Need to Read" (Chapter 2).

- A section on *sentence combining* is included in Chapter 8 to help students add flavor and style to their writing after they have mastered compound and complex sentences.

- The former "Roundup of Problem Areas" has been revised and expanded to strengthen understanding of the many "internal" problems of the sentence, and has been retitled "Nouns, Pronouns, Adjectives, and Adverbs" (Chapter 11). Some of the problems originally handled in the roundup chapter have been moved to other chapters.

- New idea-stimulating articles, pictures, and cartoons are provided in the first, second, and last chapters, and *student-written* paragraphs and themes have been added to Chapters 12 and 13.

Write Your Own Prescription

Flexibility is one of the chief attributes of THE WRITING CLINIC. Instructors can write their own prescriptions or follow the text's carefully ordered plan. It is possible to adapt the text to the classroom for quarters or semesters, to individualized or group instruction in the classroom, and to tutorial systems.

Chapter 2, "Directions, Details, and the Need to Read," might be the best starting place for instructors who want to open their courses with motivational material and a few chuckles.

Some instructors like to start with Chapter 11, "Nouns, Pronouns, Adjectives, and Adverbs," and follow it with the very thorough study of tense in Chapter 10, "The Time Machine," before beginning the six-chapter sequence on sentence building. This sequence opens with one-word sentences in Chapter 3 and culminates in sentence combining in Chapter 8. Chapter 4 interrupts the sequence to provide intensive treatment in subject-verb agreement before wrong usage habits become too ingrained.

Other instructors prefer to focus on rhetoric by starting with Part IV, "Expository Writing." As students' compositions reveal symptoms in need of attention, these instructors refer students to grammatical and mechanical "cures" in pertinent parts of the Clinic.

Detailed suggestions for using the text in different ways will be found in the Instructor's Manual. The manual also contains summaries of each chapter as well as tests. Answer keys are supplied for the assignments and tests in the textbook as well as for tests in the manual.

The Writing Clinic Approach

The book takes nothing for granted. It starts with the most basic grammatical and rhetorical problems and methodically progresses to the more complicated.

Grammatical theory and terminology are kept to a minimum. Every effort has been made to eliminate those aspects of grammar needed only for a theoretical understanding of the language (aspects which can be reserved for more specialized courses) and to concentrate on the grammar needed to write good sentences. Also eliminated are aspects of grammar that cause no problems for most students, and those that can be bypassed because of this text's three-fold approach to teaching the three basic sentence types:

1. It focuses on *structure,* starting from the simplest sentence patterns and working to the most complex.
2. It emphasizes how words *function* in sentences rather than what parts of speech they are.
3. It uses and defines terms *as necessary* instead of starting with lists of definitions.

This approach makes it possible to teach the three basic sentence types—simple, compound, and complex—using primarily three sentence parts: subjects, verbs, and conjunctions. Once the student has learned these key elements, many other sentence parts fall naturally into place. Work with parts of speech and tense can thus be reserved for later, when the student has developed a good sense of what a sentence is.

Emphasis is placed on writing sentences in context. Many students who can write individual sentences correctly lose their sentence "sense" when they write paragraphs and themes. To counter this tendency, THE WRITING CLINIC provides writing assignments in its first and last three chapters so that the instructor can diagnose the students' sentences in context at the beginning of the course and measure their improvement at the end. Other paragraph assignments are interspersed throughout the book. This approach helps avoid the frustrations which occur when students succeed in short answer exercises only to fail in the grammatical and mechanical aspects of sentence writing when they write the longer units.

The book provides a carefully structured sequence of instructional and supportive materials. Because language learning is partially automatic, and because many students have developed deeply ingrained nonstandard responses, this text uses a variety of learning activities to reinforce the standard forms it teaches. Emphasis is placed on *practice* and *performance* rather than on just instruction reading and rule memorization.

Comprehension Checks. Since many students with writing problems also have reading problems, comprehension checks are provided to focus their attention on what they have just read. This helps them avoid the tendency many students have of merely looking at words instead of reading for understanding.

Practices. These are exercises based on immediately preceding instructions. Students practice the skills they have just read about—mostly on the *recognition* level.

Keys. The text gives students answers for the comprehension checks and the practices. Having answers readily available aids both motivation and comprehension. It involves students more fully in the teaching/learning process by encouraging them to make judgments about their own work and by providing immediate feedback. Students who are not mature enough to use keys effectively may require initial monitoring. *When they answer questions incorrectly, they should be encouraged to restudy the lesson or to ask questions before proceeding to the assignments.*

Assignments. No keys are given for these exercises. They serve two functions: (1) They usually require students to answer with their own words, thus moving them from recognition to *performance.* (2) Since no keys are available, these exercises provide the instructor with measures of the students' progress. (It is suggested that students be encouraged to refer to the instructions and examples when doing the assignments to get them in the habit of referring to the text for answers.) For this edition some assignments have been moved to the Instructor's Manual to give teachers greater control over the process.

Tests.   These appear at the ends of some chapters and in the Instructor's Manual to test mastery.

Profusion of Material.   The extent and variety of exercises give instructors flexibility to work effectively with a wide range of students. *Only the weakest students, however, are likely to need the entire "treatment." More able students should be allowed to skip unnecessary lessons and move ahead at their own speed.*

The instructor's judgment cannot be programmed. Most students with writing problems need the stimulation of regular class attendance and/or periodic assistance from carefully trained tutors to help them get the most from this book. It takes highly skilled, experienced instructors to deal with writing problems, especially when they persist at the adult level. A scattering of short answer tests and infrequent compositions tell little about a student's writing ability. On the other hand, experienced instructors working with carefully planned lessons can nurture the positive elements in students' work even as they diagnose patterns of recurring errors and suggest appropriate remedies. If instructors also are given time to meet with students individually, they can add the crucial personal touch that often makes the difference between student success or failure.

Part I

Although most college students have attained a high degree of oral language ability, their compositions suffer from many weaknesses because there are more rules and formalities to follow in writing. Writing is more exacting than speech, more precise. Chapter 1 provides writing experiences so that your instructor can find what "ails" your compositions and prescribe treatment. Chapter 2 discusses the importance of following directions, attention to detail, close listening, and extensive reading—all vital to improving your compositions' health. Turn the page and

CHECK INTO THE CLINIC

ADMISSIONS
THE WRITING CLINIC
A VERY SICK LOOKING PAPER...
LOOK AT ALL THOSE RED MARKS!
WE'D BETTER GET IT TO THE CLINIC-RIGHT AWAY!
ADMISSIONS
A. JASPERSON '82

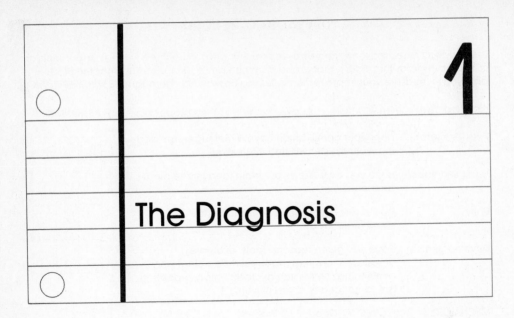

The Diagnosis

The assignments in this chapter give you something to write about. Your writing will demonstrate how well you organize and express your ideas and how you handle the form of the language—such things as grammar, spelling, and mechanics. "Mechanics" refers to punctuation, capitalization, and possession.

WRITING SUGGESTIONS

1. Read the directions for each assignment carefully.
2. Since all the assignments provide choices, choose those which interest you most.
3. Pace yourself so that you can finish your work in the allotted time.
4. Limit your idea. It is better to develop one idea in depth than to state many ideas superficially.
5. Before starting to write, jot down your main idea and supporting points.
6. If time permits, write a rough draft.
7. Do not try to impress the instructor with fancy language. Keep your wording simple and straightforward.
8. When writing an in-class paper, allow at least five minutes for corrections. Read it through twice: first to see if it makes good sense and holds together well, then to check your grammar, spelling, and mechanics. Spend more time on homework papers, of course. You are usually expected to do a more polished job on these than on papers written in class.

3

DIAGNOSTIC RECORD

Use this chart to record the strong and weak points of your first three writing assignments as indicated by your instructor's marks and comments. A similar chart in Chapter 14 will enable you to measure your improvement after you have worked through *THE WRITING CLINIC.*

CONTENT AND ORGANIZATION: Answer Yes or No in the proper box.

ASSIGNMENTS
1   2   3

Reader Interest: Does your composition have a message—an idea—that your reader will find interesting?

Topic Sentence: Have you expressed your main idea in one clear sentence?

Unity: Do the rest of your sentences stick to the same main idea?

Development: Have you given reasons, facts, examples, or explanations that make your idea clear and convincing? (Have you avoided simply repeating the same idea in different words?)

MECHANICS: Indicate G for Good, P for Problems, or N.E. for No Evidence (if, for example, you didn't use past tense, possession, or contractions).

Fragments, comma splices, run-ons

Present tense verbs (*has, have; does, do; is, are;* etc.)

Past tense and past participles of verbs (*walked; broke, broken;* etc.)

Singular and plural forms of nouns (*boy, boys; woman, women;* etc.)

Pronouns (*I, me, they, he,* etc.)

Apostrophes (*didn't, can't; girl's, girls';* etc.)

Easily confused words (*there, their, they're; to, two, too; its, it's; your, you're;* etc.)

Capitalization

Spelling

INSTRUCTOR'S COMMENTS:

Assignment 1: _____

Assignment 2: _____

Assignment 3: _____

Reacting to Pictures, Cartoons, Poems, and Essays

In your first writing assignments you will probably wish to respond to one picture, poem, or essay at a time, although you may tie two or more together if you wish. It should be interesting to write about subjects such as television, ecology, and women's liberation in reaction to the brief materials in this chapter and then read more about the same subjects in Chapter 14. Needless to say, the more you read about a subject the more you will be able to write about it. Later, you will write longer papers about these subjects in response to assignments in Chapter 14.

ASSIGNMENT 1: React to Pictures and Cartoons

Write a paper of about 200 words in which you react to one or more of the pictures on the following pages. Review the writing suggestions on page 3 and read "what to write about" in each assignment before starting to write.

what to write about

This is not a wise old owl but a bald eagle, the symbol of the U.S.A. Does the picture suggest that we have become more intelligent or more shortsighted? Does it suggest power and wisdom or old age or foolishness? Would you want the eagle with spectacles to be a symbol of *your* way of life? Select one of these ideas—or what the eagle suggests to you—and write about it.

Courtesy of The Chase Manhattan Bank.

By permission of William Steig.

what to write about

Write about fruitless arguments, frustrations, bottled up feelings, or people who don't listen. (See "Ten Keys to Effective Listening" in Chapter 14.)

IMPORTANT: When writing assignments, be sure that you write fully developed paragraphs, not merely answers to the questions. The questions are there to give you ideas, not to limit your response.

By permission of Johnny Hart and Field Enterprises, Inc.

*"Whatever liberates our spirit
without giving us self-control
is disastrous."*
—*GOETHE*

what to write about

Relate the cartoon about Bung, the alcoholic court juggler in "The Wizard of Id," to the statement by the famous German poet, Goethe. Relate them to drug abuse, alcoholism, or smoking.

what to write about

What should we do with our old folks? Should we dump them, send them to nursing homes or senior citizens' colonies, or keep them at home? Should we force them to retire early? How do you want to be treated when you grow old?

Courtesy of Doyle Dane Bernbach, Inc.

what to write about

The montage above provides a sampling of the violence depicted on TV. Discuss your views of TV violence. Describe your favorite show. Compare the kinds of programs provided by your public television station with those shown on the commercial stations. Discuss how TV can be used more effectively. What are some worthwhile programs you have seen on commercial TV? What changes might take place in your family life if you had no TV? Consider how TV can be used more effectively than it is now being used.

THE LITTLE RED SCHOOLHOUSE

Osrin in *The Plain Dealer*.

what to write about

Describe in detail a paddling you experienced in school or at home. How did the paddling affect your attitude toward the paddler? Did it improve your behavior?

Do you or would you use corporal punishment on your child? What method of discipline do you advocate? Explain.

Does paddling teach children to behave or does it teach them to use force to solve problems? Discuss.

You may wish to get a copy of the 1977 Supreme Court Decision on School Paddling (or more recent decisions, if any) to get a more complete understanding of the Court's decision.

TAXES FOR WAR

what to write about

If you feel that huge expenditures for war weigh us all down and keep us from solving the problems of hunger, disease, pollution, and educational inequities, write in support of this cartoon. If you feel that the cartoonist is wrong, and that the U.S. doesn't spend enough on armaments, argue against the cartoon.

what to write about

Envision yourself as a medical or dental technician, computer operator, or drafts-man. Plan to be a research scientist, doctor, lawyer, geologist, chemist, professional musician, dancer, actor, or athlete. Describe your day in any of these fields: your work, accomplishments, contributions, satisfaction. Discuss how you will reach your goal. Consider your past experiences, your personal strengths, your motivation. If you have reached some of these goals, tell how you got there, describe what you do, and project your plans for the future.

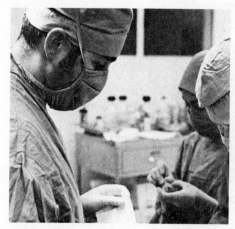

UPI photo

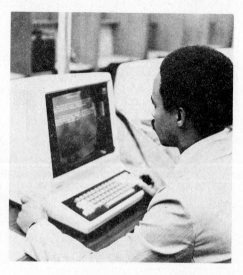

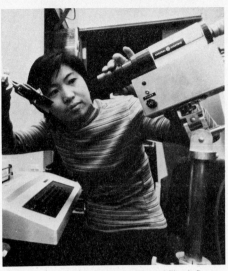

Courtesy of General Electric Company

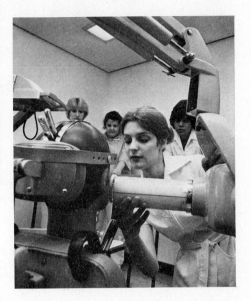

Drawing by Frascino, © 1973 The New Yorker Magazine, Inc.

"I want you to know, gentlemen, that at this moment I feel
I have realized my full potential as a woman."

what to write about

How do you feel about this woman? Are you amused or scornful? Do you feel that she is an oddball or unfeminine, or is she a capable, resourceful person? Take a position on this statement: "Women do (do not) have a right to take 'men's' jobs."

ASSIGNMENT 2: React to Poems

Write a paper of about 200 words in which you react to one or more of the poems on the following pages. If you use more than one poem, be sure that you do not write two separate themes. Keep your work unified. Review the writing suggestions on page 3 before starting to write.

CAUTION: Do not write a poem. Write a paragraph giving your reactions to the poetry you have chosen.

A Women's Liberation Movement Woman

—JUDITH VIORST

When it's snowing and I put on all the galoshes
While he reads the paper,
Then I want to become a
Women's Liberation Movement woman.
And when it's snowing and he looks for the taxi
While I wait in the lobby,
Then I don't.

And when it's vacation and I'm in charge of
    mosquito bites and poison ivy and car sickness
While he's in charge of swimming,
Then I want to become a
Women's Liberation Movement woman.
And when it's vacation and he carries the trunk
    and the overnight bag and the extra blankets
While I carry the wig case,
Then I don't.
And when it's three in the morning and the
    baby definitely needs a glass of water and I
    have to get up and bring it
While he keeps my place warm,
Then I want to become a
Women's Liberation Movement woman.
And when it's three in the morning and there is
    definitely a murder-rapist in the vestibule and
    he has to get up and catch him
While I keep his place warm,
Then I don't.
And after dinner, when he talks to the company
While I clean the broiler
(because I am a victim of capitalism,
    imperialism, male chauvinism, and also
    Playboy magazine),
And afternoons, when he invents the telephone
    and wins the Dreyfus case and writes War
    and Peace
While I sort the socks
(because I am economically oppressed, physically
    exploited, psychologically mutilated, and also
    very insulted),
And after he tells me that it is genetically
    determined that the man makes martinis and
    the lady makes the beds
(because he sees me as a sex object, an earth
    mother, a domestic servant, and also dumber
    than he is),
Then I want to become a
Women's Liberation Movement Woman.

And after I contemplate
No marriage, no family, no shaving under my
    arms,
And no one to step on a cockroach whenever I
    need him,
Then I don't.

Judith Viorst's poem takes a lighthearted approach to a subject which is very serious for many women and men. How does the poet deal with the serious issues? Why? Discuss the poem from one of these points of view: male chauvinist, women's liberation, anti-liberationist woman. Does the poem reflect the views of a middle class or working class woman? How might the two differ?

Ex-Basketball Player

—JOHN UPDIKE

Pearl Avenue runs past the high school lot,
Bends with the trolley tracks, and stops, cut off
Before it has a chance to go two blocks,
At Colonel McComsky Plaza. Berth's Garage
Is on the corner facing west, and there,
Most days, you'll find Flick Webb, who helps Berth out.

Flick stands tall among the idiot pumps—
Five on a side, the odd bubble-head style,
Their rubber elbows hanging loose and low.
One's nostrils are two S's, and his eyes
an E and O. And one is squat, without
A head at all—more of a football type.

Once, Flick played for the high school team, the Wizards.
He was good: in fact, the best. In '46,
He bucketed three hundred ninety points,
A county record still. The ball loved Flick.
I saw him rack up thirty-eight or forty
In one home game. His hands were like wild birds.

He never learned a trade; he just sells gas,
Checks oil, and changes flats. Once in a while,
As a gag, he dribbles an inner tube,
But most of us remember anyway.
His hands are fine and nervous on the lug wrench.
It makes no difference to the lug wrench, though.

Off work, he hangs around Mae's Luncheonette.
Grease-grey and kind of coiled, he plays pinball,
Sips lemon cokes, and smokes those thin cigars;
Flick seldom speaks to Mae, just sits and nods
Beyond her face towards bright applauding tiers
Of Necco Wafers, Nebs, and Juju Beads.

Discuss the advantages of being a great professional basketball player or other top athlete. Write about the dangers of putting all your eggs in one "basket." Write about players you know who went all out for professional athletics and won—or lost.

Incident

—COUNTEE CULLEN

Once riding in old Baltimore,
Heart-filled, head-filled with glee,
I saw a Baltimorean
Keep looking straight at me.

Now, I was eight and very small,
And he was no whit bigger,
And so I smiled, but he poked out
His tongue, and called me, "Nigger."

I saw the whole of Baltimore
From May until December;
Of all the things that happened there
That's all that I remember.

what to write about

Describe an incident in which *you* suffered the sting of bigotry or hurt someone else with prejudice.

Words

—E. B. DE VITO

There are words that make us
    Shudder, wince:
Wormwood, persimmon,
    Alum, quince.

There are words that soothe
    And tranquilize:
Slumbering, rainbows,
    Butterflies.

There are words that tighten,
    Words that roil:
Tension, turmoil,
    Chaos, spoil.

There are words that shimmer,
    That beguile:
Stars, ships, peacocks,
    Firelight, smile.

And always, words
    That make life full:
Love, laughter, home,
    Peace, beautiful.

> *"The difference between the right word*
> *and the almost right word*
> *is the difference between lightning*
> *and the lightning bug."*
>
> —*MARK TWAIN*

what to write about

Write about words that sound funny, ominous, silly, or sad; write about how you feel about words. Using a dictionary, write about the endless variety of words. Give examples.

ASSIGNMENT 3: React to Essays

Write a paper of about 200 words in which you react to one of the essays on the following pages. Review the writing suggestions on page 3 before proceeding.

College Is OK If You Do It by Degrees

—DAVE BARRY

Many of you young persons out there are seriously thinking about going to college. (That is, of course, a lie. The only things you young persons think seriously about are loud music and sex. Trust me: these are closely related to college.)

College is basically a bunch of rooms where you sit for roughly 2,000 hours and try to memorize things. The 2,000 hours are spread out over four years; you spend the rest of the time sleeping and trying to get dates.

Basically, you learn two kinds of things in college:

• *Things you will need to know in later life (2 hours).* These include how to make collect telephone calls and get beer-and-crepe-paper stains out of your pajamas.

• *Things you will not need to know in later life (1,198 hours).* These are the things you learn in classes whose names end in "ology," "osophy," "istry," "ics," and so on. The idea is, you memorize these things, then write them down in little exam books, then forget them. If you fail to forget them, you become a professor and have to stay in college for the rest of your life.

It's very difficult to forget everything. For example, when I was in college, I had to memorize—don't ask me why—the names of three metaphysical poets other than John Donne. I have managed to forget one of them, but I still remember that the other two were named Vaughan and Crashaw. Sometimes, when I'm trying to remember something important like whether my wife told me to get tuna packed in oil or tuna packed in water, Vaughan and Crashaw just pop up in my mind, right there in the supermarket. It's a terrible waste of brain cells.

After you've been in college for a year or so, you're supposed to choose a major, which is the subject you intend to memorize and forget the most things about. Here is a very important piece of advice: *Be sure to choose a major that does not involve Known Facts and Right Answers.*

This means you must *not* major in mathematics, physics, biology or chemistry, because these subjects involve actual facts. If, for example, you major in mathematics, you're going to wander into class one day and the professor will say: "Define the cosine integer of the quadrant of a rhomboid binary axis, and extrapolate your result to five significant vertices." If you don't come up with *exactly* the answer the professor has in mind, you fail. The same is true of chemistry: If you write in your exam book that carbon and hydrogen combine to form oak, your professor will flunk you. He wants you to come up with the same answer he and all the other chemists have agreed on. Scientists are extremely snotty about this.

So you should major in subjects like English, philosophy, psychology and sociology—subjects in which nobody really understands what anybody else is talking about, and which involve virtually no actual facts. I attended classes in all these subjects, so I'll give you a quick overview of each:

English: This involves writing papers about long books you have read little snippets of just before class. Here is a tip on how to get good grades on your English papers: *Never say anything about a book that anybody with any common sense would say.* For example, suppose you are studying "Moby Dick." Anybody with any common sense would say Moby Dick is a big white whale, since the characters in the book refer to it as a big white whale roughly 11,000 times. So in *your* paper, *you* say Moby Dick is actually the Republic of Ireland. Your professor, who is sick to death of reading papers and never liked "Moby Dick" anyway, will think you are enormously creative. If you can regularly come up with lunatic interpretations of simple stories, you should major in English.

Philosophy: Basically, this involves sitting in a room and deciding there is no such thing as reality and then going to lunch. You should major in philosophy if you plan to take a lot of drugs.

Psychology: This involves talking about rats and dreams. Psychologists are *obsessed* with rats and dreams. I once spent an entire semester training a rat to punch little buttons in a certain sequence, then training my roommate to do the same thing. The rat learned much faster. My roommate is now a doctor.

Studying dreams is more fun. I had one professor who claimed everything we dreamed about—tractors, Arizona, baseball, frogs— actually represented a sexual organ. He was very insistent about this. Nobody wanted to sit near him. If you like rats or dreams, and above all if you dream about rats, you should major in psychology.

Sociology: For sheer lack of intelligibility, sociology is far and away the No. 1 subject. I sat through hundreds of hours of sociology courses, and read gobs of sociology writing, and I never once heard or read a coherent statement. This is because sociologists want to be considered scientists, so they spend most of their time translating simple, obvious observations into a scientific-sounding code. If you plan to major in sociology, you'll have to learn to do the same thing. For example, suppose you have observed that children cry when they fall down. You should write: "Methodological observation of the sociometrical behavior tendencies of pre-maturated isolates indicates that a causal relationship exists between groundward tropism and lachrymatory, or 'crying,' behavior forms." If you can keep this up for 50 or 60 pages, you will get a large government grant.

what to write about

Did anything funny ever happen to you in high school or college? Were any of the courses unusual, humorous, or worthless? Do you have any zany advice to give to young students?

El Hoyo

—MARIO SUAREZ

From the center of downtown Tucson the ground slopes gently away to Main Street, drops a few feet, and then rolls to the banks of the Santa Cruz River. Here lies the section of the city known as El Hoyo. Why it is called El Hoyo is not very clear. In no sense is it a hole as its name would imply; it is simply the river's immediate valley. Its inhabitants are *chicanos* who raise hell on Saturday night and listen to Padre Estanislao on Sunday morning. While the term *chicano* is the short way of saying Mexicano, it is not restricted to the *paisanos* who came from old Mexico with the territory or the last famine to work for the railroad, labor, sing, and go on relief. *Chicano* is the easy way of referring to everybody. Pablo Gutierrez married the Chinese grocer's daughter and now runs a meat department; his sons are *chicanos*. So are the sons of Killer Jones who threw a fight in Harlem and fled to El Hoyo to marry Cristina Mendez. And so are all of them. However, it is doubtful that all these spiritual sons of Mexico live in El Hoyo because they love each other—many fight and bicker constantly. It is doubtful they live in El Hoyo because of its scenic beauty—it is everything but beautiful. Its houses are simple affairs of unplastered adobe, wood, and abandoned car parts. Its narrow streets are mostly clearings which have, in time, acquired names. Except for some tall trees which nobody has ever cared to identify, nurse, or destroy, the main things known to grow in the general area are weeds, garbage piles, dark-eyed *chavalos,* and dogs. And it is doubtful that the *chicanos* live in El Hoyo because it is safe—many times the Santa Cruz has risen and inundated the area.

In other respects living in El Hoyo has its advantages. If one is born with weakness for acquiring bills, El Hoyo is where the collectors are less likely to find you. If one has acquired the habit of listening to Octavio Perea's Mexican Hour in the wee hours of the morning with the radio on at full blast, El Hoyo is where you are less likely to be reported to the authorities. Besides, Perea is very popular and sooner or later to everyone "Smoke In The Eyes" is dedicated between the pinto beans and white flour commercials. If one, for any reason whatever, comes on an extended period of hard times, where, if not in El Hoyo are the neighbors more willing to offer solace? When Teofila Malacara's house burned to the ground with all her belongings and two children, a benevolent gentleman carried through the gesture that made tolerable her burden. He made a list of five hundred names and solicited from each a dollar. At the end of the month he turned over to the tearful but grateful señora one hundred dollars in cold cash and then accompanied her on a short vacation. When the new manager of a local store decided that no more *chicanas* were to work behind the counters, it was the *chicanos* of El Hoyo who, on taking their individually small but collectively great buying power elsewhere, drove the manager out and the girls returned to their jobs. When the Mexican Army was en route to Baja California and the *chicanos* found out that the enlisted men ate only at infrequent intervals, it was El Hoyo's *chicanos* who crusaded across town with pots of beans and trays of *tortillas* to meet the train. When someone gets married, celebrating is not restricted to the immediate friends of the couple. Everybody is invited. Anything calls for a celebration and a celebration calls for anything. . . .

Perhaps El Hoyo, its inhabitants, and its essence can best be explained by telling a bit about a dish called *capirotada.* Its origin is uncertain. But, according to the time and the circumstance, it is made of old, new or hard bread. It is softened with water and then cooked with peanuts, raisins, onions, cheese, and *panocha.* It is fired with sherry wine. Then it is served hot, cold, or just "on the weather" as they say in El Hoyo. The Sermeños like it one way, the Garcias another, and the Ortegas still another. While it might differ greatly from one home to another, nevertheless it is still *capirotada.* And so it is with El Hoyo's *chicanos.* While being divided from within and from without, like the *capirotada,* they remain *chicanos.*

what to write about

Write a paper which describes the unique qualities of the people who live on your street. Describe the people at a neighborhood dance, party, picnic, religious service, or clambake.

The Lakotas, Lovers of the Earth

—CHIEF LUTHER STANDING BEAR

The Lakota was a true naturist—a lover of nature. He loved the earth and all things of the earth, the attachment growing with age. The old people came literally to love the soil and they sat or reclined on the ground with a feeling of being close to a mothering power. It was good for the skin to touch the earth and the old people liked to remove their moccasins and walk with bare feet on the sacred earth. Their *tipis* were built upon the earth and their altars were made of earth. The birds that flew in the air came to rest upon the earth and it was the final abiding place of all things that lived and grew. The soil was soothing, strengthening, cleansing, and healing.

That is why the old Indian still sits upon the earth instead of propping himself up and away from its life-giving forces. For him, to sit or lie upon the ground is to be able to think more deeply and to feel more keenly; he can see more clearly into the mysteries of life and come closer in kinship to other lives about him. . . .

Kinship with all creatures of the earth, sky and water was a real and active principle. For the animal and bird world there existed a brotherly feeling that kept the Lakota safe among them and so close did some of the Lakotas come to their feathered and furred friends that in true brotherhood they spoke a common tongue.

The old Lakota was wise. He knew that man's heart away from nature becomes hard; he knew that lack of respect for growing, living things soon led to lack of respect for humans too. So he kept his youth close to its softening influence.

what to write about

What is your attitude toward nature? Have you ever marveled at the beauty of a night sky full of stars or at powerful waves beating against huge rocks? Have you seen a flower that had poked through a crack in the sidewalk and wondered how the fragile thing could survive? Write about such an experience. Or write about the negative attitude that many people have toward the land. Describe your feelings about hiking deep into a forest only to find a pile of rusted cans and broken bottles. After you have written your paragraph, you may want to read "Trash Explosion" in Chapter 14.

Everyone Suffers Slipped Disciplines

—ANDY ROONEY

I saw the driver of a panel truck throw a paper cup and a napkin out the window onto a New York street yesterday and it angered me. I was driving myself, so I pulled up beside him at the next light and yelled, "You dropped something back there!"

"Whaddya want me to do, take it to the dump? This whole town's a dump," was his reply.

That "everyone else is doing it" seems to be the single most persuasive reason most of us give ourselves for doing something we really shouldn't do. If enough people do something that's wrong, it often becomes acceptable practice.

A U.S. corporation tries to sell a few hundred million dollars worth of its product to a foreign country with a corrupt government. It offers the potentate in charge of buying things a few million dollars to keep for himself if he'll buy the goods because, the corporation explains to itself, "that's the way everyone does business over here."

A competitor sends a salesman to the same country and he reports that everyone is making under-the-table deals and that isn't considered unusual there. It's the same paper cup and the napkin thrown in the street.

The college football season is starting and nowhere are ethical procedures more consistently violated. College teams should be made up of students who come to a school for an education and who play football for fun. The very first time one of the teams in a hot college rivalry lowered its standards just a hair to admit a high school boy who failed biology but ran the 100-yard dash in 9.8 seconds, amateur football was done for in that league.

In the news business, the newspaper that embellishes the truth and emphasizes the stories that appeal to our lesser instincts will invariably sell the most papers. In England, the London newspapers compete with lurid stories that make our supermarket tabloids look like the Wall Street Journal by comparison.

There is a constant edginess among executives in network television news organizations because if one of them ever decides to lower its journalistic standards and give people what they'd like to watch instead of what they ought to know, that network will very soon take the major part of the audience.

I don't know why "everyone else is doing it" is such an attractive idea to a nation that prides itself on individuality.

what to write about

Did you ever get yourself into trouble because someone convinced you that "Everyone is doing it"? Did you later find that everyone didn't? Is it a good excuse? Why does Mr. Rooney mention individuality in this context?

School Should Be a Place for Praise and Laughter

—GEORGE EPPLEY

Some 16 years ago I was teaching a graduate-level course on the philosophy of education at St. John College. I told the class I would expect two papers at the end of the semester. One paper was to be the students' personal philosophy of education; the other was to be the philosophy of education which they would espouse if they were ever the principal of a school.

I usually regretted giving this double assignment when it came time to read and return the papers with appropriate comments because there were always 20 or 25 students in the class. One evening, however, the task of correcting became pure joy. A middle-aged woman who taught in a Cleveland public school had written "If I were principal, my school would be a place where laughter flows through the curriculum."

That sentence leaped out at me. Had she written nothing else, I would have given her an A.

A couple of days later, I returned the papers to the class. It was imposible to comment on all of them, but I did single out the one about laughter in the curriculum. I read it to the class and said I wished I had written it.

The class and I had a lively discussion about laughter and its place in the school. I dismissed them with some parting comments about the final exam which they would be taking the following week.

The night of the final I arrived rather early and was pacing up and down the corridor next to the classroom. Suddenly I was confronted by the woman who had written about laughter in the curriculum. She was wearing a large hat, carrying books in one arm and an oversized handbag in the other.

"How do you like my handbag?" she asked

"Oh, it's nice," I said, not wanting to let her know that I'm not big on big handbags.

"It's genuine Mexican leather. It cost $55!"

"Fifty-five dollars?"

"Yes, $55, and you're the cause of my buying it."

"Me? I don't recall my telling you or anyone to buy a $55 handbag."

"Of course, you didn't tell me to buy it. But you praised me in our last class, and I felt so good about it that I went to Halle's after class and bought the handbag. You know, that was the second time I had ever been praised in school. The last time was in the third grade!"

At the time I showed no emotion. But I was so moved by that incident that later that evening I silently wept—not only for her but for the countless students I had taught but had never publicly praised.

I have often thought about that teacher and what she said. Unfortunately, I did not keep in contact with her, so I am not sure whether she is still living and still teaching and still striving to be in charge of a school where laughter could flow through the curriculum.

When one reads about problems in the public schools, there is little cause for laughter. Who can laugh about teachers not being paid? Who can laugh about truancy, absenteeism and apathy? Who can laugh about teachers and children being denied books and materials so essential to the teaching/learning process?

But who can laugh at the sins of commission and omission of another day? A middle-aged graduate student in the 1960s remembers that in eight years of grammar school, four years of high school, four years of college and two years of graduate school, she was publicly praised by teachers only twice.

In rebuilding our school system, we must certainly listen to fiscal, administrative and curriculum experts on the national, state and local levels. We must listen to those for whom the system has worked.

Above all, we must listen to those for whom the system has not worked. Those especially who can say through their suffering and tears that school should be a place where "laughter should flow through the curriculum."

what to write about

Under what conditions do you learn best? Give some examples from past experience. How important is laughter in school and in other areas of your life?

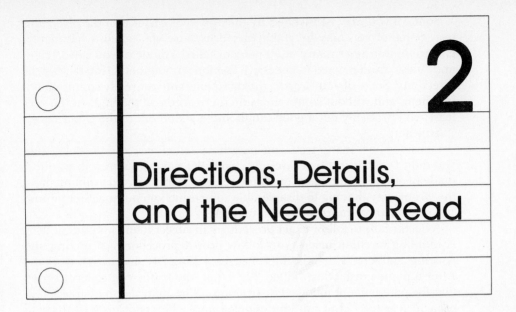

Directions, Details, and the Need to Read

Directions Test

This is a test in following directions. It is important that you read everything on this page before answering anything. Following directions in college can often mean the difference between passing or failing a course. On the job, your ability to follow directions can mean the difference between success or failure. In some jobs it can become a matter of life or death.

Check One

	True	False
1. This is a test about life or death.	——	——
2. Following directions is unimportant.	——	——
3. Following directions is important only in business and industry.	——	——
4. In college, following directions can mean passing or failing a course.	——	——
5. I was supposed to read everything on this page before answering any questions. (See sentence 2 of directions.)	——	——

If you have read this far without answering any questions, your grade is A. If you answered any, your grade is F. Write your grade in the blank to the right. ——

Some of you may be insulted by the apparent easiness of the directions test. Some of you may be embarrassed because you failed it. (In actual classroom testing as many as 50 percent failed.) Some of you saw "true" and "false" and reacted in knee-jerk fashion without bothering to read the directions. Some of you "read" the directions without really comprehending them, and without comprehension there is no real reading. At the very least, you probably got a good laugh and a lesson out of the experience.

So what?

Consider how many tests you may have failed over the years because you didn't read directions carefully. Consider how many mistakes you've made in other situations for the same reason: ruining a cake, mixing paint the wrong way, having to disassemble something you put together wrong.

Consider these more serious situations:

A doctor fails to follow exact procedures in surgery, and his patient dies. A building foreman neglects to follow proper procedures in mixing and pouring concrete. The building collapses, killing 20 construction workers. After a plane crash which killed 90 people, the traffic controller asserted that the pilot had not followed instructions. The controller had given "approach clearance" but not landing clearance. The pilot insisted that approach clearance means that it is safe to descend, but the controller insisted that such clearance does not exempt a pilot from maintaining a safe altitude. Because of lack of clarity in giving or receiving instructions, 90 people died.

You aren't likely to kill anyone at college by not following directions. But college is a training ground for the professions you hope to enter soon. In many of them a mistake on your part can mean the loss of a great deal of money and, worse, the loss of lives.

This textbook, like most others, is full of directions. Some of these directions may seem difficult, some tedious. If you read and follow them carefully, you should be able to "cure" your compositions in this course and transfer this directions-following capability to other studies. Eventually, you will use it in your profession—where you will not only follow but *give* directions. Lack of seriousness about following directions may keep you from ever achieving that profession.

for discussion

Discuss situations in which your failure or that of someone else to follow directions resulted in a problem: a child's toy wouldn't work, a meal was spoiled, a destination wasn't reached, an engine wouldn't start. Perhaps, *your* mistake caused an accident.

A COMPUTER ISN'T SMART ENOUGH TO MAKE A MISTEAK.

Most students understand that if a key punch operator punches the wrong figure, a computer may bill 50,000 bank customers incorrectly. The error is the operator's, not the computer's. When space engineers aim a projectile at the moon, an error in their calculations of one-thousandth of an inch can send the missile far off course. If an eye surgeon errs by a fraction of an inch, a human being may be blinded.

We recognize the importance of attention to detail in many areas of our highly technical, ultra-scientific, extremely complex industrial society. But what has this to do with English? Do stupid little things like commas or periods or misspelled or wrong words here or there make a difference?

The following headline appeared on the front page of a big city newspaper. Remove the second comma and see what happens to the judge.

LEVINE IS INNOCENT, INSANE, JUDGE RULES

Would it make much difference if you switched *raze* and *raise* in the following headline about two schools?

Raze the Old, Raise the New

News Item

The car of Elmo Sawbridge was stolen from a parking lot in August. Police recovered the car two days later and attempted to contact the owner through the serial number. Three months later the owner of the parking lot where the car was stored tried again—and succeeded. The person who had checked the car the first time had listed the serial number as 182496G-5824 instead of as 182496J-5824. By the time the rightful owner was notified, he owed so much for towing and storage charges that he couldn't afford to retrieve the car from the storage company.

One-digit Error Means a Day Without Gas

—JERRY MASEK

A single-digit mistake in the address of an East Ohio Gas Co. cutoff order made Frankie Bailey's heart skip a beat.

A gas company serviceman told Mrs. Bailey he was cutting off her service "because your house is being demolished."

Mrs. Bailey envisioned a wrecking ball coming down the street any minute, and she quickly started making phone calls, including one to Ward 18 Councilwoman Artha Woods.

East Ohio finally admitted its error and restored service, but not before the Baileys and their 16-year-old daughter spent Monday night with no gas.

News Item

James R. Smith sued a loan company because they accused him of owing them $400 and garnisheed his wages. In court it was found that James Robert Smith was in debt to the loan company, not James Roland Smith, the man whose wages were garnisheed. James Roland Smith was awarded $20,000 by the court for the loan company's mistake.

News Item

In an Illinois hospital a boy by the name of Ryan and another by the name of Bryan were scheduled for surgery at the same time. Ryan had his urinary tract enlarged and Bryan had his tonsils and adenoids removed. After surgery it was discovered that each had undergone the other's operation. Both had to be operated on again.

Legal Details—You Be the Judge

In a Philadelphia court a judge had to interpret the following statement in the will of a deceased farmer:

"My property is deeded to George Henderson, and Fred Hampton and Helen Hampton, his wife."

Did each of the inheritors get one-third of the property, or did Henderson get one-half and the Hamptons the other half?

The judge decreed that Henderson should get one-half and each of the Hamptons should get one-fourth of the property because of the way the sentence was written. Had it said, "My property is deeded to George Henderson, Fred Hampton, and Helen Hampton," each would have received a third of the property.

In Oregon a judge was asked to divide the property of Orwell Tett. His will said, "My estate is to be divided equally between my four sons and my twelve nieces and nephews."

Did each recipient get one-sixteenth of the estate, or did the four sons get half and the nieces and nephews the other half?

The judge ruled that "between" was the key word. Half the property went to the four sons and the other half to the nieces and nephews. Had the deceased used the term "among," each of the litigants would have received one-sixteenth of the property.

A Modern "Comedy of Errors"

The following collection of classified ads purportedly shows the results of a typographical error and the disastrous (hilarious?) attempts to correct it.

(Monday) FOR SALE—R.D. Jones has one sewing machine for sale. Phone 948-0707 after 7 p.m. and ask for Mrs. Kelly who lives with him cheap.

(Tuesday) NOTICE—We regret having erred in R.D. Jones' ad yesterday. It should have read: One sewing machine for sale. Cheap. Phone 948-0707 and ask for Mrs. Kelly who lives with him after 7 p.m.

(Wednesday) NOTICE—R.D. Jones has informed us that he has received several annoying telephone calls because of the error we made in his classified ad yesterday. His ad stands correct as follows: FOR SALE—R.D. Jones has one sewing machine for sale. Cheap. Phone 948-0707 p.m. and ask for Mrs. Kelly who loves with him.

(Thursday) NOTICE—I, R.D. Jones, have NO sewing machine for sale. I SMASHED IT. Don't call 948-0707, as the telephone has been taken out. I have NOT been carrying on with Mrs. Kelly. Until yesterday she was my housekeeper, but she quit.

This book is full of details. You will learn when to add *s* to your verbs so that they will agree with your subjects, or to nouns to make them plural; when to add *ed* for the past tense, and when to use commas and periods. If you don't have the patience to deal with such details, you should go fishing. But then, of course, you would have to deal with those darn little worms.

for discussion

Consider the kinds of errors reported above. Do they remind you of similar errors that you've read about or experienced? Recall situations in which something very small made a big difference. It might have been a test error which caused you to fail, a mistake in an address which made you miss an appointment, a misreading of a phone number or map. Discuss how failure to pay attention to details can create problems or cause serious accidents.

ASSIGNMENT: Attention to Detail Test

Copy the first paragraph below on a sheet of paper, making sure to copy everything accurately. If you make a simple error, copy paragraph 2 as a retest. If you still make any mistakes, do paragraph 3, and this time get it perfect.

(1) The new racing car runs perfectly. Yesterday, the driver parked his Volkswagen near the track, clambered into his chartreuse racer, and raced it around the track until it seemed as if its tires would disintegrate. "They're not making many of them like this anymore," he said. "There are too many slipshod machines on the tracks. Their engines can't stand up under high speeds. The manufacturers go through the motions, but they're not thorough enough in their quality control departments."

(2) The lady truck driver got into her huge vehicle, The Jolly Juggernaut, turned on the ignition, put it in gear, and quickly accelerated it. In a fraction of a minute she was barreling down Sea Shore Freeway. She had previously been employed as an electrician but didn't like staying in one place. In the past two weeks she has been to Kalamazoo, Michigan; Cincinnati, Ohio; and Kennebunk, Maine. Now she's going to New Haven, Connecticut.

(3) The two little ragamuffins were screaming at one another, working themselves up to a fight.

"That's mine, not yours," shouted one, grabbing for a dilapidated bicycle.

"It ain't yours! It's theirs," countered the smaller one, nodding his head toward his two sobbing brothers. "And it's mine, too!" With that he flailed out at his opponent.

The two were so angry and excited that neither was conscious of their mother's presence until they were pulled apart and escorted home.

WHY READING IS IMPORTANT

Following directions and paying attention to detail will be of great help to you as you work your way through *The Writing Clinic* and other textbooks. In addition, it's important that you read as much as possible. Reading a wide range of books, magazines, and newspapers will increase your knowledge of the world and enhance your appreciation of life. It will broaden your vocabulary and give you a better grasp of your language.

If you don't enjoy reading, maybe it's because you read so slowly that you become bored. Or perhaps your mind wanders because you don't fully grasp the meaning. Maybe you have other reading problems for which you should seek help.

Reprinted by permission of Tribune Company Syndicate, Inc.

Many people use words to prey on others. They are advertisers who use slick prose and fancy packages to induce others to buy things they don't need at prices they can't afford to pay; they are high pressure salespeople who offer "irresistible" contracts, and politicians who try to enlist your support for issues or candidates, sometimes against your own best interests.

Your main protection is knowledge. Most knowledge comes from reading. Read widely for knowledge, for self-fulfillment, for self-protection, and for enjoyment. Read to improve your writing.

Read. Read! READ!!!

for discussion

What is the importance of reading in everyday life? Relate your discussion to education, health, job opportunities, child care, marital relations, entertainment, and travel. Can television, radio, and the movies substitute for wide reading?

NOTE: For an interesting discussion of a subject closely connected with the material in this chapter, turn to "Ten Keys to Listening" in Chapter 14.

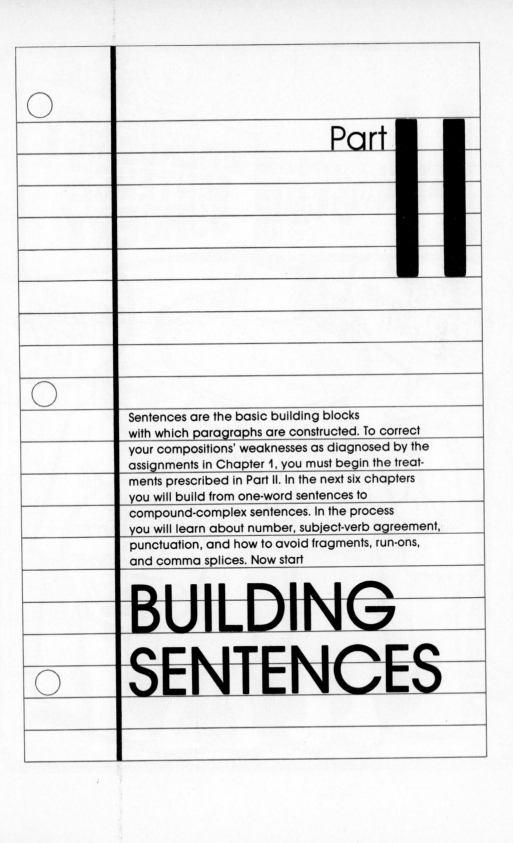

Part **II**

Sentences are the basic building blocks
with which paragraphs are constructed. To correct
your compositions' weaknesses as diagnosed by the
assignments in Chapter 1, you must begin the treatments prescribed in Part II. In the next six chapters
you will build from one-word sentences to
compound-complex sentences. In the process
you will learn about number, subject-verb agreement,
punctuation, and how to avoid fragments, run-ons,
and comma splices. Now start

BUILDING SENTENCES

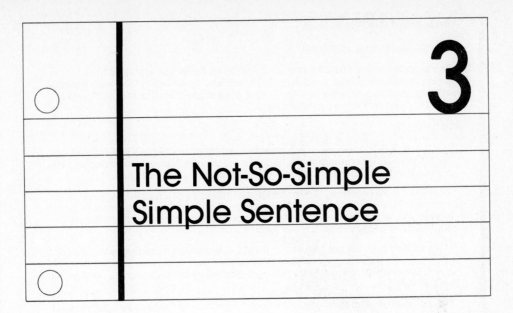

The Not-So-Simple Simple Sentence

(1) *Laugh!*

(2) *After the graduation ball, Fred, the son of a Presbyterian minister, and Mattie, one of the best singers in the church choir, sat in Fred's car in the church parking lot until it was almost time for breakfast.*

The two examples above are both simple sentences.

Simple sentences are called "simple" because they are readily defined by the three criteria listed below, and because they form the base for all other sentences. They are "not so simple" because their length is virtually unlimited and their structure permits a wide range of variations.

THE SUBJECT-VERB CORE

Generally speaking, sentences are formed by the interaction between subjects and verbs. Since most sentence-writing problems center upon the subject-verb relationship, this book focuses a great deal of attention on what it calls the *subject-verb core*. Every sentence you write must contain the basic elements of the simple sentence; once you have mastered the simple sentence, you should have less trouble with the others.

how to do the exercises

COMPREHENSION CHECKS

The purpose of the comprehension checks is to make you stop and think about what you've read. It is all too easy to look hurriedly at words without really absorbing their meaning. Use the keys at the end of each chapter to check your answers. *Correct any errors before proceeding.*

PRACTICES

The practice exercises give you a chance to apply what you have just studied—to reinforce your understanding. Sometimes repetitious, they are intended to help break old, non-standard verbal habits and build new, standard ones.

Answers for all practices are in the keys at the ends of chapters. *Always grade and correct a practice before proceeding.* If you don't understand why your answer was wrong, review the pertinent page or pages immediately preceding the practice.

Many of the practices are branching, that is, they provide more than one quiz on a given unit of instruction. For example, Practice 1 in this chapter has two parts, A and B. Grade and correct A before doing B. Sometimes there are study hints in the keys to help you.

The ✔ will be used throughout the book to remind you to *check and correct* your answers before proceeding with your work.

ASSIGNMENTS

The assignments are more complicated than the practices and usually require more writing. *No keys are provided.* Write the answers on your own paper and give the paper to your instructor. Most assignments are based on the instructions and examples immediately preceding them. Refer to them for help while you are doing the work.

NOTE: Avoid doing the work all at once—mindlessly, mechanically. Do short segments thoughtfully and carefully with other work sandwiched in between.

WHAT IS A SIMPLE SENTENCE?

A simple sentence has the following characteristics: (a) it must contain at least one verb and a subject which is either stated or implied (understood), and (b) it must contain a complete idea. You will better understand what a complete idea is as we go along.

A sentence may consist of only one word, a verb in the present tense: *Stop. Go. Hurry!* On the other hand, you may string together a thousand words which make sense in sequence, but if they do not contain a subject (either stated or understood) and a verb which interacts with the subject, you have not written a sentence.

Subject. A subject is the word or words which combine with the verb to form the core of the sentence. The subject can be a **person** (*plumber, Tom Thumb*), a **group** (*jury, dozen*), a **thing** (*Volkswagen, butterfly*), a **place** (*Gulf of Mexico, Broadway and 42nd Street*), a **quality** or **idea** (*hate, honesty, democracy, justice*), or an **activity** (*diving, reading*).

Any of the words that are usually called "nouns" and any of the words and groups of words that can substitute for nouns can be subjects. (This book uses the term "subject" as some books use the term "simple subject." The simple subject is the one word with which the verb must agree in number, that is, singular or plural.)

Verb.   A verb is the word or words which combine with the subject to form the core of the sentence. A verb can **describe an action** (*run, bleed, breathe, advertise*), **indicate existence** (the forms of the verb *be*), **express feeling** or **sensory reactions** (*smell, taste, feel, sound*), or **indicate possession** (*have, keep, own*).

NOTE: Before doing the comprehension check below, read the instructions on HOW TO DO THE EXERCISES.

COMPREHENSION CHECK 1

Write out your answers to the following questions.

1. Sentences are formed by the interaction between what two sentence parts?
2. Every sentence must contain within it the basic elements of _____.
3. Why does this book place emphasis on the subject-verb core?
4. A one-word sentence must consist of _____.
5. What is the subject of a sentence?
6. List six kinds of subjects.
7. What is the verb of a sentence?
8. List four things that a verb can do.

✔ *CHECK YOUR ANSWERS.   CORRECT YOUR WORK.   THE KEY IS AT THE END OF THE CHAPTER.*

THE SUBJECT OF A SENTENCE

Words do not become subjects until they are *used* as subjects in sentences. To be a subject, a word (or words) must combine with a verb in a sentence that makes sense.

Characteristics of Subjects

1. Subjects work together with their verbs.
2. The other words in the sentence describe the subject, tell what it is doing, or say something about it.
3. If you delete the subject, you usually get a response such as "*Who* did that?" "*What's* this about?" or "*Which* one are you describing?"

Study the subjects in the sentences below. Note how they work together with their verbs. Also note that subjects are not always people, places, or things. Then cover each with a finger while you read the rest of the sentence, applying the *who, what,* and *which* test. Subjects are underlined once; verbs are underlined twice. (*This system is followed throughout the book.*)

Types of Subjects

PERSON, PLACE, and THING Subjects

George was a fine person.
The rusty, rickety, dirt-covered old car suddenly collapsed.
Each is capable of doing the job.
No one has volunteered.
That is my zebra.
She grows chick peas.

GROUP Subjects

The band has arrived.
The herd of cattle will be here tomorrow.
Members of the team will speak at the rally.
All of them are here.
The committee has promised to vote.

IDEA or QUALITY Subjects

Democracy is the best form of government.
Religion is a comfort to many people.
His principles are not being questioned.
Honesty may not always be profitable.
Faithfulness is considered a virtue.
Youth is highly valued by Americans.

ACTIVITY Subjects

Running the mile[1] is a difficult feat.
To act promptly can save many lives.
To retreat at this moment would be wise.

NOTE: Before doing the practice below, see "Practices" in HOW TO DO THE EXERCISES, p. 38.

---

[1] The phrase "Running the mile" is actually the subject of the sentence. However, in order to master the problem of agreement of subject and verb, you must learn to recognize the single word that works with the verb. For example, in the sentence: "Running many miles is a difficult feat," the verb must agree with the word "running" (singular), not with the word "miles" (plural). Chapter 5 concentrates on the problem of subject-verb agreement.

PRACTICE 1: Recognizing Subjects

In the exercises below, the subjects have been omitted. To complete each sentence, choose an appropriate word from the choices given and insert it where it makes the best sense. (Some words don't fit at all.) Don't use any word twice. In the first five sentences, a caret (∧) shows where the subject belongs.

EXAMPLE: The car ∧ refused to sell imported cars.
             salesman

CHOICES: bills, are, Hockey, peace, frantic, fishing, president, ugly, Beer, doctor, ran, virtue, Roger, fish, giggle, salesman.

1. Hospital ∧ are ridiculously high.
2. ∧ is a game full of surprises.
3. During the war ∧ was always on our minds.
4. In the summertime ∧ is his favorite hobby.
5. The ∧ was inaugurated on a cold, January day.
6. is a favorite beverage of many Americans.
7. The examined my injured knee.
8. Her is not being questioned by the minister.
9. can fix almost anything.
10. Some eat worms.

✔ The answer key is at the end of this chapter. Be sure to grade this practice and correct your work before proceeding.

Pronouns as Subjects

Pronouns are words used instead of nouns (see Chapter 11). These words can substitute for subjects and, therefore, become subjects themselves. In each of the following pairs of sentences, a pronoun is used in the second sentence to substitute for the subject in the first sentence. The pronoun is printed in italics.

> George was a fine person. *He* will be remembered for many years.
> The dancer has arrived. *She* will dance tonight.
> Fish swim upstream when mating. *They* are very talented.

PRACTICE 2: Using Pronouns as Subjects

Use the five most appropriate pronouns from the following list as subjects in the sentences below.

CHOICES: she, all, mine, it, I, each, he, you.

1. My name is Oscar. _____ am very good-looking and intelligent.
2. Members of the band came in from the storm. _____ were shivering from the cold.

3. The team traveled in an old bus. _____ had only three good tires.
4. John's dog died of old age last week. _____ was killed by a truck yesterday.
5. The sorority women contributed $500 to Gloria's campaign. _____ won the election.

✔ CHECK YOUR ANSWERS.   CORRECT YOUR WORK.

"You Understood" as Subject

One of the exceptions to the rule that every sentence must have a subject is the "*you* understood" exception. When verbs are used in the *present tense* as commands, directives, or strong requests, we accept the fact that the *you* is understood, and that the sentence is complete with only the verb or with the verb and its modifiers (the predicate).

The constructions below are considered sentences because each has a verb which makes sense with "*you* understood" as the subject.

Go! Look at her. Please do not eat the daisies. Take the pastrami sandwich with you. Demand your rights! Sign here. Keep your children in the barn. Stop! Practice your piccolo for two hours.

PRACTICE 3: Recognizing "*You* Understood" as a Subject

Insert *(y.u.)* after each sentence in which "*you* understood" is the subject.

EXAMPLE: Donna, please slice the peach carefully.   *(y. u.)*

1. Gerry eats onions raw.
2. Start the engines.
3. Pour catsup on the meatballs.
4. The president hates stew.
5. Gargling with salt water cures his sore throat.
6. Please send us the funny pictures.
7. Many residents are alcoholics.
8. Feed the chipmunks the green peanuts.
9. After supper, take your medicine.
10. Come to see me after the earthquake is over.

✔ CHECK YOUR ANSWERS.   CORRECT YOUR WORK.

Nouns of Address Are *Not* Subjects

Nouns of address are proper nouns used in direct oral communications. They can appear in various parts of the sentence and are separated from the body of the sentence by commas. On paper they look like this:·

John, come here. Come here, *Stephen.* Take this, *Dolores,* to your mother. The answer, *Watson,* is elementary.

The nouns of address (John, Stephen, Dolores, Watson) are *not* the subjects of the above sentences. The subject in the first three is *"you understood."* In the last sentence the subject is *answer. Note that commas always separate the noun of address from the rest of the sentence.*

PRACTICE 4: Recognizing Nouns of Address

Circle the nouns of address in the sentences below. If *"you* understood" is the subject of the sentence, write *(y.u.)* after it. (Both can occur in the same sentence.)

EXAMPLE: Mike, don't slurp your soup.

(Mike,) don't slurp your soup.   *(y.u.)*

1. Sam, come home right now.
2. Sam comes home regularly.
3. Come home now, Sam.
4. His name, Gertrude, is Alexander.
5. Kenny leaves early every day.
6. Kenny, don't leave early anymore.
7. Francine jogs three miles three times a week.
8. The bankers agree to give every citizen $12,000, Mr. President.
9. Give the money to Theresa.
10. Smile, Oliver, for the photographer.

✔ *CHECK YOUR ANSWERS.   CORRECT YOUR WORK.*

Subject Review

In the comprehension check, the practices, and the assignment that follow, you will put together all you have learned about recognizing the various types of subjects mentioned on page 38 as well as *"you un-derstood"* and pronoun subjects. You'll also be reminded about nouns of address.

COMPREHENSION CHECK 2

Fill in the blanks.

1. Subjects work together with their _____.
2. When checking for subjects, try the _____, _____, or _____ test.
3. The other words in the sentence describe the _____, tell what the _____ is doing, or say something about the _____. (*The same word goes in all the blanks.*)

4. Words do not become subjects until they are _____ as subjects.
5. To be a subject, a word (or words) must combine with a _____ in a _____ that makes _____.
6. Nouns of address cannot be _____ of sentences.
7. _____ are words that can substitute for previously mentioned _____.
8. In a sentence in the present tense in which someone is asked or told to do something, the subject is usually "_____."

✔ CHECK AND CORRECT YOUR WORK.

PRACTICE 5

Underline the subjects in the following sentences. To help you, verbs are double underlined in Part A. When the subject is "*you* understood," write *(y.u.)*. Circle nouns of address.

Part A

1. The girls threw eggs at the boys.
2. Some are wearing green hats.
3. The freshmen are having tryouts.
4. Do not go there.
5. The team arrived at eight.
6. His mother voted for Blodget.
7. It will cost twenty yen.
8. The gruesome-looking, three-headed thing attacked.
9. Everyone walked across campus.
10. Benjamin ate sixteen hamburgers.

✔ CHECK AND CORRECT YOUR WORK.

Part B

1. His sincerity can be questioned.
2. The soldiers stopped the jeep abruptly.
3. John, go to the store.
4. The plane landed safely.
5. Go!
6. The boys threw yams at the girls.
7. Breathing is a reflex action.
8. Despair descended on them.
9. The women attended the meeting together.
10. Mr. President, our city needs help.

✔ CHECK AND CORRECT YOUR WORK.

NOTE: Before doing the assignment below, see "Assignments" in HOW TO DO THE EXERCISES, p. 38.

ASSIGNMENT 1: Recognizing Subjects

Copy the sentences below on a sheet of paper to be handed in. Underline the subjects of each sentence. If "*you* understood" is the subject, write (*y.u.*). Circle the nouns of address.

Part A

1. Those hats are mine.
2. These are yours.
3. Linda brought me a paper.
4. Linda, please bring me a paper.
5. Governor, the people disagree with your plan.
6. Eat your apricots now.
7. The truth is hard to find.
8. Running tires me quickly.
9. To argue with him is useless.
10. The cows stampeded.

Part B

Write ten simple sentences of your own. Underline the subjects.

Part C

Write a brief paragraph based on a funny, embarrassing, or frightening experience. Try to use only simple sentences. Underline your subjects.

THE VERB IN A SENTENCE

Words do not become verbs until they are *used* as verbs in sentences. To be a verb, a word (or words) must combine with a subject in a sentence that makes sense.

In this section you will study the overall characteristics of verbs, see how they function with subjects, and learn how they can be changed to other parts of speech and back to verbs again. You will also learn how to use auxiliaries correctly.

Characteristics of Verbs

1. Verbs work with their subjects to provide the core meanings of sentences.
2. Verbs adapt to their subjects so that they can agree in number, one verb form being used when the subject is singular (one person or thing) and another verb form being used when the subject is plural (more than one).
3. Verbs help set the time of sentences. (Tense is discussed in great detail in Chapter 10.) One way to identify verbs is to look for the word

that would change if the time of the sentence were changed. This does not include words like *now, today, yesterday, tomorrow*. For example: *The sun is (was) bright. He looks (looked) good. She has (had) a nice smile. The horse runs (ran) rapidly.* Sometimes the change is in the auxiliary (helping) verb. *He is (was) exercising regularly. She is (was) changing the tire.* (Auxiliaries are discussed later in this chapter.)

Because of the verb's function in setting time, it is necessary to know how to change each verb so that it correctly indicates the past, present, future, or in-between times (the perfect and progressive tenses).

Both of these characteristics of verbs, agreement and tense, are discussed in detail later.

Types of Verbs

In this text we recognize four types of verbs: (1) existence verbs, (2) possessive verbs, (3) action verbs, and (4) feeling or sensory verbs. The sentences below illustrate the four types and show how the verbs (underlined twice) work together with their subjects (underlined once).

EXISTENCE (State of Being) VERBS

This category is comprised of the forms of the verb *be: is, am, was,* and *were.* They are among the most frequently used words in the language. While other words used as verbs can also function as parts of speech other than verbs, the various forms of *be* are **always** used as verbs or auxiliaries.

The chipmunks are here often.
Matilda is living in France.
Several hundred Boy Scouts were here yesterday.
The inspectors have been there several times.
Twelve Martians will be our guests tomorrow.

POSSESSIVE VERBS

The company has many subsidiaries.
They had more before the depression.
Their wives own stock in the company.
Their children possess many admirable qualities.

ACTION VERBS

Frank died.
He thought about it for days.
Cleotis bought twelve books.
The pitchman guessed her weight.
Jack and Betty eloped.

VERBS of FEELING or SENSORY REACTIONS

The <u>rose</u> <u><u>smelled</u></u> good.
Those <u>apples</u> <u><u>taste</u></u> rotten.
Her <u>children</u> <u><u>feel</u></u> neglected.
Their <u>music</u> <u><u>sounds</u></u> absolutely beautiful.

Other texts may classify verbs somewhat differently, and you may find that some overlap in the above method of classification. The important point is that you should learn to recognize verbs by their *function* in the sentences you write. *They always operate as part of a subject-verb core.*

COMPREHENSION CHECK 3

Fill in the blanks.

1. _____ work with their _____ to provide the core meanings of sentences.
2. Verbs adapt to their _____ so that they can agree in _____, one verb form being used when the subject is _____, and another verb form being used when the subject is _____.
3. Verbs help to set the _____ of sentences. For this reason it is necessary to know how to change each verb so that it correctly indicates the _____, _____, _____, or in-between times.
4. List the four types of verbs according to this text.
5. Words used as verbs must combine with the _____ in a _____ that makes sense.

PRACTICE 6

Double underline each verb in the following sentences. To help you, the subjects are indicated in Part A.

Part A

1. <u>They</u> ate a big meal.
2. The <u>kitchen</u> is pink.
3. <u>Smoke</u> poured from the barn.
4. The <u>bus</u> left early.
5. <u>Senators</u> give many speeches.
6. <u>She</u> traveled by bus, train, and plane.
7. <u>Jim</u> and <u>Charley</u> opened a restaurant.
8. A pretty <u>girl</u> won the "ugliest man" contest.
9. Seventy-eight <u>men</u> died in the mine.
10. Mine <u>workers</u> protested.

✔ *CHECK AND CORRECT.*

Part B

1. Someone tripped the burglar alarm.
2. Many policemen reported to work late.
3. The old man had diabetes.
4. To run tonight is futile.
5. Clara was one of the youngest patients.
6. No one knows.
7. Enemy troops ambushed our forces.
8. The mayor spoke slowly.
9. Two holdup suspects escaped.
10. Gentle George plants tulips every spring.

✔ CHECK AND CORRECT.

Part C

Since verbs help change the time of sentences, one way of recognizing them is to find the word that makes the change. The sentences below are written in the present tense. Change the verbs to put them into the past tense. All but two of the verbs can be changed by adding *d* or *ed*. (Three of these must first drop the final *s*.)

EXAMPLE: Steve works hard all day.   (worked)

1. The seal barks at the ringmaster.
2. Computers operate entire factories.
3. The whole family enjoys the movies.
4. They deliver coal on Sundays.
5. She eats only one meal a day.
6. The child jumps into the pond.
7. He changes the weather of the whole world.
8. They believe in sex education.
9. Mexico is an oil rich nation.
10. He lives in Iran.

✔ CHECK AND CORRECT YOUR WORK   From this point on only the check mark will be used to remind you to check your answers and correct your work.

ASSIGNMENT 2: Recognizing Verbs

A. Copy the following sentences on a sheet of paper; then double underline the verbs.

1. Blow the clarinet softly.
2. Benny, drive the car home.
3. To jump across that creek is impossible.
4. She resisted his advances.
5. Smoking is bad for your heart.

6. He ran all the way home.
7. She followed the thief to his hideout.
8. We are almost late.
9. They recovered the money.
10. Sleeping is good for you.

B. Write ten simple sentences of your own. Underline the subjects once and the verbs twice.

VERB PHRASES

You may have noted in earlier examples that in some sentences more than one word has been double underlined. These words are *verb phrases*. The last word in the phrase is always the *main verb*. The other words in the verb phrase are *auxiliaries* (helping verbs).

Study the list of auxiliaries below; then see how they work in typical sentences.

Auxiliaries

can	shall[1]	be	have
may	will	am	has
could	ought (to)	is	had
would	do	are	might
should	does	was	must
	did	were	
		been	

Now, see how the auxiliaries combine with verbs and other auxiliaries to form verb phrases. Note that some of the auxiliaries can also be used as main verbs, and some can be used as *simple verbs* (alone).

SIMPLE VERBS

John walks to school.
The penguins are hurt.
May dates Joe.
Be careful.
Francine does well.
They have problems.
The Marines were outnumbered.

VERB PHRASES

Georgiana is working. Frank can jog six miles. Anne may have driven home.
Caryn does eat enough.
The mail may have been stolen from the train. One thief may be escaping. The other had been hurt in a previous shootout.
Celia ought to have gone with Ben.

---

[1] *Shall* is rarely used today. *Will* seems to have replaced it almost completely.

COMPREHENSION CHECK 4

1. When one or more auxiliaries are joined to a verb, the group of words is called a _____ _____.
2. The last word is called the _____ _____.
3. The helping verbs are called _____.
✔ 4. When a verb is used alone, it is called a _____ verb.

PRACTICE 7

Revise the sentences by inserting in the proper place the auxiliaries given in parentheses. You may have to change the form of the main verb.

EXAMPLES

He works hard. (can) He can work hard.
She is teaching. (might) She might teach. (or) She might be teaching.

1. He spilled the beans. (did)
2. The landlord is sleeping. (may)
3. Juanita arrives on time every morning. (ought to)
4. Gregory was attending a concert that night. (had been)
5. They visited him at the hospital. (would)
6. He works very carefully. (must)
7. Louise spells every word correctly. (should)
8. The children drank milk. (ought to)
9. Zenobia is madly in love with Christopher. (might)
✔ 10. Hector crossed the Danube in a canoe. (will)

ASSIGNMENT 3

Using the following auxiliaries, write six sentences containing verb phrases. Keep the sentences simple. Underline subjects once and the verb (verb phrase) twice. *From this point on when instructed to underline the verb, always underline the verb phrase.*

can, should, must, will, ought to, has been, might be, am, was, did, had

WHEN A "VERB" IS NOT A VERB
(How to "Freeze" or Deactivate a Verb)

As you do the following exercises, keep in mind our earlier statements that words are considered subjects or verbs of sentences because of the way they *function* in given sentences. Words commonly used as verbs can often be used in other ways. This can be confusing if you are not aware of how this happens. There are three ways to "freeze" a so-called action verb so that it no longer functions as a verb in a sentence:

1. By using *to*
2. By adding *ing* without an auxiliary
3. By using *ed* or various irregular endings without auxiliaries

When verbs are thus "frozen," other verbs must be supplied to make the sentence complete. Let's see how this works.

Effect of "to"

When the preposition *to* is placed in front of an action verb like *run* or *sing,* the *to* deactivates the verb and the two words together (*to run, to sing,* etc.) are called an infinitive. An infinitive can function as subject or as direct object in a sentence, but it cannot act as a verb. In the examples below, notice how the infinitive is used either as subject or as direct object (shown in brackets). The direct object receives the action of the verb. It answers the questions *what* or *whom.* For example, "I hit [what?] the *ball.*" "We saw [whom?] the *man.*"

> To sing is fun.
> He loves [to sing].
> To congregate in large groups can be exciting.
> People like [to congregate] in large groups.

Remember, when you place *to* before a verb, it is no longer a verb; it is an infinitive. In such cases another word must act as verb, or you don't have a sentence. A verb tells time through tense. An infinitive can't function as a verb because it no longer tells time.

PRACTICE 8

A. Underline subjects once and verbs twice.

1. He loved to ride.
2. To ride for hours was his favorite sport.
3. The explorers tried to find the gold.
4. To betray her country was unthinkable.
5. The astronauts attempted to reach Mars.

B. Underline subjects once and verbs twice.

1. They tried to sink the Titanic.
2. To sink the Titanic was their aim.
3. The Titanic refused to sink.
4. They decided to try again.
5. To try again proved impossible.

Effect of "ing"

Ing added to an action verb "freezes" it by forming words such as *reading* and *wishing,* which are called *present participles.* (See Chapter 10.) To function as verbs, these words must be used with auxiliaries (*is* reading, *have been* wishing, etc.). Alone, *inged* words are not verbs. Instead, they can be used as adjectives (to modify or describe nouns or pronouns) or as direct objects. In the following sentences, watch the verbs change to subjects, then to adjectives, and finally to direct objects. *Note that in each case a different word takes on the verb function.*

The congressman decided to vote for the bill.
Deciding was difficult.
The deciding votes were cast by absentee ballot.
He hated deciding such questions.

The old lady presided at the meeting.
Presiding at the meeting was no novelty for her.
The presiding officer was given a bouquet.
She loved presiding at that meeting.

PRACTICE 9

A. Underline the subjects and verbs in the sentences below.

1. The child is laughing happily. The laughing child is hungry. Laughing is good for children. Children enjoy laughing.
2. The drunkard was cursing his wife and children. The cursing was heard in the street. The cursing man was arrested. His wife hated the cursing.
3. The boiling kettle was steaming the walls and windows. Steaming is one way of removing wallpaper. The steaming kettle exploded.
4. The mourning will continue all day. The family is mourning the dead child. She hated the crying and mourning. The mourning parents are pale and silent.
5. The examining physician is doing a careful job. He is examining the head wound with special care. Examining a patient is a highly responsible job.

B. Underline subjects once and verbs twice.

1. Swimming is good exercise.
2. Dripping water can increase water bills.
3. The water is dripping steadily.
4. The floor is caving in.
5. Leaking roofs can be repaired.
6. Shaving is a pain in the neck.
7. Bathing regularly is necessary.

8. She is bathing the crocodile.
9. The swimming pool is closed.
✔ 10. The opening in the heart valve has been repaired.

Effect of "ed," "en," etc.

Regular verbs in the past tense and past participle end in *ed*. (See *past participles* in Chapter 10.) They can be used as adjectives when they are placed properly in a sentence and when no auxiliary is used. Irregular verbs vary in their past participle form. (See list in Chapter 10.) These, too, can be adjectives when no auxiliary is used.

Watch the words below switch from verb functions to adjective functions. *Note that in each case another word takes up the job of the verb.* Remember that you can identify the verb by its relationship with the subject—the subject and verb working together in the subject-verb core.

The dog *hunted* for rabbits.
The *hunted* rabbit escaped.   (*Hunted* describes *rabbit*.)

The soldier *fired* the rifle.
The rifle *fired* by the soldier exploded.   (*Fired* describes *rifle*.)

The car was *stolen* yesterday.
The *stolen* car was stripped by the thief.   (*Stolen* describes *car*.)

PRACTICE 10

A. Underline subjects once and verbs twice. Circle verbs changed to adjectives.

1. The man accused his wife of infidelity. The accused woman wept bitterly.
2. The car wrecked the baby buggy. The wrecked buggy was discarded.
3. Sheila dyed her hair orange. Her boyfriend likes dyed hair.
4. The boy was spanked for cheating. The spanked boy was sent home.
✔ 5. The convict escaped from Alcatraz. The escaped convict was caught.

B. Use the following words in the blanks below: *wrecked, towed, demolished, purchased, stolen.* Underline subjects and verbs. Circle words used as adjectives.

1. The motorist _____ the car. The _____ car was towed by the wrecker.
2. The wrecker _____ the car to the junkyard. There, the _____ car was demolished.
3. A steel company bought the _____ car.
4. The motorist _____ a new car. The newly _____ car was stolen.
✔ 5. The _____ car was never recovered. The motorist bought a bicycle.

ASSIGNMENT 4: Switching Verbs into Adjectives

With the examples in P-10 as models, write four pairs of sentences using the following words: *startled, canned, painted, boiled.* In the first sentence of each pair, use the word as a verb; in the second sentence, use it as an adjective. Underline all subjects and verbs. Circle your adjectives.

what you have learned in chapter 3

This chapter has centered on the study of subjects and verbs because this understanding is the key to all your work with sentences. Remember that *words act as subjects and verbs only when they work together in sentences as subject-verb cores.*

SUBJECTS are of six kinds: *person, place, thing, group, idea or quality,* and *activity.* You have learned to recognize *"you* understood" as the subject of certain sentences; you know that the "noun of address" is *not* the subject.

VERBS may be classified as *possessive, action, existence* verbs, and verbs that express *feeling* and *sensory* reactions. AUXILIARIES are helping verbs.

(If you still feel "shaky" about subjects and verbs, the best medicine now is to keep going. Things will become clearer in the next two chapters.)

C—Key 1

(1) Sentences are formed by the interaction between subjects and verbs. (2) Every sentence must contain within it the basic elements of the simple sentence. (3) This book places emphasis on what it calls the "subject-verb" core because most sentence-writing problems center around the subject-verb relationship. (4) A one-word sentence must consist of a verb in the present tense. (5) The subject of a sentence is the word or words which combine with the verb to form the core of the sentence. (6) Person, group, thing, place, quality or idea, and activity. (7) The verb of a sentence is the word or words which combine with the subject to form the core of the sentence. (8) Describe an action, indicate existence, express feeling or sensory reactions, indicate possession.

P—Key 1

Verbs (double underlined) are included here to show the subject-verb relationship.

(1) bills are   (2) Hockey is   (3) peace was   (4) fishing is   (5) president was inaugurated   (6) Beer is   (7) doctor examined   (8) virtue is (9) Roger can fix   (10) fish eat

P—Key 2

(1) I   (2) All   (3) It   (4) Mine   (5) She

P—Key 3

"*You* understood" is subject in sentences 2, 3, 6, 8, 9, 10.

Study Hint: If you missed more than one answer, review your work. Note how *you* makes sense with *start, pour, send, feed, take,* and *come.*

P—Key 4

Nouns of address:

(1) Sam, *y.u.* (3) Sam, *y.u.* (4) Gertrude (6) Kenny, *y.u.* (8) Mr. President (9) *y.u.* (10) Oliver, *y.u.*

C—Key 2

NOTE: When the exact order of the answers doesn't matter, a slash will be placed between them instead of a comma.

(1) verbs (2) who / what / which (3) subject (4) used (5) verb, sentence, sense (6) subjects (7) pronouns, subjects (8) "*you* understood"

P—Key 5

A. (1) girls (2) Some (3) freshmen (4) *y.u.* (5) team (6) mother (7) It (8) thing (9) Everyone (10) Benjamin

Study Hint: If you selected any word after the verb, you were wrong. Most verbs follow their subjects. Don't look for any verbs to precede their subjects until we discuss *inversions.* If you missed #4, see page 42. In #6 *his* didn't vote; *mother* did vote. In #8 *thing* did the attacking. The other words merely describe the thing.

B. (1) sincerity (2) soldiers (3) *John,*[1] y.u. (4) plane (5) y.u. (6) boys (7) Breathing (8) Despair (9) women (10) *Mr. President,* city

Study Hint: To help you better understand which words are the subjects, their verbs are listed below. Match them, and see how they work together.

(1) can be questioned (2) stopped (3) go (4) landed (5) Go! (6) threw (7) is (8) descended (9) attended (10) needs

C—Key 3

(1) Verbs / subjects (2) subjects, number, singular / plural (3) time, past / present / future (4) existence / possessive / action / feeling or sensory reactions (5) subject, sentence

[1] Nouns of address are shown here in italics.

P—Key 6

A. (1) ate (2) is (3) poured (4) left (5) give (6) traveled (7) opened (8) won (9) died (10) protested

Study Hint: If any of your answers in Part A are incorrect, apply the hint given for Practice 5B above. Match the verb with the subject and see how they work together.

B. (1) tripped (2) reported (3) had (4) is (5) was (6) knows (7) ambushed (8) spoke (9) escaped (10) plants

Study Hint: Remember that all forms of *have* (#4) are always verbs or parts of verb phrases. *To run* (in #4) is, of course, the subject.

C. (1) barked (2) operated (3) enjoyed (4) delivered (5) ate (6) jumped (7) changed (8) believed (9) was (10) lived

C—Key 4

(1) verb phrase (2) main verb (3) auxiliaries (4) simple

P—Key 7

(1) did spill (2) may be sleeping / may sleep (3) ought to arrive (4) had been attending (5) would visit (6) must work (7) should spell (8) ought to drink (9) might be (10) will cross

P—Key 8

A. (1) He loved (2) To ride was (3) explorers tried (4) to betray was (5) astronauts attempted

B. (1) They tried (2) To sink was (3) Titanic refused (4) They decided (5) To try proved

P—Key 9

A. (1) child is laughing, child is, Laughing is, Children enjoy
(2) drunkard was cursing, cursing was heard, man was arrested, wife hated
(3) kettle was steaming, steaming is, kettle exploded
(4) mourning will continue, family is mourning, She hated, parents are
(5) physician is doing, He is examining, Examining is

B. (1) Swimming is (2) water can increase (3) water is dripping (4) floor is caving (5) roofs can be repaired (6) Shaving is (7) Bathing is (8) She is bathing (9) pool is closed (10) opening has been repaired.

A.　(1) man accused, *accused* woman wept　(2) car wrecked, *wrecked* buggy was discarded　(3) Sheila dyed, boyfriend likes *dyed* hair　(4) boy was spanked, *spanked* boy was sent　(5) convict escaped, *escaped* convict was caught

B.　(1) motorist wrecked, *wrecked* car　(2) wrecker towed, *wrecked / towed* car was demolished　(3) company bought, *wrecked / demolished* car (4) motorist purchased, *purchased* car was stolen　(5) *stolen* car was recovered, motorist bought

4

Simple Sentence Patterns

In Chapter 3 we concentrated on subjects and verbs in the simple sentence. In this chapter, first we will study the interaction of subjects and verbs in various patterns; then we will expand the simple sentence by adding words and phrases to the core.

A simple sentence has only one subject-verb core. Those we worked with in Chapter 3 contained only one subject and only one verb. But a core may contain any number of subjects and verbs, provided that (a) the subjects are *consecutive,* that is, they do *not* alternate with the verbs; and (b) each subject relates to all the verbs, as in the sentence: *Al, Joe, and Mae ate, drank, and sang* (SSS-VVV pattern).

The following sentence is *not* simple: *Al ate, Joe drank, and Mae sang.* The subjects alternate with the verbs and each subject relates to only one verb. It is a compound sentence and can, in fact, be divided into three separate sentences: *Al ate. Joe drank. Mae sang.*

Once subjects and verbs *alternate* within a sentence (S-V, S-V, S-V), new cores are formed, and the sentence is no longer simple; then new mechanical and grammatical problems arise. Since our goal is to build from simple sentences to compound and complex forms, we must know simple sentence structure thoroughly before moving ahead.

The following table shows the simple sentence patterns with examples of each. Study them. All the exercises in this chapter are based on these patterns.

SIMPLE SENTENCE PATTERNS		EXAMPLES
subject understood—verb	—V	Go!
single subject—single verb	S—V	Dictators dictate.
multiple subject—single verb	SSSSS—V	The President, his wife, members of the Cabinet, the White House staff, 22 reporters, and the President's bodyguards have gone on a picnic.
single subject—multiple verb	S—VVVVV	The Olympic athlete ran the 100-yard dash, threw the discus, vaulted 16 feet, swam in the 100-meter backstroke, participated in the cross-country relay, and then slept for 36 hours.
multiple subject—multiple verb	SS—VVV	Sadie and Tom married, divorced, and remarried.

PRACTICE WITH THE SUBJECT-VERB CORE

If you are not sure of your subject and verb, you cannot control your sentence structure. This may well lead to errors in punctuation, in agreement of subject and verb, and to run-on sentences, comma splices, and fragments—a very sick composition. For this reason we will now focus solely on the subject and verb relationship to reinforce your understanding of its function and its importance.

Single-Word Sentences ("*You* Understood")

In a single-word sentence the word must be a verb in the *present tense.* The subject, *you,* is understood in each case. Here are examples of one-word sentences: *Run! Stop! Kiss. Eat. Charge! Give. Look. Retreat!* Study the examples and then do the quiz.

PRACTICE 1

Circle the number of those words that can be one-word sentences.

Part A

1. Sit
2. March
3. Egg

4. Ran
5. Sing
6. Instructor
7. Orange

8. Underwear
9. Beg
10. Surprising

✔ *Remember to check and correct your work whenever you see the check mark.*

Part B

1. Teach
2. Scream
3. Groundhog

4. Pitch
5. Went
6. Hello
7. Porcupine

8. Ride
9. Blink
10. Lied

✔

COMPREHENSION CHECK 1

Write out your answers to the following questions.

1. How many subjects and verbs can a simple sentence contain?
2. What changes a simple sentence into a compound or complex sentence?
3. One of our aims is to build from _____ sentences to _____ and _____ forms.
4. Define *consecutive* as used in the second paragraph of this chapter.
5. Define *alternate* as used in the second and third paragraphs.

ASSIGNMENT 1

Write ten of your own one-word sentences. Punctuate them.

Single-Subject, Single-Verb Sentences

Below are examples of two- and three-word sentences which follow the S-V pattern. Study the examples; then do the quizzes.

Men fight.
A woman sobbed.
He is sitting.
It died.

Horses snort.
The boy escaped.
The cow was mooing.
Some cats scratch.

PRACTICE 2

Make single-subject, single-verb sentences by inserting the most appropriate words from the choices given. Underline subjects and verbs. Punctuate.

CHOICES: warms, electrocutes, giggled, swim, crowed, dance, development, blowing, gallop, instructor, blow, moistens, activity, smelled, lovely

1. Horses _____
2. The child _____
3. Rain _____
4. A rooster _____
5. Winds _____

6. Dancers _____
7. Fish _____
8. Heat _____
9. Electricity _____
10. Her perfume _____

PRACTICE 3

Make single-subject, single-verb sentences by inserting the most appropriate words. Underline subjects and verbs.

CHOICES: The pickets, Merry-go-rounds, Lovely, Understand, Lovers, Bigots, Unnecessary, A prisoner, Dynamite, Rioters, Advertisers, Students, A child

1. _____ advertise.
2. _____ picketed.
3. _____ riot.
4. _____ explodes.
5. _____ hate.

6. _____ love.
7. _____ escaped.
8. _____ revolve.
9. _____ were studying.
10. _____ was playing.

PRACTICE 4

Rewrite each set of scrambled words to make a good sentence having one subject and one verb. Underline subjects and verbs.

1. mangoes farmers huge African grow
2. Plymouth colonists at Rock the landed
3. you good vegetables for fresh are
4. headed is for the Mars rocket
5. to children camping love go many

ASSIGNMENT 2

Part A: Make complete sentences by writing verbs or verb phrases to go with the following subjects.

1. Reptiles _____
2. The penguins _____

3. Musicians _____
4. Apricots _____

5. An American _____   8. Mathematicians _____
6. Birds _____   9. Miners _____
7. The bride _____   10. Satellites _____

Part B: Make complete sentences by writing subjects to go with the following verbs.

1. _____ steal.   6. _____ paint.
2. _____ buy.   7. _____ stinks.
3. _____ develop.   8. _____ study.
4. _____ fainted.   9. _____ curses.
5. _____ destroy.   10. _____ filed.

Part C: Write ten single-subject, single-verb sentences of your own.

Multiple-Subject, Single-Verb Sentences

In the exercises you have just completed, sentences follow the S-V pattern. They have one subject and one verb. Here are two examples of simple sentences that have more than one subject:

Joan and Henry were married.
Flies, fleas, and mosquitoes love me.[1]

PRACTICE 5

Unscramble the words to make a sentence with two or more subjects and one verb. Write out the sentences and underline subjects and verbs.

1. underwater swim fish toads and
2. day moles every and celery eat rabbits
3. stars early usually movie ballplayers and marry
4. and feed their nation farmers families the
5. boys young alligators girls eat and

ASSIGNMENT 3

Write five multiple-subject, single-verb sentences.

Single-Subject, Multiple-Verb Sentences

Some sentences have one subject and more than one verb. Here are two examples:

Playing strengthens and relaxes the patients.
The cat crouched, ran, and pounced on the mouse.

[1] Note the use of commas to separate words in a series.

PRACTICE 6

Unscramble the words to make a sentence with one subject and two or more verbs. Don't change the form of any words. Some scrambles may lend themselves to more than one sentence.

1. and grunted Ivan swore
2. lawn Ignazio the seeded fertilized and
3. the shores militia our defends the keeps peace and
4. chirp all eat and sparrows flutter day
✔ 5. car and Igor some borrowed rented money a

ASSIGNMENT 4

Write five single-subject, multiple-verb sentences. Underline subjects and verbs.

Multiple-Subject, Multiple-Verb Sentences

Remember that in simple sentences with multiple subjects and multiple verbs every subject is connected with every verb. See for yourself how, in the examples below, all subjects interact with all verbs.

The prime minister and his wife swore, screamed, and fainted. (The prime minister swore, screamed, and fainted. His wife swore, screamed, and fainted.)

The crocodiles, alligators, rhinos, and flamingos sunned themselves on the beach, waded in the water, and sounded their mating calls. (Each of them sunned, waded, and sounded.)

ASSIGNMENT 5

Write five multiple-subject, multiple-verb sentences.

THE PATTERN IN REVERSE: INVERTED SENTENCES

The subject-verb pattern in the English language is so common that exceptions to the pattern are given a special name. When the verb is placed before the subject, or when the subject is placed between the verb and its auxiliary, the sentence is said to be in reverse or *inverted* order. This occurs in three situations.

1. In most questions
2. When the expletive *there* is used
3. When the sentence starts with an adverb or an adverbial phrase[1]

[1] An adverb is a word that modifies an adjective, verb, or another adverb. See Chapter 11.

Questions that Invert

When forms of the verb *be* are used, the verb changes places with the subject.

You were busy. ⟶ Were you busy?
She is his wife. ⟶ Is she his wife?
They are at home. ⟶ Are they at home?

When other types of verbs are used, they combine with auxiliaries to form questions. The subjects are then placed between the auxiliaries and their verbs.

You are coming with us. ⟶ Are you coming with us?
He will help us. ⟶ Will he help us?
They can do the job well. ⟶ Can they do the job well?

Note that question words in inverted sentences are not subjects and don't introduce subjects. Also note the punctuation.

How busy were you? *Why* are you in school?
How often does he ask that? *Which* copy should I keep?

PRACTICE 7

In the sentences below, underline the subjects once and the verbs twice.

1. Are the girls coming with us?
2. Can you untie this knot?
3. Will the party be held at your house?
4. Have they won any games this year?
5. John Smetz is coming here?
6. Olga has lumbago?
7. When will the eclipse take place?
8. Why did she marry him?
9. Did the dog have rabies?
10. Who is he?

Questions that Don't Invert

You can ask a question without inverting the sentence by merely raising your voice at the end of the sentence: *He is coming? They are here?*

You also don't invert the sentence when you use the question words *who, whose, which,* and *what* if they are the subject of the verb or if they introduce the subject.

What is going on?
Who went with him?
Which one is guilty?
Whose friend disappeared?

"There" as an Expletive: Another Type of Inversion

The word *there* is commonly used to mean "in that place." When used in this way, it is called an *adverb*. In such sentences subjects and verbs are not inverted. Here are some examples:

Place the carton over there.   He lives there.   Leave the money there.
Our friends boarded there many years ago.   There he is.

Sometimes *there* does not act as an adverb but as an *expletive*—a kind of "hook" on which to hang a sentence. In these cases *there* displaces the subject and shoves it over to the other side of the verb. When writing such sentences, one must realize that the subject and the verb have been inverted. In the following examples, notice that *there* does not tell *where*.

In the room there are twelve people. During the Civil War there were many casualties. There are thirty days in November. There will be many June weddings this year.

PRACTICE 8

Underline subjects once and verbs twice. Circle *there* when it is used as an adverb.

1. He placed the fish heads there.
2. There are 600 red beans.
3. There is a milch cow in his barn.
4. In the auditorium there are many angry people.
5. He is right there.
6. They are sitting there by their parents.
7. After the party there is always a mess to clean up.
8. There by their well there are three pails.
9. There he is.
10. Put it over there.

Introductory Adverbial Phrases: A Third Type of Inversion

In order to vary your writing, you may wish to invert your sentences in the following manner:

Out of the cave came the six convicts.
Over the fence jumped the rhinoceros.

Through the hot, festering jungle tramped the exhausted men.
Seldom have I won at bingo.
Rarely have they found such a big pearl in an oyster.

EXPANDING THE SIMPLE SENTENCE

The simple sentence can be expanded indefinitely and remain simple as long as no new subject-verb cores are added. Once new cores are included, the sentence becomes compound or complex. When a new subject-verb core is added to a simple sentence, each core and the words associated with it are called *clauses*. This is explained more fully in the chapters on compound and complex sentences.

The exercises in this half of the chapter are designed to help you expand your sentences while at the same time keeping you aware of their subject-verb cores. We will add words before the subject, between the subject and the verb, and after the verb.

The chart below shows the simple sentence patterns with blanks to indicate where words and phrases will be added. Some of the longer patterns are omitted because they do not present new problems; their only difference lies in the number of subjects and/or verbs. Study the chart carefully; then go on to the exercises.

EXPANDED SIMPLE SENTENCE PATTERNS

1. *The "you understood" pattern:*

   After supper, wash the dishes.

   _____ **V** _____ .

2. *Words before the subject:*

   Early in the spring, George proposed.

   _____ **S**   **V.**

3. *Words between the subject and verb:*

   George, my darling husband, proposed.

   S _____ **V.**

4. *Words after the verb:*

   George proposed to my best friend.

   S   **V** _____.

5. *Words before the subject, between the subject and verb, and after the verb:*

Early in the spring George, my darling husband, proposed a fishing trip.

_____ **S** _____ **V** ____ .

6. *Pattern 5 with multiple subjects:*

Before doing their homework each day, Don, Gene, and Leon, eager and ambitious, sold large boxes of candy to melancholy housewives.

_____ **SSS** _____ **V** _____ .

7. *Pattern 5 with multiple subjects and multiple verbs:*

Under the old house, a skunk, a raccoon, and a bearded vagabond, unconscious of the blizzard, snored, fidgeted, and belched throughout the night.

_____ **SSS** _____ **VVV** _____ .

Check for yourself. You will find no more than one subject-verb core in any of the above patterns. They are all *simple* sentences.

You have seen that many words can be added to a simple sentence, and it can remain simple. When you add an S-V core without being aware of it, you may create problems with punctuation and make your meaning unclear. The following exercises are designed to make you aware of the presence of more than one S-V core.

PRACTICE 9

Under each of the six subject-verb cores below there are five choices. Circle the letter of those choices that do *not* contain additional S-V cores.

Part A

1. The senators debated . . .
   a. the representatives adjourned.
   b. loudly, bitterly, and angrily.
   c. with the highly opinionated lobbyists.
   d. until the late hours of the morning.
   e. the president slept.

2. The explorers arrived . . .
   a. late at night.
   b. the treasure was gone.

c. at an ancient Aztec village in the jungle.

d. Jake was never seen again.

e. in time to find 80 cans of bean soup, 20 cases of rice pudding, and thousands of heartburn pills.

3. Many people talk . . .

a. a great deal about life and death.

b. long into the night.

c. who listens?

d. others keep quiet.

e. no one knows the answers.

✔ Grade and correct your work before proceeding.

Part B

1. The pitcher pitched . . .

a. a spitball.

b. the catcher was ready.

c. a long, looping, deceptive curve.

d. the catcher fumbled.

e. two no-hit games.

2. Margaret sang . . .

a. her husband objected.

b. completely out of tune.

c. at the Sunday evening church picnic.

d. her voice was delightful.

e. to the group of noisy children.

3. The attorneys for the defense argued . . .

a. for the prisoner's release.

b. the prosecutor was angry.

c. the judge banged his gavel.

d. very convincingly.

✔ e. the defendant wept.

Adding Words to Expand the S-V Core

The following exercises provide practice in expanding the simple sentence from very brief subject-verb combinations to much longer and more complicated patterns. You are asked to add words before subjects, between subjects and verbs, and after verbs. You are not given the technical terms for the various words and phrases but are told that they should *not include new subject-verb patterns*.

Remember that we are concentrating on the basic structure of simple sentences because, once you have learned to recognize and handle the subjects and verbs, you tend to make few other errors. Such errors as you are likely to make will be examined at later points in this book.

Adding Words before the Subject

PRACTICE 10

From the choices (1–17) below, select three phrases for each subject-verb core which will make the cores into good, sensible, simple sentences. Do *not* select clauses. (Clauses, remember, contain S-V cores and would make the sentences compound or complex.) *Suggestion:* First, read over all of the choices to eliminate the clauses; then match the phrases. Some of the phrases may fit more than one core.

1 a. _____ priest knelt before the altar.

   b. _____ " " " " "

   c. _____ " " " " "

2 a. _____ Litt exposes graft effectively.

   b. _____ " " " "

   c. _____ " " " "

3 a. _____ he was attending school.

   b. _____ " " " "

   c. _____ " " " "

4 a. _____ jewels are very expensive.

   b. _____ " " " "

✔   c. _____ " " " "

CHOICES:

1. Nobody knew that
2. They hired a guard because
3. Old, white-haired, and black-frocked, the
4. According to the May issue of *Crime,*
5. Unlike his trouble-making friends,
6. After many hours of indecision, the
7. Despite great sacrifices,
8. The president realizes that the
9. During the most difficult years of the Depression,
10. Modern in style, beautifully arranged, the
11. Until dawn the
12. His mother was so happy that
13. The girl's

14. In *Hold Tight,* the author's first book on crime,
15. Before the police arrived, the
16. She objected bitterly because the
17. When the congregation had left, the

Inserting Words between the Subject and the Verb

Various words and phrases can be placed between the subject and the verb of a simple sentence without making it compound or complex. There are only two basic restrictions: (1) that no new subject-verb cores be injected; (2) that the additional words be pertinent to the idea of the sentence and make sense.

Here are some examples:

The old man walked down the street.
The old man, reeking with whiskey, walked down the street.
The old man, my father's friend, walked down the street.
The old man from my father's town walked down the street.

Note that commas are added when the added words are not essential in identifying the subject and when the added words interrupt the flow of the idea.

PRACTICE 11

Select phrases from the list below and insert them in the spaces between the subjects and the verbs. Read all of the sentences and all of the phrases before you start. Select the most apt phrase for each sentence. Add commas where necessary.

PHRASES:

half drowned
attending the convention
sightless eyes staring blankly ahead
ever helpful
still shouting for women's rights

typing feverishly
my best friend
wearing a floppy red hat
in the middle of the lake
a career soldier

1. The foreign correspondent _____ wrote the story from memory.

2. Boy Scouts _____ came to his assistance.

3. The Suffragettes _____ marched down the street.

4. The delegates _____ listened to the chairman's speech.

5. After the storm the sailor _____ staggered to his bunk.

6. The blind beggar _____ suddenly collapsed.

7. The lieutenant _____ reenlisted.

8. The rowboat _____ was overturned.

9. Juan _____ loaned me the money.

✔ 10. The fat woman _____ rode gaily down the street.

FINAL TEST

Part A: *Individual Simple Sentences*

Write ten simple sentences with words preceding the subjects, words between the subjects and verbs, and words following the verbs. In at least three of these sentences, use multiple subjects and multiple verbs. Select your words carefully and try to make each sentence distinct and meaningful. Underline your subjects once and your verbs twice.

Part B: *Simple Sentences in Context*

Using one of the topics suggested below, write a ten-sentence paragraph containing *only simple sentences.* BE CAREFUL. Many students who can write good individual sentences lose their sentence sense or "feel" when they write paragraphs. That is one reason for all the drill that you have been subjected to. When you have completed your paragraph, examine each sentence as a separate unit. Underline your subjects and verbs. If any of your sentences are incomplete, correct them. If they are not simple sentences, make them simple.

NOTE: You will find it difficult to write a paragraph full of simple sentences. It is more natural to use a variety of sentences. This exercise is aimed at making you aware of your sentence structure in context.

TOPICS:
My Old Car Was Better than My New Car
Women (Men) Cannot Be Trusted
TV Commercials Should (Should Not) Be Banned
You Are What You Eat
Pornographic Words Should (Should Not) Be Used in School
    Publications
Old Folks Are People Too

what you have learned in chapter 4

Starting with sentences containing one verb and "*you* understood" as the subject, this chapter has explored many simple sentence patterns. It has demonstrated that neither the number of subjects and verbs nor the total number of other words in the sentence changes its basic structure. As long as all subjects are together and all subjects relate to all verbs, the sentence is simple. Once the subjects and verbs *alternate,* the sentence usually (there are a few exceptions) becomes compound or complex. Sure knowledge of the simple sentence provides the groundwork for building more complicated sentences because all sentences depend on simple sentences as part of their basic structure.

P—Key 1

A. Sit, March, Sing, Beg

Study Hint: *Ran* is a verb, but it is in the past tense. Remember that you are looking for verbs in the present tense. Someone is telling/asking someone else to do something. Try adding "please." You might say, "Please sing," or "Please run." You wouldn't say, "Please underwear," "Please ran," or "Please surprising."

B. Teach, Scream, Pitch, Ride, Blink

C—Key 1

(1) A simple sentence can contain any number of consecutive subjects and consecutive verbs as long as they form only one S-V core. (2) A simple sentence becomes a compound or complex sentence when subjects and verbs *alternate*, S-V, S-V. (3) simple, compound/complex (4) *Consecutive* means following one after the other without interruption. (5) *Alternate* means to follow each other by turns.

P—Key 2

(1) gallop (2) giggled (3) moistens (4) crowed (5) blow
(6) dance (7) swim (8) warms (9) electrocutes (10) smelled

P—Key 3

(1) Advertisers (2) The pickets (3) Rioters (4) Dynamite
(5) Bigots (6) Lovers (7) A prisoner (8) Merry-go-rounds
(9) Students (10) A child

P—Key 4

(1) African farmers grow huge mangoes (or) Huge African farmers grow mangoes. (2) The colonists landed at Plymouth Rock. (3) Fresh vegetables are good for you. (4) The rocket is headed for Mars (or) Mars is headed for the rocket. (5) Many children love to go camping.

P—Key 5

(Subjects may be in any order.)
(1) Fish and toads (toads and fish) swim underwater. (2) Moles and rabbits eat celery every day. (3) Movie stars and ballplayers usually marry early. (4) Farmers and their families feed the nation. (5) Young boys and girls eat alligators (or) Young girls and alligators eat boys. (or?)

P—Key 6

(Verbs may be in any order.)
(1) Ivan <u>swore</u> and <u>grunted</u> (<u>grunted</u> and <u>swore</u>). (2) Ignazio <u>fertilized</u> and <u>seeded</u> the lawn. (3) The militia <u>defends</u> our shores and <u>keeps</u> the peace. (4) Sparrows <u>eat</u>, <u>chirp</u>, and <u>flutter</u> all day. (5) Igor <u>borrowed</u> some money and <u>rented</u> a car.

P—Key 7

(1) <u>girls</u> <u>are coming</u> (2) <u>you</u> <u>can untie</u> (3) <u>party</u> <u>will be held</u> (4) <u>they</u> <u>have won</u> (5) <u>John Smetz</u> <u>is coming</u> (6) <u>Olga</u> <u>has</u> (7) <u>eclipse</u> <u>will take place</u> (8) <u>she</u> <u>did marry</u> (9) <u>dog</u> <u>did have</u> (10) <u>he</u> <u>is</u>

P—Key 8

(1) He <u>placed</u> (2) beans <u>are</u> (3) cow <u>is</u> (4) people <u>are</u> (5) He <u>is</u> (6) They <u>are sitting</u> (7) mess <u>is</u> (8) pails <u>are</u> (9) he <u>is</u> (10) "*you* under-stood" <u>put</u>
There is used as an adverb in 1, 5, 6, 8 (There by . . .), 9, 10.

P—Key 9

A. (1) b, c, d   (2) a, c, e   (3) a, b
B. (1) a, c, e   (2) b, c, e   (3) a, d

P—Key 10

(1) 3/6/11/13   (2) 4/5/7/9/14   (3) 4/5/7/9   (4) 4/10/13/16

P—Key 11

(1), typing feverishly,   (2), ever helpful, (3), still shouting for women's rights,   (4) attending the convention   (5), half drowned,   (6), sightless eyes staring blankly ahead,   (7), a career soldier,   (8) in the middle of the lake   (9), my best friend,   (10) wearing a floppy red hat

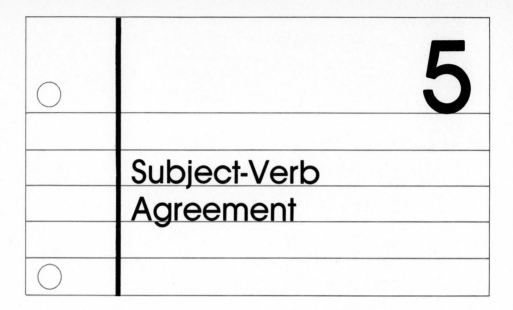

Subject-Verb Agreement

Before moving from simple sentences to compound and complex sentences, we will examine a weakness that afflicts many sentences—errors in subject-verb agreement. In every sentence the verb must agree with the subject in number and person; therefore, students who have trouble with subject-verb agreement tend to write papers with many flaws.

THE THREE ELEMENTS OF SUBJECT-VERB AGREEMENT

Agreement involves three distinct elements:

1. NUMBER.   You must know how to write singular and plural subjects, and you must be aware that they are singular or plural.
2. PERSON.   You must know whether your subject is in first, second, or third person.
3. VERB FORM.   You must be able to match the correct form of the verb to your subject.

We will examine each of these elements in turn.

Know the Subject's Number: Singular or Plural

When a word (or words) is used as a subject, it is considered a noun or noun form. (Nouns are defined in Chapter 11.) Most nouns can be made singular or plural. Some are identical in the singular and plural.

Listed below are most of the methods by which nouns are made plural, with examples of each. They are divided into four categories: (1) regular—those that can be learned by memorizing a particular rule; (2) irregular—those for which there is no rule; (3) those that can be either singular or plural; and (4) nouns that are only singular.

Study these rules and examples, especially those that give you trouble.

1. **Regular plural formation—according to rules.**

   A. Most common nouns form the plural by adding *s:*

frog	frogs	aspirin	aspirins
banana	bananas	toe	toes
trio	trios	pickle	pickles
bicycle	bicycles	night	nights
chief	chiefs	handkerchief	handkerchiefs
attorney	attorneys	turkey	turkeys
radio	radios	tobacco	tobaccos

   B. Most proper nouns add *s* or *es,* so that the basic spelling of the names is not changed. Proper nouns are specific names: George, Kleinmetz High School, *The Saturday Review,* Lake Huron.

Burke	Burkes	Jones	Joneses
Wiley	Wileys	Smith	Smiths
Will	Wills	Cohen	Cohens
DiFranco	DiFrancos	Skrscynski	Skrscynskis

   C. Nouns that end with *sh, ch, s,* or *x* add *es:*

box	boxes	church	churches
brush	brushes	fish	fishes[1]
gas	gases	glass	glasses

   D. Nouns that end in a consonant plus *y* drop the *y* and add *ies:*

secretary	secretaries	fly	flies
sky	skies	baby	babies
ally	allies	enemy	enemies
variety	varieties	boundary	boundaries

2. **Irregular plural formation—rules don't always apply. Use dictionary when in doubt.**

   A. Some nouns ending with a consonant followed by an *o* add *es;* some just add *s;* some can be spelled both ways:

silo	silos	volcano	volcanoes (os)
veto	vetoes	potato	potatoes
cello	cellos	embargo	embargoes

---

[1] The usual plural of *fish* is *fish: I have other fish to fry.* When referring to different species, the plural is *fishes: The lake was stocked with fishes of many varieties.*

B. Some nouns change their final *f* or *fe* to *ves*:

loaf	loaves	half	halves
elf	elves	thief	thieves
knife	knives	leaf	leaves
wife	wives	calf	calves

C. Some nouns change their internal spelling:

louse	lice	goose	geese
mouse	mice	man	men
foot	feet	woman	women
		tooth	teeth

3. Some nouns are identical in the singular and plural. The context of the sentence tells the reader which number is intended: *He saw one Japanese. He saw ten Japanese. He saw a group of Japanese.*

moose	moose	Chinese	Chinese
deer	deer	sheep	sheep

4. Some nouns are used only in the singular.

The *furniture* is here. The *wheat* was planted. The *rice* has been harvested. His *courage* is great.

NOTE: Pronouns may also be singular or plural. They must agree in number with the nouns they are replacing and also with their verbs. Pronoun problems are discussed in Chapter 11.

Handling Your Numbers Problem

The following exercises are intended to give you practice and to make you aware of the numbers problem. *The best rule is: when in doubt about a word, look it up.* Most standard dictionaries give irregular plurals and indicate whether a word is used as a plural or collective noun.

PRACTICE 1

Write the plural form of the following nouns:

1. mouse	9. company	17. goose
2. fish	10. dynamo	18. pea
3. bird	11. turkey	19. potato
4. secretary	12. box	20. tooth
5. administrator	13. bus	21. man
6. city	14. embryo	22. thief
7. deer	15. enemy	23. variety
8. antelope	16. jelly	24. boundary

25. embargo	34. church	43. attorney
26. ally	35. Japanese	44. quantity
27. baby	36. calf	45. Murphy
28. moose	37. foot	46. house
29. radio	38. sheep	47. stone
30. child	39. key	48. Smith
31. loaf	40. lady	49. ox
32. engineer	41. studio	50. study
33. Jones	42. veto	

Write the singular form of the following nouns:

1. eggs	18. cantaloupes	35. locomotives
2. astronauts	19. fraternities	36. lettuce
3. peas	20. Abercrombys	37. liabilities
4. bottles	21. subsidies	38. globes
5. tomatoes	22. countries	39. elves
6. ladies	23. nations	40. revenues
7. moose	24. O'Briens	41. G-men
8. Chinese	25. belles	42. Fitches
9. apples	26. stevedores	43. diamonds
10. Frenchmen	27. trophies	44. ditties
11. receivers	28. penguins	45. phenomena
12. studies	29. cherries	46. estuaries
13. shelves	30. committees	47. plagues
14. benches	31. Longfellows	48. freemen
15. astronomers	32. attorneys	49. ducks
16. classes	33. journeys	50. localities
17. peasants	34. women	

✔ CHECK YOUR ANSWERS.   CORRECT YOUR ERRORS.

Know the Subject's Person: First, Second, or Third

There are three persons: first, second, and third. They may be either singular or plural in number.

FIRST PERSON.   The speaker(s) or writer(s).

FIRST PERSON SINGULAR: I
FIRST PERSON PLURAL: we

SECOND PERSON.   The person or persons being spoken to.

SECOND PERSON SINGULAR: you
SECOND PERSON PLURAL: you

THIRD PERSON.   Anyone or anything else.

THIRD PERSON SINGULAR: she, he, it, the cat, the pot, etc.
THIRD PERSON PLURAL: they, the Baltimore Orioles, the apricots, etc.

NOTE: It should be easy to remember that *I* and *we* are first person, *you* is second person, and all the rest are third person. All nouns are third person.

COMPREHENSION CHECK 1

1. The three types of persons are: _____, _____, and _____.
2. The two types of number are: _____ and _____.
3. Provide the following pronouns:

first person singular: _____   second person plural: _____

first person plural: _____   third person singular: _____

✔ second person singular: _____   third person plural: _____

Match the Subject with the Correct Verb Form

Once you know whether your subject is singular or plural and whether its person is first, second, or third, you are ready to mate it with the proper form of the verb.

Verbs that Add *s* or *es*

All verbs, except the various forms of *be* and some helping verbs, end in *s* or *es* in the *third person singular* of the *present tense.*[1] *Remember:* When the subject is singular, the verb ends in *s;* no *s* when the subject is plural.

	SINGULAR	PLURAL
FIRST PERSON	I do too much. I sometimes stutter. I go there often.	We do too much. We sometimes stutter. We go there often.
SECOND PERSON	You do too much. You sometimes stutter. You go there often.	You do too much. You sometimes stutter. You go there often.
THIRD PERSON	She does too much. He sometimes stutters. The turtle goes there often.	They do too much. Boys sometimes stutter. The turtles go there often.

[1] Verbs ending in *y* (*dry, deny, apply,* etc.) change the *y* to *i* and add *es: dries, denies, applies.* Tense is discussed in detail in Chapter 10. For the purposes of this chapter you need only know about the present and past tenses. Take careful note of the examples given for each exercise and you should have no problem.

In the preceding examples, note that the only ending changes take place in the verbs that match the third person singular subject. Also note that all of the verbs are in the *present tense.* The changes do not occur in other tenses except in the *be* verbs.

Study the following examples, bearing in mind that the *s* ending is found only in the *third person singular:*

I travel every year.   (first person singular)
You travel on Sundays.   (second person, singular or plural)
She travel*s* frequently.   (third person singular)

We love you.   (first person plural)
You love us.   (second person, singular or plural)
They love you.   (third person plural)
Pedro and Josette love you.   (third person plural)

The cowboy ride*s* into the sunset.   (third person singular)
The team win*s* regularly.   (third person singular)
The bats fly at midnight.   (third person plural)
The companies buy our car.   (third person plural)

PRACTICE 2

Part A. Underline the correct verb in the following sentences.

1. The turtle (swim, swims) fairly rapidly.
2. Porpoises (swim, swims) fast.
3. The hens (lays, lay) over 140 eggs per week.
4. Crocodiles and alligators (eats, eat) fish.
5. The lawyers (speaks, speak) to the jury.
6. You (runs, run) too slowly.
7. The roosters (crows, crow) every morning.
8. They (fertilizes, fertilize) their grass too often.
9. I (buy, buys) a new car every twenty years.
10. They (arriving, arrive, arrives) tomorrow.

Part B. In the first five sentences change the subjects to the first person (I or we) and in 6-10 change them to the second person (you). Change the verbs if necessary. Underline your subjects and verbs.

EXAMPLE: The hare hops rapidly about. I hop rapidly about.

1. The freight train passes through here every morning.
2. The planes take off on time.
3. The student studies five hours a day.
4. He adjusts the microscope carefully.
5. She manipulates the boat with great dexterity.

6. The child catches the ball very well.
7. Who claims to know everything?
8. My neighbors go to work early.
9. He does the dishes every night.
✔ 10. The cows are sleeping in the sun.

Part C. The paragraph below is written in past tenses. Rewrite it in present tenses. Change only the verbs. Underline them. The first sentence should be changed to read: "I find the old man at home."

I found the old man at home. As usual, he was sitting on the front stoop waiting for me. We sat and talked awhile. He invited me to dinner. I decided to join him. His dog, Joe, ate with us. Jake tossed him bones and some bread. Joe chewed the bones and also chewed my shoes. Jake ate slowly. He talked a great deal. We traded jokes and stories. We thoroughly enjoyed each other's company. Jake said goodbye glumly. I saw him through the window for the last time. He had filled his pipe and was sitting ✔ by the fireplace rocking slowly back and forth.

ASSIGNMENT 1

Write 20 simple sentences using the subjects indicated. Use the subject first in its singular form and then in its plural form. Mate each subject with a different verb in the PRESENT tense. Use no *be* forms.

EXAMPLE:

(boat) a. The boat leaks.
b. The boats sail well.

1. car
2. I
3. man
4. prune
5. girl
6. horse
7. factory
8. deer
9. knife
10. piccolo

ASSIGNMENT 2

Write 20 simple sentences in the PRESENT tense. Use each word below as a verb twice: (a) in the first person singular, and (b) in the third person singular.

EXAMPLE:

(eat) a. I eat apples.
b. She eats worms.

1. do	6. want
2. desire	7. claim
3. stay	8. box
4. go	9. receive
5. deny	10. play

Verbs that Change in Various Ways

As demonstrated in the last few pages, most verbs change only in the third person singular of the present tense. The *be* verbs, however, change in *all three singular persons* in both *present* and *past tenses*. In the table below, these forms are matched with their subjects in person and number. Memorize this table. It is important to know these forms by heart because they are the most frequently used in the language, not only by themselves but also as auxiliaries.

	SINGULAR	*Present*	*Past*	PLURAL	*Present*	*Past*
FIRST PERSON:	I	am	was	We	are	were
SECOND PERSON:	You	are	were	You	are	were
THIRD PERSON:	He, she, it etc.	is	was	They	are	were

Study the examples below to identify the *be* forms as to person (first, second, or third), number (singular or plural), and tense (past or present). In some sentences they are used as auxiliaries.

PRESENT TENSES

SINGULAR
First person: I *am* early.   I *am going* to pay you now.
Second person: You *are* a good friend.   You *are working* too hard.
Third person: He *is* a forger.   The food *is* excellent.   The weather *is* terrible. The rabbit *is running* away.   She *is screaming*.

PLURAL
First person: We *are* on time.   We *are assuming* power.
Second person: You *are* a fine group.   You *are playing* a great game.
Third person: They *are* sick.   They *are leaving* now.

PAST TENSES

SINGULAR
First person: I *was* a friend of hers.   I *was chasing* a rabbit.
Second person: You *were* her best friend.   You *were driving* too fast.
Third person: He *was* sick.   She *was* unfriendly.   It *was* red.   The company *was* bankrupt.   The potato *was* rotten.   A truce *was arranged*.

PLURAL

First person: We *were* there last year.   We *were singing* all night.   We *were delivering* the supplies.

Second person: You *were* slow in getting started.   You *were moving* erratically.

Third person: They *were* very happy.   They *were fishing* all night.

PRACTICE 3

Part A. Underline the correct word.

1. You three men (are, is) to come with me.
2. The company (were, was) recently incorporated.
3. I (am, are) leaving immediately.
4. Sam and I (am, are) forming a partnership.
5. Australia (are, is) sending a delegation.
6. You (is, are) expected to go to the party.
7. Thelma and Julia (is, are) kissing Edward and Frank now.
8. I (is, am, are) arriving on the noon plane.
9. The men and women (am, is, are) here in the conference room.
10. Lena and Egbert (is, was, were) with us.

Part B. Underline the correct word.

1. The soldiers (is, are, were) disembarking now.
2. The bakers (am, are, is) baking day and night.
3. We (were, was) in Afghanistan last week.
4. They (is, are, were) fighting all last week.
5. They (was, were, is) playing.
6. We (are, is) on the island now.
7. I (were, was) going to town.
8. You (was, were) with them at the time.
9. You (was, is, were) riding in the back seat.
10. I (was, am, were) there yesterday.

PRACTICE 4: A Review

Part A. Read this paragraph; then answer the questions below.

(1) The Cochran family likes to watch TV. (2) Mr. Cochran watches his favorite soap opera every day. (3) Mrs. Cochran likes the science fiction programs. (4) George, the son, catches every football game. (5) The daughters prefer basketball games and variety shows.

Below, list the subjects and verbs for each sentence.

1. _____

2. _____

3. _____

4. _____

5. _____

6. List the singular subject(s). _____

7. List the plural subject(s). _____

8. The paragraph is written in the _____ tense.

9. Most verbs (but not forms of *be*) end in _____ when their subjects are singular.

10. Most plural subjects end in _____ or _____.

11. The verb *prefer* in the last sentence of the paragraph does not end in

✔ _____ because the subject is _____.

Part B. Rewrite the paragraph below in the present habitual tense—as if it happens every day. In this paragraph some *be* verbs are used. Underline the verbs you write. The first sentence should read:

Evelyn <u>chops</u> wood for the stove, <u>cooks</u> breakfast, and <u>kisses</u> Randy goodbye.

Evelyn chopped wood for the stove, cooked breakfast, and kissed Randy goodbye. He was going to the sawmill. He worked there every day. For lunch she and a neighbor were planning to catch fish in the brook. After lunch she cleaned the cabin, chopped some more wood, weeded the vegetable garden, and set some rabbit traps. She brought home the rabbit caught the previous day, skinned it, and cooked it for supper. Later in the evening Randy got home tired from work at the mill. He told her how easy ✔ she had it at home.

ASSIGNMENT 3

Read this paragraph; then follow the directions below.

The typical harbor tugboat has a crew of about six men besides the captain. The mate helps the captain. A deckhand takes care of the huge ropes used on a tug. The chief engineer has charge of the engines. The oiler oils them and keeps the engine room clean. The fireman feeds the engines fuel. The cook, of course, cooks. The crew quickly learns the necessary teamwork to operate the boat efficiently.

Part A. Complete the following:

1. This paragraph is written in the _____ tense.
2. Each subject is _____.
3. Therefore each verb ends with _____.

Part B. (4–10) Rewrite the paragraph so that all of the subjects are plural. Your paragraph will begin: "Typical harbor tugboats have crews of about six men besides the captain." Underline all subjects. Double underline the verbs.

ASSIGNMENT 4

NOTE: Underline subjects and verbs in all parts of this assignment.

Part A. Write a total of six simple sentences. In each sentence use a different *be* verb in the first, second, third person singular and plural, PRESENT tense.

Part B. Write six sentences as above in the PAST tense.

Part C. Compose ten simple sentences by completing the terms below. Use the correct form of *is, are, am, were, was* as auxiliaries or as individual verbs. You may use each verb more than once.

1. The camels
2. Apples, lemons, and bananas
3. The companies
4. Lulu and I
5. The governors
6. After the earthquake, the people
7. Despite the warning, the club
8. The girl
9. We
10. The inhabitants of the island

Part D. Write five pairs of sentences of your own using *is, are, am, were, was.* In the first sentence of each pair, use the verb alone; in the second sentence, use it as an auxiliary.

BRINGING IN PREPOSITIONAL PHRASES

In Chapter 3 you learned to insert words and phrases between subjects and verbs without losing track of the subjects and verbs. The type of phrase most frequently used in this in-between position is the *prepositional phrase.* These phrases are groups of words which start with a preposition and end with a noun or noun form called the object of the preposition: *over the hill, under the dam, beyond the horizon.*

When the prepositional phrase is written between the subject and verb, the writer sometimes confuses the object of the preposition with the subject of the sentence and makes errors in agreement of subject and verb. This happens when the subject and object differ in number. For example, if the subject is plural but the object of the preposition is singular, you might make the mistake of using a singular verb:

Incorrect: The ships in old Boston Harbor was small.
Correct: The ships in old Boston Harbor were small.

When checking your sentences for agreement of subject and verb, it is especially valuable to be able to recognize prepositional phrases because they *never* contain the subject or verb of the sentence.

COMPREHENSION CHECK 2

1. A prepositional phrase must contain at least two words, a _____ and its _____.
2. A group of words which starts with a preposition and ends with its object is called a _____.
3. The prepositional phrase is often placed between the _____ and _____ of a sentence.
4. The _____ of a preposition is a noun or a _____ form.
5. The prepositional phrase is mentioned here in particular because its _____ is sometimes confused with the _____ of the sentence.
6. Prepositional phrases may contain words other than the _____ and its _____, but they never contain the _____ or the _____ of the sentence.
7. If you confuse the object of your _____ with the subject of your _____, you may write the wrong form of the verb.
8. This problem in agreement arises because the subject of the sentence may be different in _____ from the _____.

Prepositional Phrases

Few students err in writing prepositional phrases. The greatest value in knowing about them is that they help you to see which words in a sentence are *not* your subject or your verb. If you have no trouble with your subjects and verbs, you have little to worry about in regard to prepositional phrases.

In all of the prepositional phrases below, the first word is the preposition and the last word is its object. Notice, first of all, how common these phrases are, and then remember that there are no subjects or verbs in them.

about time	to the house	beneath the starry sky
above your head	without help	beside the lovely lady
across the field	for you	up the creek
after the storm	in place	by way of introduction
against the wall	during the night	to bed

along the path	as for your question	through the window
among the people	at night	from the post office
between the trees	before sunrise	from him
but Fred	behind the shed	except Snodgrass
concerning your father	below the deck	down the drain

In the sentences below at least one prepositional phrase is inserted in brackets between each subject and verb. Read them carefully and note how a careless writer might confuse the object of the preposition (the last word of the prepositional phrase) with the subject of the sentence.

1. The crate [of apples] was shipped yesterday.
2. His team [of horses] works hard.
3. The men [on top] [of the red roof] are drunk.
4. Butchers [from the eastern part] [of Nova Scotia] are holding a convention.
5. The child [in the blue suit and brown shoes] is crying.
6. One [of those dangerous criminals] is at large.
7. Each [of the contestants] still has a chance to win.
8. The children [in the big red house] [on the other side] [of the dark and muddy river] wave [at us] every day.
9. None [of the men] has signed the contract.
10. The ladies [in the clubhouse] are fighting.

PRACTICE 5

Rewrite the paragraph below in the PRESENT tense as you did in Practice 4B. In this exercise the emphasis is on correct subject-verb agreement in sentences whose subjects and verbs are separated by prepositional phrases. Your first sentence should read: *Computer specialists from many countries regularly attend a conference in San Francisco.* In the second sentence add "usually" after "meeting." Otherwise, change only the verbs.

(1) Computer specialists from many countries attended a conference in San Francisco. (2) The delegates at the business meeting voted on some important issues. (3) Questions by one of the delegates confused the new chairman. (4) Most of the delegates were bored by the speeches. (5) One of them, over the objections of several diehards, made a motion for adjournment. (6) The chairman, under pressure, called the question. (7) Almost everyone in the room voted to end the meeting. (8) The chairman, with the overwhelming support of the delegates, provided welcome news. (9) Cocktails were being served in the lobby.

ASSIGNMENT 5

Complete the sentences below. Keep them SIMPLE and in the PRESENT tense. Underline your subjects once and your verbs twice. Put brackets around the prepositional phrases. Warning: In two sentences prepositional phrases precede the subjects of the sentences.

1. The men on the tree-covered island in the middle of the lake
2. Somebody in the upper stands
3. Children under the age of six, in the company of an adult
4. The old man in the tobacco-stained, baggy suit
5. In spite of their troubles, the people of Upper Slobovia
6. The girls in the class of 1942
7. Neither of the two terror-stricken teenagers
8. The team of carefully-trained firefighters
9. In early May members of the most famous marching band in the country
10. The friendly, hungry, chattering birds in our tree house

The following exercise is designed to show you how other words and phrases as well as prepositional phrases can get between the subjects and the verbs. Keep in mind that we are continuing to work with *simple* sentences. The ground rules are that any number of words which enhance the meaning of the sentence may be added except those which form new subject-verb cores.

PRACTICE 6

Underline the subject of each sentence once; then double underline the proper verb from the choices in parentheses.

Part A

1. The veteran, tired, worn, and discouraged, (is, are, am, were) going home.
2. Professor Limbo, wishing to be friendly, (tell, tells) three jokes to his early morning classes every Monday.
3. The astronauts, daring and resourceful men, (am, is, was, are) planning to land on the moon.
4. The highbrows, filled with dreams of social improvement or self-aggrandizement, (are, is, am, was) leaving the universities.
5. In early autumn the leaves, saturated with the colors of the sun, slowly (drop, drops) from the trees.
6. The miser, hated by many, finally (give, gives) his money to the poor.
7. His childhood, full of sweet and sour memories, (comes, come) back to him on days like this.

8. India, with its countless starving and its royal rich, its myriad views, its starkness and its pageantry, (beckon, beckons) the adventurous traveler.
9. The milk in the pot, bubbling furiously, (spill, spills) on the floor.
✔ 10. The actress, gay and charming, (have, has) a deep baritone voice.

Part B

1. The rabbi, deep in meditation, (do, does) not hear the thunder.
2. The soldier, obeying his orders, (shoot, shoots) the stranger.
3. The children, dressed in Nature's own apparel, (dive, dives) into the pool.
4. Computers, precise, efficient, accurate-appearing, (is, am, are, was) far from perfect.
5. The house on the corner of Bog and Jay Streets (lean, leans) to one side.
6. Elephants, gray, lumbering, quizzical beasts, (lie, lies) in the shade of the tree.
7. There by the pond (are, is, am, was) ten nuts.
8. There, but for the grace of God, (go, goes) I.
9. Where (is, are) the man in the yellow shirt?
✔ 10. The Ancient Mariner, starved and tortured, (cry, cries) for help.

ASSIGNMENT 6

Part A. Underline the subjects once in the phrases below and complete the sentences. Underline your verbs twice. Keep all of your writing in the PRESENT tense. Do not use any form of *be*.

1. The maniac, screaming and shouting,
2. In the late afternoon, the dog in the apartment next door
3. The baritone, bowing from the waist,
4. Fishermen in small, unseaworthy boats
5. Jane, ill for many months,
6. The rescue squad, sirens shrilling,
7. Winston Churchill, speaking before Parliament,
8. The boa constrictor, its body curled tightly around the antelope,
9. Love and peace, together
10. His car, rusty and dilapidated,

Part B. Write ten simple sentences of your own in which your subjects are separated from your verbs by words or prepositional phrases (no new subject-verb cores). Use different subjects and verbs in each sentence. Keep them all in the PRESENT tense. Underline your subjects once and your verbs twice.

Part C. Rewrite the paragraph below changing the verbs to PRESENT tense. In this exercise various phrases separate subjects and verbs. The first sentence should say: *Elathia Dopp is disappointed.* Be sure to copy correctly.

(1) Elathia Dopp was disappointed. (2) She, as the latest in a long line of beauty queens, had been quickly disillusioned by it all. (3) The queen, instead of being treated like a queen, was being "packaged and sold" like any other commercial product. (4) Her manager, a gruff, overdressed publicist, rushed her constantly. (5) On many days Elathia was scheduled for six to eight personal appearances. (6) Advertising agencies in every city had contracted for her time. (7) Photographers, hurrying to meet deadlines, were often rude. (8) Despite traveling almost constantly and getting little rest, she at all times was required to look fresh and beautiful. (9) Elathia, already feeling like an old queen, was anxious to be dethroned.

what you have learned in chapter 5

Making subjects and verbs agree involves an understanding of *number* (singular and plural) and of first, second, and third *person.* Most verbs change only in the *third person singular* of the *present tense,* but *be* verbs require special study because they change into various forms, and they change in the *past* as well as the *present tense.* It is also important to recognize prepositional phrases because, often coming between subject and verb, they cause agreement problems.

(If you are still uncertain about subjects and verbs, the subject-verb core, the simple sentence, or agreement of subject and verb, review the necessary sections of chapters 3, 4, and 5 before proceeding to Chapter 6.)

P—Key 1

Plural

1. mice	18. peas	35. Japanese
2. fish, fishes	19. potatoes	36. calves
3. birds	20. teeth	37. feet
4. secretaries	21. men	38. sheep
5. administrators	22. thieves	39. keys
6. cities	23. varieties	40. ladies
7. deer	24. boundaries	41. studios
8. antelopes, antelope	25. embargoes	42. vetoes
9. companies	26. allies	43. attorneys
10. dynamos	27. babies	44. quantities
11. turkeys	28. moose	45. Murphys
12. boxes	29. radios	46. houses
13. buses, busses	30. children	47. stones
14. embryos	31. loaves	48. Smiths
15. enemies	32. engineers	49. oxen
16. jellies	33. Joneses	50. studies
17. geese	34. churches	

Singular

1. egg	3. pea	5. tomato
2. astronaut	4. bottle	6. lady

7. moose	22. country	37. liability
8. Chinese	23. nation	38. globe
9. apple	24. O'Brien	39. elf
10. Frenchman	25. belle	40. revenue
11. receiver	26. stevedore	41. G-man
12. study	27. trophy	42. Fitch
13. shelf	28. penguin	43. diamond
14. bench	29. cherry	44. ditty
15. astronomer	30. committee	45. phenomenon
16. class	31. Longfellow	46. estuary
17. peasant	32. attorney	47. plague
18. cantaloupe	33. journey	48. freeman
19. fraternity	34. woman	49. duck
20. Abercromby	35. locomotive	50. locality
21. subsidy	36. lettuce	

C—Key 1

(1) first, second, third   (2) singular / plural   (3) I; we; you; you; she / he / it; they

P—Key 2

A.   (1) swims   (2) swim   (3) lay   (4) eat   (5) speak   (6) run   (7) crow   (8) fertilize   (9) buy   (10) arrive

B.   (1) I / We pass   (2) I / We take   (3) I / We study   (4) I / We adjust   (5) I / We manipulate   (6) You catch   (7) You claim   (8) You go   (9) You do   (10) You are sleeping.

C.   I find. . . . he is sitting. . . . We sit and talk. . . . He invites. . . . I decide. . . . His dog. . . eats. . . . Jake tosses. . . . Joe chews. . . . chews. . . . Jake eats. . . . He talks. . . . We trade. . . . We enjoy. . . . Jake says. . . . I see. . . . He fills / has filled . . . is sitting . . .

P—Key 3

A.   (1) are   (2) was   (3) am   (4) are   (5) is   (6) are   (7) are   (8) am   (9) are   (10) were

Study hint: If you missed any of the above, review page 81 before proceeding.

B.   (1) are   (2) are   (3) were   (4) were   (5) were   (6) are   (7) was   (8) were   (9) were   (10) was

P—Key 4

A.   (1) family likes   (2) Mr. Cochran watches   (3) Mrs. Cochran likes   (4) George catches   (5) daughters prefer   (6) family, Mr. Cochran,

Mrs. Cochran, George   (7) daughters   (8) present   (9) *s*   (10) *s/es*
(11) *s, plural*

B.   Evelyn <u>chops</u> . . . <u>cooks</u> . . . and <u>kisses</u>. . . . He <u>is going</u>. . . . He <u>works</u>.
. . . <u>she</u> and a neighbor are <u>planning</u>. . . . she <u>cleans</u> . . . <u>chops</u> . . .
<u>weeds</u> . . . and <u>sets</u>. . . . She <u>brings</u> . . . <u>skins</u> . . . and <u>cooks</u>. . . . Randy
<u>gets</u>. . . . He <u>tells</u>. . . . she <u>has</u>. . . .

C—Key 2

(1) preposition, object   (2) prepositional phrase   (3) subject / verb   (4) object, noun   (5) object, subject   (6) preposition, object, subject / verb
(7) preposition, sentence   (8) number, object of the preposition.

P—Key 5

(1) specialists . . . attend   (2) The delegates . . . vote   (3) Questions . . . confuse   (4) Most . . . are bored   (5) One . . . makes   (6) The chairman
. . . calls   (7) everyone . . . votes   (8) The chairman . . . provides
(9) Cocktails are being served

P—Key 6

A.   (1) <u>veteran</u> <u>is going</u>   (2) Professor <u>Limbo</u> <u>tells</u>   (3) <u>astronauts</u> <u>are planning</u>   (4) <u>highbrows</u> <u>are leaving</u>   (5) <u>leaves</u> <u>drop</u>   (6) <u>miser</u> <u>gives</u>
(7) <u>childhood</u> <u>comes</u>   (8) <u>India</u> <u>beckons</u>   (9) <u>milk</u> <u>spills</u>   (10) <u>actress</u> <u>has</u>

B.   (1) <u>rabbi</u> <u>does hear</u>   (2) <u>soldier</u> <u>shoots</u>   (3) <u>children</u> <u>dive</u>   (4) <u>Computers</u> <u>are</u>   (5) <u>house</u> <u>leans</u>   (6) <u>Elephants</u> <u>lie</u>   (7) <u>nuts</u> <u>are</u>   (8) <u>I</u> <u>go</u>
(9) <u>man</u> <u>is</u>   (10) <u>Ancient</u> <u>Mariner</u> <u>cries</u>

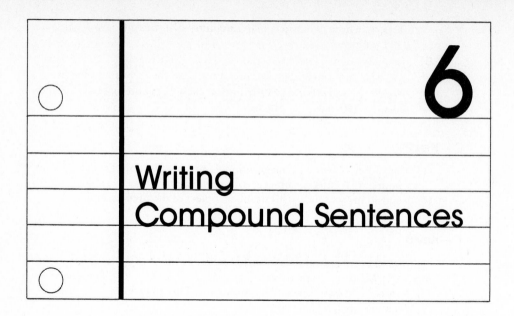

6

Writing Compound Sentences

In mastering the simple sentence and subject-verb agreement, you have come a long way. But mature writers must also master compound and complex sentences. Your problem now is to continue to keep control of your sentences as you write more complicated patterns.

The purpose of this section is to give you practice with expanding simple sentences into compound sentences. The many exercises in this section will help you recognize and eliminate sentence faults such as run-ons and comma splices by making you more aware of how compound sentences are structured.

WHAT IS A COMPOUND SENTENCE?

A compound sentence consists of two or more simple sentences joined together by one or more coordinate conjunctions or by a semicolon. Various patterns are possible, as shown in the diagrams below.

Main (Independent) Clauses. The parts of compound sentences that separately would be considered simple sentences are called *main clauses*. In other words, once two or more simple sentences have been combined to make a compound sentence, the simple sentences become main clauses.

Coordinate Conjunctions. Key parts of the compound sentence are coordinate conjunctions like *and, or, so,* and *however.* They are used to tie two or more main clauses together. *However* and a group of similar conjunctions are usually called *conjunctive adverbs.* They are discussed later in this chapter.

COMPOUND SENTENCE PATTERNS: Four Ways to Connect

Main clauses (simple sentences) can be joined in four ways to form compound sentences:

1. the "and—but" pattern
2. the "either . . . or" pattern
3. the "semicolon—however" pattern
4. the "semicolon alone" pattern

We will examine each of these patterns and look at some examples.

1. **The "and—but" pattern.**

, and   , but   , or   , nor   , for   , yet   , so

These are the most common coordinate conjunctions. When they are used to connect main clauses (except very short ones), they are preceded by commas. (They also connect words and phrases, for example: cat *or* dog; into the house *and* over the new rug; kind *but* firm.) *So* is considered a coordinate conjunction when *and* can be substituted. "It stopped raining, *so* we went home." "The temperature was 90, *so* we stayed up late." (See p. 104, note 1.)

	coordinate	
MAIN CLAUSE	conjunction	MAIN CLAUSE
S-V	, (CC)	S-V

The President arrived early, *yet* he missed the Prime Minister.
Gregory went to the beach, *but* he did not find Vivian.
She didn't invite you, *nor* does she plan to.
(Note the inverted subject and verb.)

There can, of course, be more than two subject-verb cores. In this case the conjunction is added before the last clause in the series.

| S-V | , | S-V | , | S-V | ,CC | S-V | . |

Some bury their dead in tombs, some burn their dead, some throw the bodies into the river, *and* some give their dead to the vultures.

2. **The "either . . . or" pattern.**

either . . . or   not only . . . but (also)   neither . . . nor

In this pattern one of the paired conjunctions is placed at or near the beginning of the sentence, and the other is placed between the clauses. Note that in the third example, where the clauses are longer, a comma is used.

CC _____ S-V _____ *CC* _____ S-V _____ .

Either John will go to Mary *or* Mary will come to John.
Neither did the enemy appear *nor* did the fog lift.
Not only did the delegation reach Iran quickly, *but* they *also* brought good news with them.
(Notice the inversion of subjects and verbs in the two examples above.)

Avoid pattern 2 when the simple sentence form would be more effective:

Preferred: Either Ben or Louise will go.
Acceptable: Either Ben will go, or Louise will go.

3. **The "semicolon—however" pattern.**   The eleven coordinate conjunctions (called *conjunctive adverbs*) below are different from other coordinate conjunctions in three respects:

a. They always work with semicolons in compound sentences.
b. They don't always stay next to the semicolons. They can be found in various positions.
c. They often begin new sentences.

; accordingly	; however	; then
; consequently	; moreover	; therefore
; furthermore	; nevertheless	; thus
; hence	; otherwise	

Commas are usually placed after some of these conjunctions when they immediately follow the semicolon.

_____ SS-V _____ ; *CC* _____ S-VV _____ .

The governor and mayor agree privately; *however*, they will not release a statement or make a speech.

The strike was called during the harvest; *consequently,* much food was spoiled.
They were invited by the President himself; *nevertheless,* they decided not to go.

Now, note how the semicolon maintains its position between the main clauses, and how the conjunction functions in other parts of the sentence. Also note the use of the commas to set off the conjunctions.

The governor and mayor agree privately; they will, *however,* not release a statement or make a speech.
The strike was called during the harvest; much food, *consequently,* was spoiled.
They were invited by the President himself; they decided not to go, *nevertheless.*
She wanted to marry John desperately; Peter had more money, *however.*

4. **The "semicolon alone" pattern.**   The semicolon alone acts as a weak period or a strong *and* in compound sentences. Writers use it between two main clauses whose ideas are closely related when they feel that the period would interrupt the idea too much and the *and* is unnecessary or inappropriate. Avoid using it too often. A period is usually better.

Hans went to Denmark; Elsa followed shortly.
The trainmen went on strike; all rail shipment was delayed.
We do not seek power; we do not seek glory.

COMPREHENSION CHECK 1

1. A _____ consists of two or more simple sentences joined together by one or more _____ or by a _____.
2. The parts of compound sentences that separately would be considered simple sentences are called _____.
3. List the seven most common coordinate conjunctions.
4. List the eleven conjunctions that are used with semicolons.
5. What punctuation mark can act like a coordinate conjunction?
6. List three coordinate conjunctions which come in pairs.
7. End punctuation, conjunctions, or semicolons are needed when the writer adds new _____ cores.

MEANINGS AND USES OF SOME COORDINATE CONJUNCTIONS

The conjunctions listed below (all of which follow the ''semicolon—however'' pattern) are grouped in three general categories:

A. Conjunctions which indicate that the ideas they introduce follow *as a result of* or *in agreement with* the preceding idea:

accordingly
I received my orders at midnight; *accordingly,* I was on my way at one A.M.

consequently
The strike took place in the middle of the harvest; much food, *consequently,* was spoiled.

hence
He did not report to work; *hence* he did not receive his pay.

thus
The peace negotiations were begun, and the major issues were settled; *thus* the war was finally ended.

therefore
We received no information; *therefore,* we did not vote.

then
The jury listened to the testimony; *then* they passed judgment.

B. Conjunctions which indicate that the ideas they introduce are *in opposition to* or *in spite of* what preceded:

nevertheless
They were shot at by a mysterious prowler; they, *nevertheless,* decided to stay in the neighborhood.

however
She wanted to marry John desperately; *however,* Peter had more money.

C. Conjunctions that suggest *in addition:*

moreover
We had wanted to travel for many years; *moreover,* we finally had the money.

furthermore
They will sue you for damages if you don't pay them; *furthermore,* they may press criminal charges against you.

PRACTICE 1

Use the correct conjunctions from the "semicolon—however" pattern in the sentences below. In some cases more than one conjunction may be used correctly.

1. The doctor gave strict orders; _____ the patient did not obey them.
2. The employers paid no attention to the demands of the workers; _____ the strike was called by the union.
3. The employers tried to negotiate with the union; _____ the strike was called.
4. We finally got the conflicting parties to the conference table; _____ we also got them to sign an agreement favorable to both sides.
5. Married for 72 years, they still seemed to be very much in love; _____ they insisted on a divorce.
6. The company is in desperate need of money; _____ its credit rating is very good.
7. The company's credit rating is very low; _____ it cannot borrow money.
8. She loved him with all her heart; _____ she reported him to the police.
9. The prosecutor could not refute the defense arguments; _____ he dropped the charges against the youth.
10. The agency will pay for the old man's bills; _____ it will provide him with shelter.

ASSIGNMENT 1

A. Write five sentences using the "and—but" pattern and five sentences using the "semicolon—however" pattern. Use different conjunctions in each sentence.

B. Write three sentences using the "either . . . or" pattern and two using the "semicolon alone" pattern.

THE RUN-ON AND THE COMMA SPLICE

The run-on sentence and the comma splice are considered incorrect writing, and they must be avoided. As the term suggests, a run-on occurs when you start a new sentence without placing a period at the end of the previous one. A comma splice occurs when you place only a comma between sentences instead of a period, a comma and conjunction, or a semicolon.

Run-on: Friendly governments contributed
                            funds relief workers fed and nursed
                            the hungry.

Comma splice:	Friendly <u>governments</u> <u>contributed</u> funds, relief <u>workers</u> <u>fed</u> and <u>nursed</u> the hungry.
Corrected with a period:	Friendly <u>governments</u> <u>contributed</u> funds. Relief <u>workers</u> <u>fed</u> and <u>nursed</u> the hungry.
Corrected with a comma and a conjunction:	Friendly <u>governments</u> <u>contributed</u> funds, and relief <u>workers</u> <u>fed</u> and <u>nursed</u> the hungry.
Corrected with a semicolon:	Friendly <u>governments</u> <u>contributed</u> funds; relief <u>workers</u> <u>fed</u> and <u>nursed</u> the hungry.

If you stay aware of your subject-verb cores, you can avoid run-ons and comma splices by using conjunctions and punctuation correctly.

PRACTICE 2

Part A. All of the following are run-on sentences or comma splices. Correct them by adding periods and the necessary capital letters only. Change commas to periods if necessary. Underline subjects once and verbs twice.

1. George, Sally, and Millie found Sam in the pond he was eating goldfish.
2. The hounds ran over the bridge, around the lake, and deep into the woods, the skunk had no chance at all.
3. Up to the square marched the protestors, singing and shouting there they ended the parade.
4. After the battle the men rested on the ground some drank French wine.
5. The psychologist listened carefully for many hours the patient talked.
6. Later in the day they had a picnic the sun set quickly.
7. Everyone ate heartily after the program they fell asleep.
8. Long after dawn the fog held tight to the ground, it kissed the grass, almost smothering it with love.
9. Come home with me, give me your hand you are my best friend.
10. The antelope darted daringly in front of the car there was a screech of brakes, Sarah screamed.

Part B. Some of these are correct. If they are, place a C to the left of the number. If they are incorrect, correct them by adding periods and capital letters only. Change commas to periods if necessary. Underline subjects once and verbs twice.

_____ 1. Dagwood went home, Selma stayed with Lucy, and Babbs left town.

_____ 2. The organization voted Millie the money after the meeting she resigned.

_____ 3. The little boy deflated the tires of his father's car all by himself his sick father reinflated them.

_____ 4. The angry settlers chased the Indians far across the plains before dawn the Indians regrouped and attacked again.

_____ 5. Write carefully and clearly, indent for paragraphs, punctuate as necessary.

_____ 6. Industry needs you; you need industry.

_____ 7. He saddled the horse and rode quickly after his brother the horse took him rapidly out of sight into the sun it sank suddenly, hiding the disappearing silhouette.

_____ 8. She was black as the night she was sweet she was kind.

_____ 9. He destroyed all before him and left the women and children sobbing in the dust.

_____ 10. The child ran home the house burned down, and the ashes glowed all night.

Part C. In the paragraphs below, correct the run-ons and comma splices by inserting periods and capital letters only. Change commas to periods if necessary. Correct each paragraph before doing the next one.

1. According to recent statistics, the anti-smoking campaigns of the 1970's helped decrease smoking in the 1980's, a researcher at the University of Michigan came to these conclusions after studying the influence of health warnings on public opinion there were many factors present in the late 1970's to cause an increase in smoking, the factors included increased smoking by women, the lowering of cigarette prices, and the introduction of more low-tar cigarettes instead of increasing, however, per capita smoking fell about one percent.

2. Breakfast is the most important meal of the day in the opinion of many authorities they cite the long wait between supper and lunch and the need for nutrition to fuel the day's activities some people actually eat a very small lunch; therefore, they get very little nutrition for long periods, many of these people also stuff themselves with junk food from evening until midnight some nutritionists actually suggest six well-planned meals a day this helps many people avoid junk food snacks.

3. The arctic explorer was alone, but he was not completely alone, he heard the sounds of an animal scuffling outside he knew of only one kind of animal in the vicinity, polar bears his rifle was beside him, but it was unloaded he was afraid to make a sound for fear of attracting the bear's attention he huddled in his sleeping bag and prayed silently, he thought of

his wife and children in Nebraska the bear ripped the tent into shreds, the explorer gave up hope, suddenly the bear left, and the traveler never knew why.

ASSIGNMENT 2

In the paragraphs below, correct the run-ons and comma splices by inserting periods and capital letters only. Change commas to periods if necessary. Do not change sentences that are correct.

(*2 run-ons, 1 comma splice*)

1. There is no need for study halls in high school they are a waste of time and effort. Some students want to study, rooms should be provided for them. Others should be allowed to take extra classes, participate in recreational activities, or go home it should be up to each student to decide for himself.

(*2 run-ons, 1 comma splice*)

2. My friend, Liza, works at St. John's Hospital in the morning she takes me to work every day, and I pay her $4.00 a week. I would like to get a job there myself, I am qualified for the work it is highly specialized.

(*2 run-ons, 1 comma splice*)

3. The draft had been a major problem in America since the 1950's. Demonstrations took place in many cities New York had one of the worst over one hundred students were arrested during one demonstration. This shocked many people, it was a very serious situation.

(*2 comma splices, 2 run-ons*)

4. Many drivers are very careless, a careful driver must be doubly on the alert. He must constantly scan the road as far ahead as possible he must check his side and rear view mirrors. He must expect someone to overlook a stop sign or ''jump'' a red light too quickly in this way he can be ready to compensate for the errors of others and help avoid an accident, this is called defensive driving.

what you have learned in chapter 6

Compound sentences are formed by adding two or more *simple sentences* together with *coordinate conjunctions.* Each simple sentence is then called a *main clause.*

To avoid writing *run-ons* or *comma splices,* you must place the proper conjunctions and/or punctuation between the main clauses. In most cases a comma *and* a coordinate conjunction are required. Sometimes a semicolon is used. When a sentence is comprised of a series of main clauses, commas are placed between each clause, and a comma and coordinate conjunction are placed before the final clause.

Writing compound sentences is simple if you have learned to write simple sentences well and have learned the coordinate conjunctions.

C—Key 1

(1) compound sentence, coordinate conjunctions, semicolon   (2) main clauses   (3) and, but, or, for, yet, so, nor   (4) accordingly, consequently, furthermore, hence, however, moreover, nevertheless, otherwise, then, therefore, thus   (5) semicolon   (6) either—or, neither—nor, not only—but (also)   (7) subject-verb

P—Key 1

(1) however or nevertheless   (2) therefore, consequently, or hence   (3) however or nevertheless   (4) moreover or furthermore   (5) however or nevertheless   (6) however or nevertheless   (7) therefore, consequently, or hence   (8) however or nevertheless   (9) therefore, consequently, or hence   (10) furthermore or moreover

P—Key 2

A.   *Check not only whether you put the periods in the right places, but also whether you underlined the S-V cores properly.*

1. George, Sally, and Millie found . . . pond. He was eating goldfish.
2. The hounds ran . . . woods. The skunk had . . . all.
3. . . . marched the protestors . . . shouting. There they ended the parade.
4. . . . men rested . . . ground. Some drank . . .
5. The psychologist listened . . . hours. The patient talked. (*Or*) The psychologist listened . . . carefully. For . . . patient talked.
6. . . . they had . . . picnic. The sun set quickly.
7. Everyone ate . . . program. They fell asleep. (*Or*) Everyone ate heartily. After . . . they fell asleep.
8. . . . fog held . . . ground. It kissed . . . love.
9. Come home with me. Give me your hand. You are my best friend.
10. The antelope darted . . . car. There was a screech of brakes. Sarah screamed.

B.
1. C
2. The organization voted . . . money. After . . . she resigned.
3. boy deflated . . . himself. His father reinflated them. (*Or*) boy deflated car. All by himself . . . father reinflated them.
4. The angry settlers chased . . . plains. Before dawn the Indians regrouped and attacked again. (*Or*) The angry . . . before dawn. The Indians . . . again.
5. Write . . . clearly. Indent for paragraphs. Punctuate as necessary.
6. C

7. He <u>saddled</u> . . . <u>rode</u> . . . brother. The <u>horse</u> <u>took</u> . . . sun. <u>It</u> <u>sank</u> . . .

8. <u>She</u> <u>was</u> . . . night. <u>She</u> <u>was</u> sweet. <u>She</u> <u>was</u> kind.

9. C

10. The <u>child</u> <u>ran</u> home. The <u>house</u> <u>burned</u> down, and the <u>ashes</u> <u>glowed</u> all night.

C. (1) According . . . 1980's. A researcher . . . opinion. There . . . smoking. The . . . cigarettes. Instead . . . one percent.

(2) Breakfast . . . authorities. They . . . activities. Some . . . periods. Many . . . midnight. Some . . . day. This . . . snacks.

(3) The . . . completely alone. He heard . . . outside. He . . . bears. His . . . unloaded. He was . . . attention. He huddled . . . silently. He thought . . . Nebraska. The bear . . . shreds. The explorer . . . hope. Suddenly . . . why.

Writing
Complex Sentences

The final step in sentence development is the building of the complex sentence. All sentences are simple, compound, complex, or a combination of these three types. Just as with the compound sentence, *complex sentence writing depends on a firm knowledge of the subject-verb core and the use of conjunctions.*

WHAT IS A COMPLEX SENTENCE?

A complex sentence consists of a main clause and at least one subordinate (dependent) clause.

Main Clause. The parts of complex sentences that separately would be considered simple sentences are called *main clauses.*

Subordinate Clause. A subordinate clause is a group of words which is usually introduced by a subordinate conjunction and which contains one subject-verb core. A *subordinate conjunction* is any word on the list below which introduces a subordinate clause and which connects that clause to a main clause.

SUBORDINATE CONJUNCTIONS

It is important to memorize the conjunctions listed below because they are the keys to the complex sentence. It is also important to note that these words can act as parts of speech other than conjunctions. *They are conjunctions only if they introduce subordinate clauses and connect them to main clauses.* You will also occasionally find other words or other combinations of the words below which act as subordinate conjunctions.

after	how	till	whether
although	if	unless	*which*
as	in order that	until	*whichever*
as if	provided that	what	while
as far as	since	whatever	*who*
as long as	so[1]	when	*whoever*
as soon as	so that	whenever	whom
because	*that*[2]	where	whomever
before	though	wherever	why

The Subordinate Conjunction—a Handy Tool

While the coordinate conjunctions add equal clauses together, the subordinate conjunctions add unequal clauses. The examples below illustrate some of the results that are possible when you combine two simple sentences into one complex sentence. Notice how important the conjunction (shown in italics) can be to the meaning of the new complex sentence.

Simple: John is a fool.
John does not like girls.

Complex: *Because* John is a fool, he does not like girls.
John is a fool *because* he does not like girls.
John, *who* does not like girls, is a fool.

Simple: Mary had been ill for weeks.
Mary went away.

Complex: *After* Mary had been ill for weeks, she went away.
Mary, *who* had been ill for weeks, went away.
Since she had been ill for weeks, Mary went away.

---

[1] The *so* used as a subordinate conjunction usually has the meaning of *so that* (in order that) as compared with the *so* used as a coordinate conjunction (see page 93). In modern writing there is a tendency to use *so* rather than *so that*. This *so* can be used to introduce the first clause in a sentence or a following clause: "*So* we could get married, I went to work." "I went to work *so* we could get married."

[2] The five conjunctions in italics (*that, which, whichever, who, whoever*) sometimes serve two functions, as will be seen later in this chapter.

Although we use mostly two-clause sentences in this chapter, note how easy it is to write more fluidly by using subordinate conjunctions to combine a group of simple sentences into one complex sentence.

Simple: Ned is in trouble again.
            Ned was my neighbor.
            Ned has been in jail before.
            Ned is worried.

Complex: *Because* he has been in jail before, Ned, *who* was my neighbor, is worried, *as* he is in trouble again.

COMPREHENSION CHECK 1

1. Sentences are of three types: _____, _____, and _____, or a _____ of these three.
2. In writing compound sentences we combine two or more _____ clauses by using _____.
3. In this section we will use _____ conjunctions to form _____ sentences.
4. A complex sentence consists of a _____ clause and at least one _____ clause.
5. A subordinate clause is a group of words which contains one _____ core and is usually introduced by a _____ conjunction.
6. When a main clause is combined with a subordinate clause, the result is a _____ sentence.
7. A _____ sentence is made up of two or more main clauses connected by one or more _____.
8. A _____ sentence is made up of a main _____ and a _____ clause. The two clauses are usually connected by a _____ conjunction.
9. A _____ conjunction is any word on the _____ conjunction list which introduces a subordinate _____ and connects that clause to a _____ clause.
10. _____ are the keys to complex sentences.
11. It is important to note that the words used as _____ conjunctions can act as _____ other than _____ conjunctions.
12. They are _____ conjunctions only if they introduce _____ clauses and connect them to _____ clauses.
✔ 13. _____ are the keys to compound sentences.

DISTINGUISHING BETWEEN A PHRASE AND A CLAUSE

A subordinate clause must be introduced by a subordinate conjunction and must contain a subject and a verb. Therefore if a word on the subordinate conjunction list is not followed by a subject and verb, it is introducing a *phrase,* not a clause.

PRACTICE 1

Part A. In the exercises below, place a C next to the clauses and a P next to the phrases. In the subordinate clauses, underline the subjects once and the verbs twice. Circle the subordinate conjunctions.

1. _____ after the fight in the old, red barn

2. _____ until they arrive

3. _____ because of the earthquake in Lower Slobbovia

4. _____ although the people of the province want peace

5. _____ while she watches the baby

6. _____ when the clock strikes

7. _____ before the early hours of misty dawn

8. _____ since the beginning of recorded time

9. _____ as deep as the deepest ocean

✔ 10. _____ whether he wishes to go

Part B. In this list are other words and phrases along with subordinate clauses. Find the subordinate clauses and underline the subjects once and the verbs twice. Circle the subordinate conjunctions.

1. slowly, carefully, inch-by-inch
2. as soon as they left
3. into the stream, over the hill, under the bridge, across the valley
4. learning about the arrival of their friends
5. as swiftly as he could run
6. jeering, chanting, shouting, screaming
7. since you were sleeping
8. though we love you dearly
9. provided that you do not fight back
✔ 10. in order that we can be sure of your loyalty

RECOGNIZING COMPLEX SENTENCES
and Reviewing the Simple and Compound

- The **simple sentence** has only one subject-verb core.
- The **compound sentence** has two or more subject-verb cores in main (independent) clauses joined by coordinate conjunctions and/or semicolons.
- The **complex sentence** must have a main clause and at least one subordinate clause introduced by a subordinate conjunction.

Study the examples; then do the exercises.

Simple: The delegates spoke at the conference.

Compound: The delegates spoke at the conference, *and* the leaders listened.

Complex: The delegates did not know *when* they should speak.

PRACTICE 2

Part A. Place an S by the simple sentences, a C by compound sentences, and a Cx by complex sentences. Underline subjects and verbs. Circle conjunctions.

1. _____ The people in the city have short tempers, and they fight a lot.

2. _____ In the winter, after the heavy snows had fallen, Jeff visited his old farm.

3. _____ She wrote to him, but he never answered.

4. _____ She loved him when others did not.

5. _____ After lunch they left.

6. _____ Before they left, they voted.

7. _____ They spent the money which their father gave them.

8. _____ Which of them will go?

9. _____ He did not know why they came.

✔ 10. _____ My friend, who lives near here, is ill.

Part B. Place a P by phrases, an S by simple sentences, and a Cx by complex sentences. Circle conjunctions. Underline subjects once and verbs twice.

_____ 1. She blushed when he pinched her.

_____ 2. Throw the ball!

_____ 3. After supper, by the beach, near the sea.

_____ 4. After eating supper.

_____ 5. After they ate supper, they hiked along the beach.

_____ 6. Stan ran far into the forest long before breakfast.

_____ 7. The Secretary of State will speak to you, provided that you disarm.

_____ 8. Since you desire peace, you must agree.

_____ 9. When I go to a sale, I get all excited.

✔ _____10. Before supper at the Lakeview Hotel in Kalamazoo.

PRACTICE 3

Write from memory the 36 subordinate conjunctions listed at the beginning of the chapter. Continue to retest yourself until you know all of them by heart.

PRACTICE 4

Try to list from memory the 20 coordinate conjunctions you learned in Chapter 6. Refer to the lists to check yourself.

ASSIGNMENT 1: Review of Sentence Types

Write 15 sentences of your own: five simple (1–5), five compound (6–10), and five complex (11–15). Underline all subjects and verbs. Circle all conjunctions.

COMPLEX SENTENCE PATTERNS

Complex sentences fall into four general patterns. In keeping with our aims in this chapter, we focus on the subject-verb cores and on the function of the subordinate conjunctions. This conjunction sometimes acts only as a connector and sometimes acts as both a connector and the subject of the subordinate clause (see all the B patterns, plus 4A, B, and C). The conjunctions that can perform this dual function form a special group of subordinate conjunctions called *relative pronouns.* They are *who, whoever, which, whichever,* and *that. What* and *whatever* (not relative pronouns) can also function as subordinate conjunctions and subjects. Understanding the function of the subordinate conjunction can help you keep better control of your complex sentences.

We will look at each of the patterns in turn; then we will work with them one at a time.

Pattern One: *The main clause comes first.* It is connected to the subordinate clause by a subordinate conjunction (*scj*).

1A. *The subordinate conjunction acts only as a conjunction.*

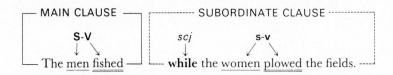

1B. *The subordinate conjunction acts as both conjunction and subject of the subordinate clause.*

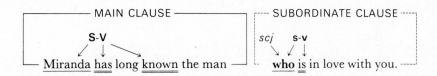

Pattern Two: *The subordinate clause comes first.* It is followed by the main clause. The conjunction is often, but not necessarily, the first word in the sentence. A comma separates the clauses when the subordinate clause is placed first.

2A. *The subordinate conjunction acts only as a conjunction.*

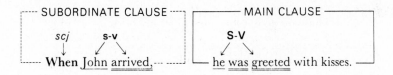

2B. *The subordinate conjunction acts both as connector and as subject of the subordinate clause.*

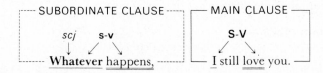

Pattern Three: *The subordinate clause is placed between the subject and the verb of the main clause.*

3A. *The subordinate conjunction acts only as a connector.*

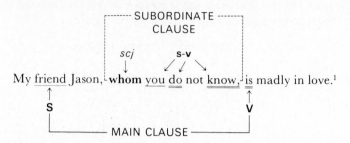

My friend Jason, whom you do not know, is madly in love.[1]

3B. *The subordinate conjunction acts both as connector and as subject of the subordinate clause.*

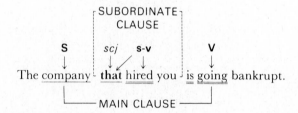

The company that hired you is going bankrupt.

Pattern Four: *An entire clause acts as a unit.* A subordinate clause *as a whole* is the subject of a sentence, the object of a preposition, or a direct object. When it functions in this manner, it is called a *noun clause.*

4A. *The subordinate clause is the subject of the sentence.*

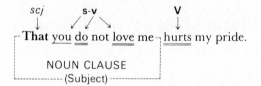

That you do not love me hurts my pride.

4B. *The subordinate clause is the object of a preposition.*

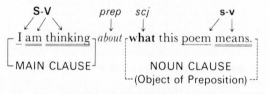

I am thinking about what this poem means.

---

[1] For an explanation of the use of commas in this sentence and no commas in 3B, see "Commas that separate non-restrictive appositives" in Chapter 9.

4C. *The subordinate clause is the direct object.*

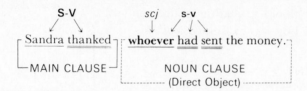

Note that in 4C the conjunction is also the subject of the clause. These patterns can also occur in 4A and 4B.

COMPREHENSION CHECK 2: Review

1. Complex sentences fall into _____ general patterns.
2. In the first pattern, the _____ clause comes first, and it is connected to the _____ clause by a _____.
3. In the second pattern, the _____ clause comes first, and it is followed by the _____ clause.
4. In the second pattern, the _____ is often the first word of the sentence.
5. In the third pattern, the _____ clause is injected between the _____ and the _____ of the _____ clause.
6. In some cases the subordinate conjunction can also act as the _____ of the _____ clause.
7. In Pattern Four complex sentences, an entire subordinate clause can act as the _____ of a sentence, the _____ of a preposition, or as a _____ object.
8. The clauses described in #7 above are called _____ clauses.
9. A complex sentence is made up of a _____ clause and a _____ clause. The two clauses are usually joined by a _____.
10. A subordinate conjunction is any word on the subordinate conjunction list which introduces a _____ clause and connects that clause to a _____ clause.
11. A clause is a group of words which contains a _____ core.

Review of Pattern One

The main clause comes first. It is connected to the subordinate clause by a subordinate conjunction.

EXAMPLES

    1. She was angry *because* George was late.
    2. The thief hid *until* the policeman left.
    3. The boy was examined *while* his parents waited.

ASSIGNMENT 2

Part A. Write five Pattern One sentences, using the conjunctions indicated. Underline your subjects once and your verbs twice.

(1) *after*   (2) *since*   (3) *that*   (4) *if*   (5) *where*

Part B. Following Pattern One, write five complex sentences using other subordinate conjunctions. Underline your subjects once, your verbs twice, and circle your subordinate conjunctions.

Review of Pattern Two

    The subordinate clause is placed *before* the main clause. Note the comma after the subordinate clause.

EXAMPLES

    1. *Before* they left, it rained.
    2. *As soon as* the message arrives from the Vatican, we will call a meeting of the Bishops.
    3. *Whoever* she is, I will not go out with her.

Don't let introductory words or phrases fool you. The next three sentences are also examples of Pattern Two complex sentences.

    4. In spite of all the complaints *that* he made, he really loved the camp.
    5. Wondering *if* help would ever come, she waited, shivering, on the narrow ledge.
    6. In our part of the country, *when* strangers arrive, we welcome them warmly.

PRACTICE 5

Part A. Rewrite the Pattern One sentences below to change them to Pattern Two, and rewrite the Pattern Two sentences to change them to Pattern One. Change only the order of the clauses and the necessary punctuation and capitalization.

1. We will stay here until we hear from you.
2. If the emergency is really great, the people will respond.
3. As long as everyone agrees, we will continue the meeting.

4. Solutions cannot be found to many of our problems while the war continues to rage.
5. They arrived in Spain after Franco had died.
✔ 6. Before the armies marched, the people prayed for peace.

Part B. The paragraph below has complex sentences. Circle the subordinate conjunctions. Underline all subjects and verbs.

(1) While she was looking into a pond, a princess dropped her golden crown into the water. (2) A frog offered to bring it back after he saw her cry. (3) The princess kissed the frog because he returned the crown. (4) As soon as she kissed him, the frog turned into a handsome prince. (5) When the queen caught them kissing, the princess told her about the frog. (6) After the queen heard that, she never again believed the
✔ princess.

ASSIGNMENT 3

Part A. Choosing any five of the conjunctions given, write five Pattern Two complex sentences. Underline your subjects once and your verbs twice. Be sure that your sentences have two subject-verb cores.

Unless	Wherever	In order that	After	So that
Whoever	Whatever	Since	Until	Before

Part B. Following Pattern Two, write five complex sentences using other subordinate conjunctions. Underline your subjects once, your verbs twice, and circle your subordinate conjunctions. Use different conjunctions in each sentence.

Review of Pattern Three

EXAMPLES

1. The man *whose* horse was stolen is here now.
2. The woman *whom* we trusted has disappeared.
3. The engine *that* was wrecked cannot be repaired.

PRACTICE 6

In the sentences below, circle the subordinate conjunctions and draw lines to connect subjects and verbs.

EXAMPLE

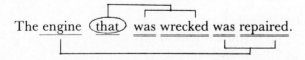

The engine (that) was wrecked was repaired.

1. The lady who left us the estate disappeared.
2. Countries where coconuts grow are usually tropical.

3. Many adult adoptees, whatever their experience has been, wonder about their natural parents.
4. The computer industry, which is growing rapidly, hires highly skilled engineers.
5. The ability to create life in a test tube, which has recently been achieved, should not be taken lightly.

ASSIGNMENT 4

Using the following conjunctions, write five Pattern Three sentences. Underline your subjects once and your verbs twice: *who   where   which   that   whatever*

Don't Confuse Pattern Three with Simple Sentences

In Chapter 4 you were told that as long as your subjects and verbs are consecutive, as long as they don't alternate, your sentence is simple. If, however, you look at the Pattern Three complex sentences, you find SS-VV, which appears to be the same as the simple sentence pattern. The difference is that, although the subjects and verbs are consecutive in Pattern Three complex sentences, each subject relates to a *different* verb. In simple sentences with multiple subjects and verbs, all of the verbs and subjects relate to each other. Note the examples below:

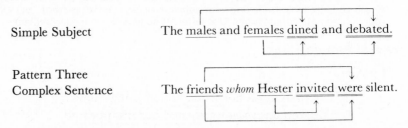

Simple Subject — The males and females dined and debated.

Pattern Three Complex Sentence — The friends *whom* Hester invited were silent.

The same test applies to those complex sentences in which the conjunction is omitted, as we shall see below.

Review of Pattern Four

EXAMPLES (The noun clause is in italics):

What he said was not clear.
Who sent the gift is still a mystery.
He believes in *what his father did.*
Clarice kept *whatever was not sold.*

PRACTICE 7

Unscramble each series of words to make Pattern Four sentences. Circle the conjunctions and underline the subjects and verbs. Place brackets around the noun clause.

1. judge what the reported was detective the to learned
   START WITH *What the detective*
2. located where is island the known is only three to explorers
   START WITH *Where the island*
3. ignored the whatever father the does child is by
   START WITH *Whatever the child*
4. mystery is city handles which the department problem a
   START WITH *Which city department*
5. the question cucumbers how can many barrel is hold the
   START WITH *How many*

ASSIGNMENT 5

Write five Pattern Four sentences of your own. Underline your subjects and verbs. Put brackets around your noun clauses.

Omitting the Subordinate Conjunction

In some complex sentences there is a tendency to omit the conjunction, especially *whom, which,* and *that.* Omitting the subordinate conjunction does not change the nature of the sentence. It is still complex. Here are some examples of complex sentences without conjunctions.

> She thinks [*that*] apricots are delightful.
> We met a couple [*whom*] we have known for many years.
> The mushrooms [*that*] they ate were poisonous.
> The opinions [*which*] I hold are shared by many other people.

PRACTICE 8

Using a caret (∧), insert the appropriate conjunction wherever it is missing.

1. The lawyer pointed to the man he hated.
2. She feels immoral movies should be banned.
3. He returned all the land he had stolen.
4. They thought dirty words should be deleted.
5. Florence believed nothing was sacred.
6. The dog he feared was dead.
7. Early last year the girl we loved so much eloped.

8. The cattle he had purchased were slaughtered.

9. Jim, the man she wanted to marry, refused to see her.

✔ 10. The animals they saw in the park were graceful.

ASSIGNMENT 6: Mid-Chapter Review

A. Write two complex sentences for each of the four major types. Underline subjects and verbs, circle subordinate conjunctions, and bracket noun clauses. Use this book to help you.

B. The story below is told in simple sentences. Rewrite it using as many different subordinate conjunctions as you can, but coordinate conjunctions are also allowed. You may use the conjunctions to combine sentences already in the story or to add new clauses that you invent. Mark your sentences in the usual manner.

EXAMPLE: *Since* our family and the Kotnik family have known and liked
each other for several years, we decided to go on a picnic together.

Our family and the Kotnik family have known and liked each other for several years. We decided to go on a picnic together. Each family was to go in its own car. We agreed on a time and place to meet. We also agreed to bring different foods to share. It rained the night before the picnic. In the morning the sun was shining brightly. The grass was still a little wet. We played volleyball and soccer. There were soft drinks for the children and beer for the adults. Sancho tried to start a fire to roast hot dogs. It began to rain. He couldn't get the fire started. We got tired and hungry. We left.

THE SENTENCE FRAGMENT

When working with compound sentences, you learned that a lack of knowledge about simple and compound sentences may cause you to write run-ons and comma splices. Similarly, a lack of understanding about phrases and subordinate clauses often leads to the writing of *fragments*. Like run-ons, fragments are considered serious errors because they usually indicate weakness in handling the basic thought unit of your language, and in many instances your writing may be unclear because of such errors.

Any group of words which is punctuated like a sentence but which does not fulfill the requirements of a sentence is a fragment. For example:

FRAGMENT	PROBLEM	SOLUTION
The diamond found on the roof.	no verb	The diamond was found on the roof. (or) The diamond found on the roof is mine.

FRAGMENT	PROBLEM	SOLUTION
Into the hot, sticky, serpent-infested jungle.	no subject or verb	Harold <u>went</u> into the hot . . . (or) Into the hot . . . <u>went</u> <u>Harold</u>.
Because he loves you very much.	no independent clause	Because <u>he</u> <u>loves</u> you very much, <u>he</u> <u>stopped</u> eating garlic.
Smuggling rum into the country.	no subject or verb	<u>They</u> <u>were</u> <u>smuggling</u> . . .
The pie tasted by the judge.	no verb	The <u>pie</u> <u>was</u> <u>tasted</u> . . . (or) The <u>pie</u> tasted by the judge <u>was</u> scrumptious.
Pedro Gonzalez, the doctor whom she met last night.	no independent clause	<u>Pedro</u> <u>Gonzalez</u>, the doctor whom <u>she</u> <u>met</u> last night, <u>proposed</u> to her.

More Examples of Fragments

We went to the theater. After the performance was over. We decided to get a bite to eat, but it was very late.

After the performance was over is, of course, a fragment. The writer obviously *thought* in terms of the complete idea. *After the performance was over, we decided to get a bite to eat, but it was very late.* He punctuated the subordinate clause, however, as if it were a complete sentence. Or, perhaps, he knew that he had written a subject-verb core, *performance was*, but he forgot that *after* is a subordinate conjunction.

PRACTICE 9

Correct the fragments below by using these proofreading marks:
   Use a slash (/) to reduce a capital letter to a small letter.
   Use a delete sign (ℐ) to remove a period.
   If you change a period to a comma, underline it (,).

EXAMPLE: Because he had been late all week. He knew that she would be angry. He loved her in a selfish way. Although he tried not to show it.

Because he had been late all week, He knew that she would be angry. He loved her in a selfish way, Although he tried not to show it.

1. They went for months at a time without sufficient food. Because they were stubborn. No one knew that they needed help. Until it was too late.

2. After the long, muggy, rainy season. Jeffrey tried to get through to the aid station. They died in agony. In spite of all his efforts.
3. They headed for cover as quickly as they could. Skidding and sliding over the icy snow they went. Until darkness covered everything.
4. When you decide. We will join you. Since you are now undecided. We will have to wait.
5. The child opened the heavy oak door. Not knowing what to expect. He trembled inwardly.

Conversational Fragments (Dialogue in Print)

Much of our normal conversation is spoken in fragments. When conversation is printed in articles and stories, these fragments are punctuated as if they are complete sentences.

(a) "How are you?"   (d) "Nothin'."
(b) "O.K."   (e) "Where d' y' live?"
(c) "What's new?"   (f) "Up th' street."

Examples *b, d,* and *f* are, of course, fragments. The usage is acceptable only for the writing of dialogue and only if the dialogue is enclosed in quotation marks and paragraphed properly.

Most students have no trouble in identifying such fragments. But they often have writing problems with the kinds of fragments listed below.

1. "When did you leave?"
   "After the show was over."
2. "Why did she fall out?"
   "Because the car turned the corner too sharply."
3. "Does your mother wear that outfit often?"
   "Whenever she goes out."
4. "When will they know?"
   "As soon as the mail arrives."

The four questions are all complete sentences; the replies are fragments. Fragments are correct when used as direct quotations in dialogue, as shown above, but they are incorrect when included as part of expository paragraphs. (The exception to this rule is discussed at the end of the chapter.) They are incorrect even though they contain S-V cores. That is because they begin with a subordinate conjunction (*after, because, whenever,* etc.) but they are not connected to a main clause. If you cover up the question in each example and read only the reply, you become aware that it is incomplete as it stands. Something is missing if you don't add a main clause.

Let's see what happens when we attach a main clause to the fragments. Compare each of the following complex sentences with the dialogue from which it was created.

1. I left *after* the show was over.
2. She fell out *because* the car turned the corner too sharply.
3. My mother wears that outfit *whenever* she goes out.
4. They will know *as soon as* the mail arrives.
5. He pleaded guilty *so that* he might get a lighter sentence.

PRACTICE 10

Convert each question-answer dialogue into a complex sentence. Underline your subjects once and your verbs twice; circle your subordinate conjunction. Don't write questions.

EXAMPLE: "Did he tell the truth?"
        "As far as I know."

        (As far as) I know, he told the truth.
        (or) He told the truth (as far as) I know.

1. "Would you vote for him for president?"
   "If he were the best man."

2. "Why did you give him the money?"
   "So that he could leave town."

3. "Will you join the fraternity?"
   "Provided that you lower the dues."

4. "Why did he commit suicide?"
   "Because no one seemed to care about his welfare."

COMPREHENSION CHECK 3

1. A lack of knowledge about _____ and _____ sentences may lead to the writing of run-ons and comma splices.
2. A lack of knowledge of phrases and _____ clauses may lead to the writing of fragments.
3. Fragments and run-ons are considered basic writing errors because they demonstrate ignorance of what a _____ is.
4. Students tend to write run-ons when they are not sure where one _____ ends and the next _____ begins.
5. A fragment results when one punctuates a _____ clause or a phrase as if it were a complete _____.

6. It is the _____ conjunctions which make it necessary to add _____ clauses.
7. The _____ conjunction makes a clause _____, therefore requiring the addition of a _____ clause.
8. A simple sentence contains one _____ core.
9. A compound sentence consists of two or more _____ connected by one or more _____.
10. A complex sentence consists of a _____ joined to a _____ by a _____.

PRACTICE 11

Identify the items below as sentences (S), run-ons (R.O.), comma splices (C.S.), or fragments (F).

1. He went to the movies, his wife went too.
2. After the long and tiresome lecture which no one understood.
3. Read this carefully.
4. Gregory delivered the mail that Lena wanted.
5. Give the mayor your carefully considered advice.
6. Despite the fact that he ignored the advice of all his friends of long standing.
7. Before he went.
8. Until you hear from me, don't answer the phone.
9. Who never believed a word.
10. He ran through the alley and into the street without thinking he was struck by a car and badly injured.
11. Kiss me.
12. Which some very lovely and scintillating person requested.
13. The delegate requested the majority to vote.
14. The armies of the Republic moved swiftly into position on the plains the enemy waited in tense expectation.
15. Men fight, women wait and sob, and children hide in fear.
16. Men fight, women wait.
17. After which everyone—man, woman, and child—on the slowly sinking ship was satisfied.
18. Whatever you, the cause of all my trouble and worries, may think.
19. So that no one, not even our enemies, will have to be hurt.
20. In the spring he entered the far end of the tunnel and worked his way toward the middle of the bats and poisonous snakes he knew little until he was attacked by them.

ASSIGNMENT 7

After correcting Practice 11, punctuate the three run-ons to make them into simple sentences and add main clauses to the eight fragments to change them into complex sentences.

When to Start Sentences with "And" or "But"

When you use coordinate conjunctions (*and, but, or, however,* etc.), you are doing so to connect a following statement with a previous one. In general, this is done *within* sentences. Sometimes, however, it is permissible to start sentences with these conjunctions. Usually this is done to emphasize the part of the sentence introduced by the conjunction:

> We will fight if we must. But we desperately want peace.
> You have been my friend for years. And I want it to stay that way.
> We have decided to send the money. However, you must guarantee its return.

It is considered substandard writing to overuse coordinate conjunctions at sentence beginnings. When you do this, you lose the effect that is gained by occasional use, your writing becomes rambling and indefinite, and you give the impression that you are not sure of your own sentence structure.

When to Use Fragments

Sentence fragments are acceptable in the same sense that sentences may occasionally be begun with coordinate conjunctions. Now and then in order to emphasize certain ideas introduced by a subordinate conjunction, it is acceptable to write a fragment. For example:

> We should allow more students into the college only under the conditions stipulated. When we have the facilities. When there is enough money. When they are eager to come.

You will see this technique used fairly often in advertising and in editorial writing. To overuse it makes your writing choppy, ineffective, and poorly structured. *As a general rule, it is wise to avoid writing fragments or starting sentences with coordinate conjunctions until you are a very skillful sentence writer.*

what you have learned in chapter 7

Complex sentences are formed by connecting *subordinate clauses* to *main clauses* with *subordinate conjunctions.*

A subordinate clause must not be treated as a simple sentence. If it is not attached to a main clause, it is considered a *fragment*. The subordinate conjunction prevents the clause from acting as an independent sentence.

Some students get confused about the difference between clauses and phrases because words used as subordinate conjunctions are also used to introduce many phrases. Simply remember that a clause contains a subject-verb core; a phrase does not.

The flexibility of the complex sentence is made possible by the various positions in which the subordinate clause can be placed: before the main clause, after it, or between the subject and verb of the main clause. Sometimes the entire subordinate clause acts as the subject of a sentence.

You now know the three basic sentence types: simple, compound, and complex. All other sentences are combinations of these three. The many exercises that you have worked with were intended to give you a *feeling* for sentence structure as well as a theoretical knowledge of it. Chapter 8 will put it all together.

C—Key 1

(1) simple / compound / complex, combination   (2) main, coordinate conjunctions   (3) subordinate, complex   (4) main, subordinate   (5) subject-verb, subordinate   (6) complex   (7) compound, coordinate conjunctions   (8) complex, clause, subordinate, subordinate   (9) subordinate, subordinate, clause, main   (10) subordinate conjunctions   (11) subordinate, parts of speech, subordinate   (12) subordinate, subordinate, main   (13) coordinate conjunctions

P—Key 1

A.   (1) P   (2) C *until* they arrive   (3) P   (4) C; *although* the people . . . want   (5) C; *while* she watches   (6) C; *when* the clock strikes   (7) P   (8) P   (9) P   (10) C; *whether* he wishes

B.   Clauses: (2) *as soon as* they left   (5) *as swiftly as* he could run   (7) *since* you were sleeping   (8) *though* we love you dearly   (9) *provided that* you do not fight back   (10) *in order that* we can be sure of your loyalty.

P—Key 2

A.   (1) C; The people . . . have . . . , *and* they fight . . .   (2) Cx; . . . *after* snows had fallen, Jeff visited . . .   (3) C; She wrote . . . , *but* he never answered.   (4) Cx; She loved him *when* others did not.   (5) S; *After* lunch they left.   (6) Cx; *Before* they left, they voted.   (7) S; They spent money *which* father gave . . .   (8) S; *Which* . . . will go?   (9) Cx; He did not know *why* they came.   (10) Cx; My friend, *who* lives . . . , is ill.

B.   (1) Cx; She blushed *when* he pinched her.   (2) S; *(You)* throw . . .   (3) P   (4) P   (5) Cx; *After* they ate supper, they hiked . . .   (6) S; Stan ran   (7) Cx; The Secretary of State will speak . . . *provided that*

you disarm. (8) Cx; *Since* you desire peace, you must agree.
(9) Cx; *When* I go . . . , I get . . . (10) P

C—Key 2

(1) four (2) main, subordinate, subordinate conjunction (3) subordinate, main (4) subordinate conjunction (5) subordinate, subject / verb, main (6) subject, subordinate (7) subject, object, direct (8) noun (9) subordinate / main, subordinate conjunction (10) subordinate, main (11) subject-verb

P—Key 5

A. (1) Until we hear from you, we will stay here. (2) The people will respond if the emergency is really great. (3) We will continue the meeting as long as everyone agrees. (4) While the war continues to rage, solutions cannot be found to many of our problems. (5) After Franco had died, they arrived in Spain. (6) The people prayed for peace before the armies marched.

B. (1) *While* she was looking . . . princess dropped. . . . (2) A frog offered . . . *after* he saw. . . . (3) The princess kissed . . . *because* he returned. . . . (4) *As soon as* she kissed . . . the frog turned. . . . (5) *When* the queen caught . . . princess told. . . . (6) *After* the queen heard that, she never again believed. . . .

P—Key 6

1. The lady *who* left us the estate disappeared.

2. Countries *where* coconuts grow are usually tropical.

3. Many adult adoptees, *whatever* their experience has been, wonder about

   their natural parents.

4. The computer industry, *which* is growing rapidly, hires highly skilled en-

   gineers.

5. The ability to create life in a test tube, *which* has been achieved recently,

   should not be taken lightly.

P—Key 7

(1) [*What* the detective learned] was reported to the judge.
(2) [*Where* the island is located] is known only to three explorers.
(3) [*Whatever* the child does] is ignored by the father.
(4) [*Which* city department handles the problem] is a mystery.
(5) [*How* many cucumbers the barrel can hold] is the question.

P—Key 8

(1) The lawyer pointed to the man *whom* he hated. (2) She feels *that* immoral movies should be banned. (3) He returned all the land *that* (which) he had stolen. (4) They thought *that* dirty words should be deleted. (5) Florence believed *that* nothing was sacred. (6) The dog *that* he feared was dead. (7) Early last year the girl *whom* we loved so much eloped. (8) The cattle *that* (which) he had purchased were slaughtered. (9) Jim, the man *whom* she wanted to marry, refused to see her. (10) The animals *that* (which) they saw in the park were graceful.

P—Key 9

1. They went for months at a time without sufficient food. Because they were stubborn. No one knew that they needed help. Until it was too late. (*or*) They went for months at a time without sufficient food. Because they were stubborn, no one knew that they needed help. Until it was too late.
2. After the long, muggy rainy season, Jeffrey tried to get through to the aid station. They died in agony. In spite of all his efforts.
3. They headed for cover as quickly as they could. Skidding and sliding over the icy snow they went. Until darkness covered everything.
4. When you decide, we will join you. Since you are now undecided, we will have to wait.
5. The child opened the heavy oak door, not knowing what to expect. He trembled inwardly. (*or*) The child opened the heavy oak door. Not knowing what to expect, he trembled inwardly.

P—Key 10

(1) *If* he were the best man, I would vote for him for president. (or) I would vote for him for president *if* he were the best man. (Each sentence in this exercise may be turned around; that is, it may begin with either the main or the subordinate clause.) (2) I gave him the money *so that* he could leave town. (3) I will join the fraternity *provided that* you lower the dues. (4) *Because* no one seemed to care about his welfare, he committed suicide.

C—Key 3

(1) simple/compound   (2) subordinate   (3) sentence   (4) sentence, sentence   (5) subordinate, sentence   (6) subordinate, main   (7) subordinate, subordinate, main   (8) subject-verb   (9) main clauses, coordinate conjunctions   (10) subordinate clause / main clause, subordinate conjunction

P—Key 11

(1) C.S.   (2) F   (3) S   (4) S   (5) S   (6) F   (7) F   (8) S   (9) F   (10) R.O.   (11) S   (12) F   (13) S   (14) R.O.   (15) S   (16) C.S.   (17) F   (18) F   (19) F   (20) R.O.

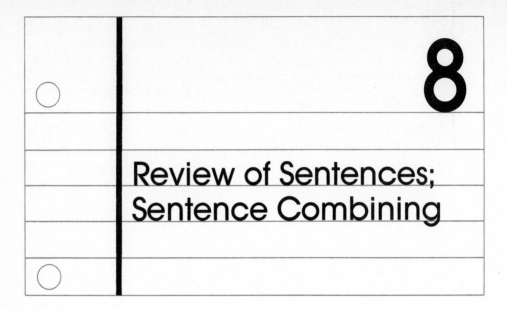

Review of Sentences; Sentence Combining

SECTION I: Sentence Structure Review

You have been building from the simplest one-word sentence to the compound and the complex. These are the basic structures. They can be combined in all sorts of ways to build compound-complex and complex-complex sentences, as we will soon see. Before we turn to more elaborate sentences, it will be helpful to review the patterns studied thus far. They illustrate the basic simplicity and flexibility of the English sentence. They reaffirm the point that if you know your subjects, verbs, and conjunctions, you can build any kind of sentence. They also show the dominance of the simple sentence in all the patterns.

THE SIMPLE SENTENCE

The simple sentence contains a subject and a verb that agree in number and person, and it must contain a complete idea. It may contain a series of subjects and a series of verbs, but these subjects and verbs may not alternate, and all subjects must relate to all verbs. Most of the possible patterns are reviewed below.

The simple sentence can be comprised of one word, a verb.   V.
It must be in the present tense. *You,* the subject, is
understood.

In all other simple sentences there must be at least one subject and one verb.	S-V.
There may be an unlimited number of subjects and one verb.	SSS-V.
There may be one subject and an unlimited number of verbs.	S-VVV.
There may be an unlimited number of subjects and an unlimited number of verbs.	SSS-VVV.
Words may precede the subject or subjects.	——S-V.
Words may be placed between the subject and the verb.	S——V.
Words may be placed after the verb or verbs.	S-V——.
Other variations are also possible.	——S——V——.

Remember: The sentence remains simple as long as the subject and verb do not alternate and all subjects relate to all verbs.

THE COMPOUND SENTENCE

The compound sentence contains two or more simple sentences (called main clauses) connected by one or more coordinate conjunctions. It does *not* contain any subordinate conjunctions.

A coordinate conjunction connects main clauses together to form compound sentences. Each main clause in a compound sentence can include all the pattern variations noted in the above description of the simple sentence.

The most common compound sentence pattern is the *"and-but"* pattern, usually with a comma added.

SUBJECT-VERB ⎹,CC⎸ SUBJECT-VERB.

In the "semicolon-however" pattern the conjunction can be placed next to the semicolon or in other parts of the clause.

SUBJECT-VERB ⎹;CC⎸ SUBJECT-VERB.

In some instances the semicolon is used without a conjunction.

SUBJECT-VERB ⎹;⎸ SUBJECT-VERB.

When there are more than two main clauses in a compound sentence, the coordinate conjunction and a comma are used only between the last two clauses. Only commas are used between the other clauses. (See page 93.)

S-V, S-V, S-V | ,*CC* | S-V.

Paired conjunctions like *"either . . . or"* and *"not only . . . but also"* form a basically different compound sentence pattern. They are considered coordinate conjunctions only if each half of the pair is followed by a subject-verb core.

CC | SUBJECT-VERB | *CC* | SUBJECT-VERB.

THE COMPLEX SENTENCE

The complex sentence contains a subordinate clause connected to a main clause by a subordinate conjunction.

Since the subordinate clause must, like the main clause, contain a subject and a verb, its basic difference lies in the presence of the subordinate conjunction. This connector sometimes acts as both conjunction and subject of the clause. The subordinate clause can contain all the patterns of the simple sentence except the *"you* understood" one.

Pattern One

The main clause comes first and the subordinate clause follows. Remember that in many complex sentences the subordinate conjunction can be used as subject of the subordinate clause as well as connector.

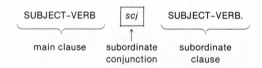

SUBJECT–VERB | *scj* | SUBJECT–VERB.

main clause   subordinate   subordinate
         conjunction   clause

Pattern Two

Here the subordinate clause comes first and the main clause follows. The comma indicates that the usual order of the clauses has been reversed.

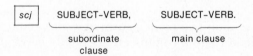

scj | SUBJECT–VERB,   SUBJECT–VERB.

      subordinate   main clause
       clause

Pattern Three

The subordinate clause is placed between the subject and the verb of the main clause. Sometimes the subordinate clause is separated from the main clause by commas.

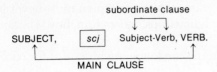

subordinate clause

SUBJECT,   │ scj │   Subject-Verb, VERB.

MAIN CLAUSE

Pattern Four

The subject of the sentence is an entire clause (known as a noun clause). A noun clause can also be a direct object or the object of a preposition.

Subject-Verb

SUBJECT — VERB.
(Noun Clause)

DIAGRAM SUMMARY OF SENTENCE TYPES

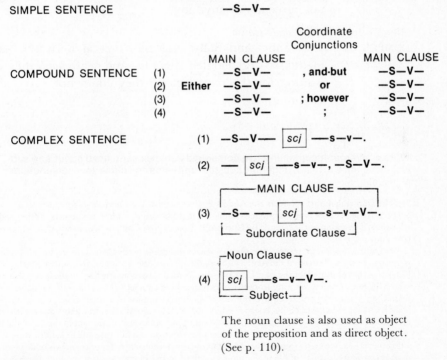

SIMPLE SENTENCE   —S—V—

			MAIN CLAUSE	Coordinate Conjunctions	MAIN CLAUSE
COMPOUND SENTENCE	(1)		—S—V—	, and-but	—S—V—
	(2)	Either	—S—V—	or	—S—V—
	(3)		—S—V—	; however	—S—V—
	(4)		—S—V—	;	—S—V—

COMPLEX SENTENCE   (1) —S—V—— │ scj │ ——s—v—.

(2) — │ scj │ ——s—v—, —S—V—.

┌——— MAIN CLAUSE ———┐

(3) —S— — │ scj │ ——s—v—V—.
└— Subordinate Clause —┘

┌Noun Clause┐

(4) │ scj │ ——s—v—V—.
└— Subject —┘

The noun clause is also used as object of the preposition and as direct object. (See p. 110).

NOTE: Sentences can be made of one or more combinations of the above and can become very complicated. Keep your sentences relatively short until you feel fully in control of them.

BUILDING ELABORATE SENTENCE STRUCTURES

By using various combinations of the basic structures, you can build longer and more elaborate sentences. New clauses can be added to modify or develop your ideas just as you might build new wings or stories on a house. The only requirement is that your architectural plan must never lose sight of the correct subject-verb relationships, no matter how elaborate your sentence gets to be.[1]

By way of illustration, examine the following blueprint for constructing compound-complex sentences.

Take one simple sentence:

SIMPLE   Jim, Sam, and Sally meditated and debated about life and death.

Add a main clause:

COMPOUND   Jim, Sam, and Sally meditated and debated about life and death, *but* they could not agree about anything.

Build in a subordinate clause:

COMPOUND-   Jim, Sam, and Sally, *who* had met at a church party,
COMPLEX   meditated and debated about life and death, *but* they could not agree about anything.

Attach a second subordinate clause:

COMPOUND-   Jim, Sam, and Sally, *who* had met at a church party,
COMPLEX   meditated and debated about life and death *while* they were waiting for the minister, *but* they could not agree about anything.

ASSIGNMENT 1

Write a paragraph containing five compound-complex sentences about any subject that comes to mind. Underline subjects and verbs and circle your conjunctions as usual.

[1] The following paragraph from the August 2, 1976 issue of *The Chronicle of Higher Education* is an extreme example of how long a sentence can be. It might be fun to underline subjects, verbs, and conjunctions. The statement was made by Norman P. Ross of New Canaan, Connecticut, at a high school ceremony.

"Having a profound respect for the academic discipline under which you, the distinguished representatives, to borrow a currently fashionable phrase, the distinguished representatives of the Class of—, have labored for the past 12 years—in crowded classrooms by day, in the lonely isolation of your bedroom at night, learning from teachers or teaching yourself—I can think of no higher compliment than to speak to you tonight within the disciplined compass of a single sentence and to say, on behalf of all my colleagues on the board of education, that we heartily congratulate you on the achievement which brings you here tonight to mark the latest milestone in your pursuit of the life of the mind, and that we warmly welcome you as you come ever closer to the full-time life of action, wherein you will discover—as we have been privileged to discover, in battle-scarred service on this board—that the most rewarding pleasures of life in community will be found in your pursuit, no matter what form it may take, in your pursuit of those elusive twin goals of both idealism and pragmatism, of both statesmanship and politics, in short, of that invigorating combination of both the life of the mind and the life of action."

THE SENTENCE IN CONTEXT

While many students have no trouble writing single sentences, they lose track of the beginnings or endings of them when they write paragraphs. This section will help you recognize other writers' sentences in context and become more aware of how to write your own correctly.

Correcting the Run-on and Comma Splice in Context

Let's review what you need to remember about these writing faults, so that you may be able to recognize and correct them in paragraphs (and, of course, to avoid them when you write your own).

1. A run-on exists when two sentences are punctuated as if they were one.
2. A comma alone is not considered sufficient punctuation between two main clauses. This error is called a *comma splice.*
3. Each sentence must contain at least one subject-verb core.
4. If more than one subject-verb core is contained in one sentence, the proper punctuation mark and conjunction must be present.
5. In a complex sentence the conjunction (subordinate) may correctly be at or near the beginning of the sentence.

PRACTICE 1

In the paragraphs that follow, you will find a given number of run-ons and/or comma splices. Correct the run-ons by inserting periods and capital letters in the proper places. Correct the comma splices by adding periods or proper conjunctions. Do not change any sentences which are punctuated correctly. Don't go about this mechanically. Use your good common sense as well as your knowledge of structure. Each sentence must make *sense. Reminder: Do one exercise at a time and correct it before doing the next one.*

1. The Failure of Lighter-than-Air Craft

(*3 run-ons, 2 comma splices*)

Lighter-than-air craft, those stately dirigibles that once sailed so smoothly through the skies, have never quite recovered from the world's two worst airship disasters, the first disaster occurred when the British R101 went down in 1930 the second happened when the German Zeppelin "Hindenburg" crashed in New Jersey in 1936. Eighty-three persons died in those crashes that number is not overwhelming in this age of jets that seat many hundreds of people, but the disasters finished the airship as a means of travel.

Plentiful supplies of nonflammable gas helium are now available for airship use, few people seem interested in building the ships. In Germany, however, an Austrian engineer recently approached the Bonn government with a proposal to build a helium-filled, nuclear-propelled airship capable of carrying 500 passengers and 100 tons of freight their aim is to attract some of the holiday tours that have been so popular in recent years.

2. College Reform

(3 run-ons, 2 comma splices)

Universities have been too slow in making changes, and campus unrest has served a purpose in helping to bring about some needed reforms this is the opinion of one prominent educator from a well-known Eastern college the educator also said that reform would probably have come to the colleges anyway, it would have come more slowly. At his university more young administrators have been hired, the administration has also included more students in decision-making committees. Students now control all of their own social activities the situation is quite different from what it was a few years ago.

3. The Courts Get Tougher on Youths

(4 run-ons, 1 comma splice)

The rebellious conduct of minors seems to be producing changes in the attitudes of the courts toward young people hitherto, the law has been gentle to minors, expecting from them only the degree of care and considerateness that is normal for persons of their age and experience in one recent case a young teenager who was playing golf was careless about the safety of other golfers he drove a ball without giving warning and severely injured another golfer. When sued for damages, the youth claimed that he could not be expected to be as careful as an adult it might be compared to a case where a young man murdered his parents and then asked for mercy because he was an orphan. The court ruled against the youth, the judge said, in effect, that a youth who participates in adult activities must take adult responsibilities.

4. The "Cheated" Woman

(4 run-ons, 2 comma splices)

Almost half of all working-age American women are working today, women comprise one-third of our labor force they are performing in almost every area of business, industry, government, the professions, and the arts despite the fact that many of them are working quite capably in these areas, their promotions and pay are not equal to those of men at identical jobs. As of 1968 about 75% of the women were working in jobs paying less than $5000 a year, most of these jobs were clerical, sales, factory, or service jobs according to recent surveys only about 2% of all the executives in this country are women, and no women are in top management positions in any major corporation. In many cases women who do the same job as men are doing get paid much less to succeed in business a woman has to be twice as good as a man—and sometimes better!

Correcting the Fragment in Context

Review the following points before you do the next exercises.

1. A fragment is usually a subordinate clause which is treated as if it were a complete sentence. It can be any group of words without an S-V core that is punctuated as if it were a sentence.
2. A careful reading will usually indicate that the fragment should have been included with the previous sentence or should be added to what follows.

PRACTICE 2

Correct the paragraphs below by incorporating the fragments properly. Use the following markings to show your corrections:

To change a capital letter to a small letter, write a slash through it: W̸
Where you change a period to a comma, underline the comma: ,
To take out unwanted punctuation, use the deletion sign: ℐ

EXAMPLE: After dinner she gave him money, W̸hich he needed badly.

1. Gandhi and the King

(*6 fragments*)

No leader relied more on symbolic gestures or achieved more with them than did Mahatma Gandhi. He asked Indians to wear homespun cloth. Because he felt that small home industry would help the Indian economy. When they did not follow his urgings. He often "punished" them by undergoing long fasts. Of course, he used his fasts more often as a political weapon against the British. Who feared that his death would cause a nationwide uprising. Another of his symbols was his loin cloth. A symbol of simplicity and poverty. When he was invited to an audience with the King of England. Gandhi entered Buckingham Palace wearing only his loin cloth. In answer to a question about the propriety of this. He replied, "The King had on enough for both of us."

2. Fair Taxes?

(*6 fragments*)

Many citizens are under the impression that people who have higher incomes pay proportionately higher taxes. This isn't necessarily true. In 1968 there were some 381 Americans with incomes of $100,000 or more. Who did not pay any income tax at all. There were even some millionaires who paid no income tax. There were also more than a thousand taxpayers with incomes over $200,000. Who paid only the same proportion of their total income as did the typical person in the $15,000 to $20,000 group. The reason for this is that there are many loopholes in the tax laws. Which help some of the very rich to avoid paying their fair share of the taxes. Some of the loopholes were brought to light at a Congressional hearing in 1969 by former Treasury Secretary Joseph W. Barr. At that time he warned. That there could be a "taxpayers' revolt." If the loopholes weren't closed.

3. When People Died Young

(5 fragments)

Not many people who are currently concerned about the generation gap, seem to realize. That the world leaders just a few centuries ago were the same age as today's college students. During the Neolithic Age the average age of the population was 25. Which means that many of the greatest inventions—the wheel, the sail, the plow—were the work of a very young population. Francis I became King of France at the age of 21. While Henry VIII became King of England at 18. Although youth today tend to blame the older generation for all the ills of the world. One can point to the past and say that young people created great inventions, beautiful poetry, *and* devastating wars. Which may indicate that it is wisdom, patience, and perhaps love that are the decisive factors, not age.

4. Letitia and the Cats

(4 fragments)

Letitia, my brother's sister-in-law, hated cats. Whenever she saw a cat, in someone else's house, at the movies, or at a formal dance. She would let out a gasp. Which sounded as if she were having a heart attack; then she would start to hiccup violently. It got so bad that my brother's brother-in-law, Letitia's husband, would call ahead to find out whether there were any cats at their point of destination. Either the host would have to vow to lock up the cat, or my brother's brother-in-law would refuse to go. This was particularly hard on people. Who loved cats. Some of them became lifelong enemies. To avoid this sort of thing, my brother's brother-in-law would often tell them that Letitia was allergic to cats. That she turned deep purple and stayed that way for several weeks at the sight of a cat. Most cat lovers accepted this. They could always understand allergies. You might say that every time Letitia came into contact with one of those friendly, furry little house pets, it was a real *cat*astrophe.

PRACTICE 3

In the following group of exercises, you will find examples of run-ons and fragments but *not* of comma splices. There is only internal punctuation, no end punctuation. You are to supply only the end punctuation. When you add a period or question mark, underline it. When you change a small letter to a capital, write the capital letter over the small letter. Check yourself with the key for each paragraph before you go on to the next one.

1. One Way to Stop War?

Do the descriptions of the horrors of war that one finds in various books and movies help people to hate the idea of war, or do they make people more callous toward the suffering of others in his book, "Nagasaki: The Forgotten Bomb," Frank W. Chinnock describes the terrible suffering of the people of Nagasaki after the atomic bomb blast an old man, for example, had bent down next to a wall to pick some weeds just when the bomb exploded before he straightened up the heat waves from the explosion killed his wife who had been standing next to him a boy who had dived into a river to find something for his sister came up to hear people all about him screaming in a burned streetcar one could see dead passengers sitting like charred mummies there are many such graphic descriptions in this book do they help to make people seek ways toward peace?

2. Teetotalling Mama

My maternal grandmother had a tendency to drink a bit too much as a result my mother refused to sip even a carbonated beverage she believed that the resultant "burp" was as sinful as a drunken stagger my brothers and I were brought up on milk, hot chocolate, lemonade, and an occasional iced punch after we grew a bit older, we once indulged in an ice cream soda at a nearby ice cream parlor, but we had to worry through a whole evening in fear that our "burps" might upset Mama and cause a major family crisis even after we were married, Mama would smell everything we drank to be sure that we weren't straying from her teachings if there was any doubt at all we would get a stern lecture this might have gone on until we were grandparents except for the fact that Mama found her Waterloo in a bowl of Hawaiian punch at the wedding reception of a family friend something attracted her to that punch for refill after refill it may have been the heat of the evening or the unusually good taste of the punch before the evening was over Mama was thoroughly "stewed" my friend swore that he had "doctored" that punch very little, but little was too much for a complete abstainer like Mama in the garden she sang several fairly risque songs in a fairly loud voice in the house she tried to unscrew several light bulbs and mix the potato chips, which were in a large cake bowl, with an electric cake mixer we took her home and put icebags on her head nobody ever said anything to Mama about how drunk she had been in turn Mama never smelled our drinks again.

3. Those Shocking Frogs

Frogs are more "shocking" creatures than most people think in 1793 Alessandro Volta saw a fellow Italian scientist take a dissected frog's leg and place it between two different metals the experiment was so arranged

that when one metal touched a nerve and the other touched a muscle, the leg twitched and contracted after many experiments Volta realized that the power came not from the frog's leg but from the metal the saline solution in the leg had acted as a conductor this experiment eventually led to Volta's invention of the storage battery in a much more recent experiment, Dr. Wolfgang Karger of the University of Ruhr in Germany demonstrated that frogs and toads carry electric energy in their skin a small amount of electric energy is generated when water is drawn into the frog's skin, enough energy to run a tiny direct current motor scientists have since found that certain human parts act in the same way this electricity may someday be used to run pacemakers these are little instruments that are used to stimulate the hearts of people with heart trouble next time you eat frogs' legs, you might meditate a little about the little fellows' contribution
✔ to human welfare it might even bring a "frog" to your throat.

4. Dyslexia

Don't make fun of the child who spells words backwards or sees numbers in reverse order these children are sometimes suffering from a special learning deficiency called "dyslexia," or specific language disability they may see the number 29 as 92 or the word "cat" as "tac" their *d*'s are written as *b*'s and their *b*'s are written as *d*'s because that is how they see them of course you should be careful not to get upset every time you notice someone occasionally making such errors some specialists claim that many children go through a brief period in early life when they "mirror" read it is only when this type of thing continues for a period of time and the child does not seem to be able to read correctly after patient prompting that one should seek professional help it is estimated that as many as six million children may suffer from this difficulty when their problem is recognized, they can be helped with special teaching techniques and a great deal of patience when it is not recognized, they often suffer terribly in school because
✔ of constant frustration and failure.

FINAL TEST ON SENTENCE STRUCTURE

Part A. Write a paragraph of about 100 to 200 words on one of the topics suggested below. Underline your subjects once, your verbs twice, and circle your conjunctions. In the process of doing this, correct any errors you may have made in sentence structure. You may modify these topics if you wish. Take either side of those that are controversial.

1. The U.S. should police the world for the good of all.
2. Beer drinking should be allowed on campus.
3. Schools and colleges should emphasize intramural sports rather than intercollegiate sports.
4. Funds for political campaigns should be greatly limited to allow people of more modest means to run for office.

5. Religion should be taught in the schools.
6. The present drug laws should be changed to. . . .
7. We should preserve more land for parks and wildlife.

Part B. Write a short theme (about 200 to 300 words) on one of the topics below. Proofread your paper carefully, keeping in mind what you have learned about sentence structure.

1. Sex education should be taught in the elementary and secondary schools.
2. The U.S. should spend less money on space and more on slums.
3. Pollution control should be made mandatory for all municipalities and all industry.
4. Drivers who are alcoholics should be relieved of their drivers' licenses permanently.
5. Obscenity laws should be made tougher.
6. Less stress should be placed on private cars, and public transportation should be greatly improved.
7. Police should use tranquilizer pellets instead of bullets.

SECTION II: Sentence Combining

Now that you've mastered the mechanics of sentence writing, it's time to begin work on style.[1] "Style" is the particular quality that you, as an individual, bring to writing. It includes your choice of words, how you combine them into sentences, and the rhythm of your language. Your style won't, of course, achieve full maturity until you do a great deal of original writing. But "playing" with words and sentences as you will do in this section should help give you a feeling for the range and flexibility of the English language.

There are several things to keep in mind as you do the following exercises:

1. There is nothing wrong with short sentences. Sometimes they are more effective than long ones. Too many consecutive short sentences, however, can seem choppy or childish and may stem the flow of thought.

2. Writers don't write long sentences to impress others. They write them to be clearer, more effective, and to make their thoughts flow.

3. In this section don't be afraid to experiment. There are no wrong answers, but your work should make sense and you should attempt to reinforce your knowledge of sentence structure, not negate it.

[1] For those students who are having trouble with such things as punctuation, tense, and agreement of pronoun and antecedent, it would be wise to proceed to Part III, "Polishing Sentences," before trying sentence combining.

This section is divided into two parts. In the first part, you will write your own sentences by selecting words from groups of basic sentences. In the second part, you will perform a similar activity, but the sentences you produce will build short paragraphs.

FORMING NEW SENTENCES

Below are 30 sets of basic sentences divided into six groups. Each group presents a somewhat different writing problem, and as you proceed, the material gets gradually longer and more complicated.

General Rules

1. Write three sentences for each basic set.
2. You may add words, but try to retain the original meaning.
3. Be sure that you write good sentences. Don't forget all you've learned about subjects, verbs, and complete ideas.

EXAMPLE: The tramp is ill.
  The tramp is tired.
  The tramp is bearded.
  The tramp is good natured.

(1) The good natured, bearded tramp is tired and ill.
(2) The bearded tramp is good natured, but he is tired and ill.
(3) Despite being tired and ill, the bearded tramp is good natured.

Group A

Set 1: The girl is young.
  The girl is slender.
  The girl is pretty.
  The girl is unhappy.

Set 2: The mother is old.
  The mother is tired.
  The mother is wrinkled.
  The mother is depressed.

Set 3: The school is hot.
  The school is crowded.
  The school is old.
  The school is noisy.

Set 4: The cake is chocolate.
  The cake is large.

The cake is layered.
The cake is delicious.

Set 5: The highway is long.
The highway is empty.
The highway is deserted.
The highway is dusty.

Group B

Set 1: The horse is wild.
The horse is running.
The horse is foaming at the mouth.
The horse is bucking.

Set 2: The children are delighted.
The children are playing.
The children are jumping rope.
The children are skipping.

Set 3: The actors are singing.
The actors are dancing.
The actors are crying.
The actors are showing many mood changes.

Set 4: The models are demonstrating the latest fashions.
The models are on the stage.
The models are smiling.
The models are posing.
The models are self-confident.

Set 5: The waiters have been rushing all evening.
The waiters have been bringing menus.
The waiters have been carrying heavy trays.
The waiters have been clearing dirty dishes.

Group C

Set 1: The thief entered the room swiftly.
The thief entered the room silently.
The thief wore green gloves.
The thief had a stocking over his head.

Set 2: The bride smiled calmly.
The bride dressed elegantly.
The bride wore a white gown.
The bride wore a long veil.

Set 3:   The worker hammered the spike.
         The worker breathed heavily.
         The worker raised the large hammer.
         The spike went into the beam.

Set 4:   The seamstresses sewed quickly.
         The seamstresses worked at the sewing machines.
         The seamstresses were skillful.
         The seamstresses sewed steadily.

Set 5:   The trail wound sharply upward.
         The trail narrowed suddenly.
         The trail was heavily covered with foliage.
         The trail led gradually to the mountain top.

Group D

Set 1:   The young mothers jumped up fearfully.
         The young mothers grabbed their children swiftly.
         The young mothers saw the car race down the street.
         The young mothers scolded their children soundly.

Set 2:   The shots rang out sharply.
         The shots rang out suddenly.
         The shots suddenly broke the silence of the night.
         The shots wounded two men slightly.

Set 3:   The cat ran up the pole.
         The cat ran onto the roof.
         The cat ran up the chimney.
         The cat fell into the fireplace.

Set 4:   The young woman stood in the doorway.
         The young woman moved slowly into the large ballroom.
         The young woman swayed to the music.
         The young woman left suddenly at eleven o'clock.

Set 5:   The immigrants stood before the officer.
         The immigrants were clad in thin clothes.
         The immigrants were wet from the rain.
         The immigrants spoke in a strange language.

Group E

Set 1:   The passengers are on the plane.
         The passengers are ready for take-off.
         The passengers are waiting.
         The plane does not fly.
         The passengers do not know why.

Set 2: The volcano erupted last year.
Its volcanic ashes spilled down the mountainside.
Its volcanic ashes covered the village below.
The eruption created havoc in the village.
The eruption threatened lives.

Set 3: Bad times were here.
Many were jobless.
Others faced lay-offs.
Almost everyone tightened his belt.
Only the very rich felt secure.

Set 4: Few Americans know foreign languages.
Knowing foreign languages can be helpful.
A knowledge of foreign languages helps in trade.
A knowledge of foreign languages helps in diplomacy.
A knowledge of foreign languages helps in understanding other cultures.

Set 5: The Metropolitan Opera is world famous.
Its performers are highly trained.
Its performers wear fancy costumes.
Its performers have magnificent voices.
Its performers are talented actors.

Group F

Set 1: Another fire-bomb exploded.
Another missile was launched.
Another plane crashed.
Another murder was committed.
The evening news was reported.

Set 2: The opossum is a marsupial.
The opossum is related to the bandicoot.
The opossum is related to the phalanger.
The opossum is related to the wombat.

Set 3: The department store marked prices down fifty percent.
People filled the aisles.
They pushed and shoved.
They examined merchandise.
They looked for bargains.

Set 4: The five-year-olds entered kindergarten.
Their mothers worried as they left the children at school.
Their mothers worried about how they would get along.
The children had a good time.

Set 5:   Morocco is a small country.
          It has rich palm groves.
          It has mountain peaks.
          The peaks are snow-covered.
          It has fields of grain.
          It has noisy, crowded towns and cities.

FORMING SENTENCES INTO PARAGRAPHS

Create a sentence of your own from each set of basic sentences below and use those sentences to construct a brief paragraph. Try to vary the structure of the sentences to produce interesting paragraphs. You might want to rewrite the paragraphs several times to create different effects.

EXAMPLE: *The Cradle of Civilization*

          The land was hot.
          The land was dry.
          The land was flat.

          The land stretched between the Tigris and Euphrates rivers.
          The land was barren.
          Only an occasional date-palm tree grew.

          People learned to irrigate this land 5,000 years ago.
          Crops flourished.
          More people were able to survive here.

          Later generations gave this region a special name.
          They called this land the "cradle of civilization."

The land was hot and dry and flat. Only an occasional date-palm tree grew on this barren land which stretched between the Tigris and Euphrates rivers. When people learned to irrigate this land 5,000 years ago, crops flourished and more people were able to survive here. Later generations gave this region a special name, the "cradle of civilization."

1. *Working Students*

The students work all day.
The students come to school at night.
They are weary.
They seek to learn new skills.

Some are married.
Some are widowed or divorced.
Many have dependents to support.

Some are middle-aged.
They may be trying to upgrade themselves on their present jobs.
They may be trying to prepare themselves for new jobs.

School is hard work for all of them.
They keep coming every evening.

2. *Job Hunting*

Daylight was just beginning to emerge.
John caught the bus at six A.M.
John rode for an hour.
John left the bus at the factory's gate.

John clutched his newspaper.
He had marked an ad.
The ad said that 200 men were wanted at the automobile factory.

It was still two hours before the employment office would open.
Lines of men stretched for blocks.
There were waiting men as far as John's eyes could see.

The evening news reported what John already knew.
The evening news said 1,500 men had come to apply for the 200 jobs.
Many had waited all night.

3. *The Train Ride*

The train pulled into the station.
The train was long.
The train had many cars.
The cars were brightly colored.
The passengers embarked quickly.

People stuffed their small bags onto the overhead rack.
People settled into their seats.
People read newspapers and magazines.
People stared out of the windows.

The sandwich-man hawked his wares.
The sandwiches held a thin slice of orange cheese between two
slices of bread.
The sandwiches were tasteless.

The city lights appeared.
The empty countryside vanished.
The train pulled into the next station.

4. *Paul's Troubles*

Paul's parents had been excellent students.
Paul's parents were now doctors.
Paul's parents had high ambitions for him.

Paul's sister was an outstanding student.
Paul's sister was now in medical school.
Paul's sister set an example that was hard to follow.

Paul's grandfather and older cousins had done very well in school.
They were now engineers.
They were very good in science and mathematics.

Paul liked to play outdoors.
Paul liked to run in the street.
Paul liked to toss a ball with his friends.

Paul barely passed his tests.
Paul did not like to study.

5. *Ice Cream*

Where she came from ice cream was rare.
It was a special treat.
It was bought and served on especially important occasions.

Ice cream at home came in two flavors.
One flavor was chocolate.
One flavor was vanilla.
There were no special trimmings.

Here ice cream was commonly used.
It came in many flavors.
It came in many shapes.
It was served with sauces.
It was served with whipped cream.
It was served with nuts.

She wondered.
What was the treat here for special occasions?
What can be special for people who eat ice cream every day?

6. *Arrival in India*

The plane landed in Bombay in the middle of the night.
The weary travellers disembarked.
The travellers entered a large, windowless room.
They located their luggage.
They moved slowly in a long line toward a desk on a platform.

An immigration officer sat behind the desk.
He looked at the travellers' passports.
He looked at the travellers' health certificates.
He asked them why they had come.

The travellers entered another large room.
Another officer examined their luggage.

One wall of the room was made of glass.
A sea of faces pressed against the glass.

The faces belonged to friends and relatives.
They were waiting for the travellers.

The travellers walked past the glass wall.
They walked into the sea of faces.
They were in India.

7. Ralph's Garden

The warm weather was just starting.
Warm weather was planting time.
Ralph began to plant his garden.

Ralph pushed a spade into the ground.
The ground was hard.
He turned the soil.
He broke up the large clumps of earth.
He cleared out the stones.

He planted a row of onions.
He planted a row of carrots.
He planted a row of peppers.
He planted a row of beans.

Ralph searched for his seed potatoes.
He could not find his seed potatoes.
He decided to let some old potatoes sprout.

It takes time for potatoes to grow sprouts.
The rains came before the potatoes grew sprouts.
The garden waited for the seed potatoes.

By late August most of the crop was ready to harvest.
There were dandelions.
There was crab grass.
There was clover.
There were plenty of potatoes.

8. *Taxes*

It's almost April 15.
Taxes are due on that date.
People are busy preparing tax returns for the deadline.

There are taxes you pay to the federal government.
There are taxes you pay to the state government.
There are taxes you pay to the local government where you live.
There are taxes you pay to the local government where you work.

There are hidden taxes.
These are the taxes you usually don't remember.

There are sales taxes on things you buy at the store.
There are special taxes included in the price of the gasoline you buy at
the gas station.
There are taxes added to your telephone bills.

There are also other kinds of taxes.
There are social security taxes deducted from your pay.
There are personal property taxes.
There are real estate taxes.
There are inheritance taxes.

Economists say you work five months out of each year without pay.
Your first five-months' wages go for taxes.

9. *At the Check-out Counter*

The cashier had been standing all day.
She was at the check-out counter.
There was a draft from the door.
The door kept opening all day.
Her feet hurt.
She was tired.
She was chilly.

She was checking out a customer.
It was her last customer.
The customer was a woman.
The customer looked mean.
The customer looked impatient.

The cashier registered the cost of each item.
The cashier was quick.
There was a loaf of bread.
There were butter and eggs.
There was some meat.

There was a head of lettuce.
There was some fruit.

The cashier filled a bag.
The bag was large.
The bag was brown.
The cashier was weary.

The customer had a purse.
She searched her purse.
She was looking for money.
She couldn't find any.
She blushed.
She hurried from the store.

The cashier cursed.
The cashier broke into tears.
She slammed the register shut.
She went home.

10. *Graduation Night*

It was graduation night.
The graduation was at the college.
Parents of the graduates were there.
Friends were there.
Relatives were there.
They filled the auditorium.

The parents were dressed in their best clothes.
The friends and relatives were dressed in their best clothes.
The parents were glowing with pride.
All were talking excitedly.

The minister rose.
The audience grew quiet.
The minister gave the invocation.

The class president spoke.
The president of the board of trustees spoke.
The president of the college spoke.
Several local politicians spoke.

The ceremony was too long.
The auditorium was hot.
The auditorium was stuffy.
Some babies started to cry.
Some people fell asleep.

The class marched off the stage.

The proud parents hugged their sons and daughters.

Friends shook their hands.

Professors congratulated them.

Everyone was happy.

what you have learned in chapter 8

Chapter 8 has given you an overview of the sentence types and a chance to develop your style through sentence combining. The sentence overview has helped you see their similarities and differences more clearly. It has shown the relationship of compound and complex sentences to the simple sentence. It has again demonstrated how the basic structure of the simple sentence depends on only two sentence parts, the subject and the verb, and how the structure of compound and complex sentences relies on three sentence parts: subjects, verbs, and conjunctions. This knowledge should help you write better sentences, punctuate them correctly, and avoid run-ons, comma splices, and fragments. Your work with sentence combining should help you write more varied and fluid sentences.

P—Key 1

(1) Lighter . . . disasters. The first . . . 1930. The second . . . 1936. Eighty-three . . . crashes. That number . . . travel. Plentiful . . . use, *but* . . . ships. In Germany . . . freight. Their aim . . . years.

(2) Universities . . . reforms. This is . . . college. The educator . . . anyway, *but* it . . . slowly. At his . . . hired, *and*[1] . . . committees. Students . . . activities. The situation . . . ago.

(3) The rebellious . . . people. Hitherto, . . . experience. In one . . . golfers. He drove . . . golfer. When sued . . . adult. It might . . . orphan. The court . . . youth, *and*[1] the judge . . . responsibilities.

(4) Almost half . . . today, *and* women . . . force. They are . . . arts. Despite . . . jobs. As of 1968 . . . year, *and* . . . service jobs. According . . . corporation. In many cases . . . less. To succeed . . . better!

P—Key 2

(1) Gandhi and the King

No leader relied more on symbolic gestures or achieved more with them than did Mahatma Gandhi. He asked Indians to wear homespun cloth, ~~B~~ecause he felt that small home industry would help the Indian economy. When they did not follow his urgings, ~~H~~e often "punished" them by undergoing long fasts. Of course, he used his fasts more often as a political weapon against the British, ~~W~~ho feared that his death would cause a nationwide uprising. Another of his symbols was his loin cloth, ~~A~~ symbol of simplicity and poverty. When he was invited to an audience with the King of England, Gandhi entered Buckingham Palace wearing only his loin cloth.

[1] A period instead of *and* would also be correct here.

In answer to a question about the propriety of this, He replied, "The King had on enough for both of us."

(2) Fair Taxes?

Many citizens are under the impression that people who have higher incomes pay proportionately higher taxes. This isn't necessarily true. In 1968 there were some 381 Americans with incomes of $100,000 or more Who did not pay any income tax at all. There were even some millionaires who paid no income tax. There were also more than a thousand taxpayers with incomes over $200,000 Who paid only the same proportion of their total income as did the typical person in the $15,000 to $20,000 group. The reason for this is that there are many loopholes in the tax laws Which help some of the very rich to avoid paying their fair share of taxes. Some of the loopholes were brought to light at a Congressional hearing in 1969 by former Treasury Secretary Joseph W. Barr. At that time he warned That there could be a "taxpayers' revolt" If the loopholes weren't closed.

(3) When People Died Young

Not many people who are currently concerned about the generation gap seem to realize That the world leaders just a few centuries ago were the same age as today's college students. During the Neolithic Age the average age of the population was 25, Which means that many of the greatest inventions—the wheel, the sail, the plow—were the work of a very young population. Francis I became King of France at the age of 21, While Henry the VIII became King of England at 18. Although youth today tend to blame the older generation for all the ills of the world, One can point to the past and say that young people created great inventions, beautiful poetry, *and* devastating wars, Which may indicate that it is wisdom, patience, and perhaps love that are the decisive factors, not age.

(4) Letitia and the Cats

Letitia, my brother's sister-in-law, hated cats. Whenever she saw a cat in someone else's house, at the movies, or at a formal dance, She would let out a gasp, Which sounded as if she were having a heart attack; then she would start to hiccup violently. It got so bad that my brother's brother-in-law, Letitia's husband, would call ahead to find out whether there were any cats at their point of destination. Either the host would have to vow to lock up the cat, or my brother's brother-in-law would refuse to go. This was particularly hard on people Who loved cats. Some of them became lifelong enemies. To avoid this sort of thing, my brother's brother-in-law would often tell them that Letitia was allergic to cats, That she turned deep purple and stayed that way for several weeks at the sight of a cat. Most cat lovers accepted this. They could always understand allergies. You might say that every time Letitia came into contact with one of those friendly, furry little house pets, it was a real *cat*astrophe.

P—Key 3

Punctuation marks that have been added to the original paragraphs are underlined in the key to aid you in checking yourself. The subjects, verbs, and conjunctions have also been indicated so that you can once again see how the subject-verb cores rule the sentence patterns. If you have punctuated certain paragraphs differently and disagree with the key, check with your instructor. You may be right. Different interpretations are sometimes possible.

(1) One Way to Stop War?
Do the descriptions of the horrors of war *that* one finds in various books and movies help people to hate the idea of war, *or* do they make people more callous toward the suffering of others? In his book, "Nagasaki: The Forgotten Bomb," Frank W. Chinnock describes the terrible suffering of the people of Nagasaki after the atomic bomb blast. An old man, for example, had bent down next to a wall to pick some weeds just *when* the bomb exploded. *Before* he straightened up, the heat waves from the explosion killed his wife *who* had been standing next to him. A boy *who* had dived into a river to find something for his sister came up to hear people all about him screaming. In a burned streetcar one could see dead passengers sitting like charred mummies. There are many such graphic descriptions in this book. Do they help to make people seek ways toward peace?

(2) Teetotalling Mama
My maternal grandmother had a tendency to drink a bit too much. As a result my mother refused to sip even a carbonated beverage. She believed *that* the resultant "burp" was as sinful as a drunken stagger. My brothers and I were brought up on milk, hot chocolate, lemonade, and an occasional iced punch. *After* we grew a bit older, we once indulged in an ice cream soda at a nearby ice cream parlor, *but* we had to worry through a whole evening in fear *that* our "burps" might upset Mama and cause a major family crisis. Even *after* we were married, Mama would smell everything we drank to be sure *that* we weren't straying from her teachings. *If* there was any doubt at all, we would get a stern lecture. This might have gone on *until* we were grandparents except for the fact *that* Mama found her Waterloo in a bowl of Hawaiian punch at the wedding reception of a family friend. Something attracted her to that punch for refill after refill. It may have been the heat of the evening or the unusually good taste of the punch. Before the evening was over Mama was thoroughly "stewed." My friend swore *that* he had "doctored" that punch very little, *but* little was too much for a complete abstainer like Mama. In the garden she sang several fairly risque songs in a fairly loud voice. In the house she tried to unscrew several light bulbs and mix the potato chips, *which* were in a large cake bowl, with an electric cake mixer. We took her home and put icebags on her head. Nobody ever said anything to Mama about how drunk she had been. In turn Mama never smelled our drinks again.

(3) Those Shocking Frogs
Frogs are more "shocking" creatures *than* most people think. In 1793 Alessandro Volta saw a fellow Italian scientist take a dissected frog's leg and place it between two different metals. The experiment was so arranged *that*

when one metal touched a nerve and the other touched a muscle, the leg twitched and contracted. After many experiments Volta realized *that* the power came not from the frog's leg but from the metal. The saline solution in the leg had acted as a conductor. This experiment eventually led to Volta's invention of the storage battery. In a much more recent experiment, Dr. Wolfgang Karger of the University of Ruhr in Germany demonstrated *that* frogs and toads carry electric energy in their skin. A small amount of electric energy is generated *when* water is drawn into the frog's skin, enough energy to run a tiny direct current motor. Scientists have since found *that* certain human parts act in the same way. This electricity may someday be used to run pacemakers. These are little instruments *that* are used to stimulate the hearts of people with heart trouble. Next time [*when*] you eat frog's legs, you might meditate a little about the little fellows' contribution to human welfare. It might even bring a "frog" to your throat.

(4) Dyslexia

Don't make fun of the child *who* spells words backwords or sees numbers in reverse order. These children are sometimes suffering from a special learning deficiency called "dyslexia," or specific language disability. They may see the number 29 as 92 or the word "cat" as "tac." Their *d*'s are written as *b*'s and their *b*'s are written as *d*'s *because* that is *how* they see them. Of course you should be careful not to get upset every time you notice someone occasionally making such errors. Some specialists claim *that* many children go through a brief period in early life *when* they "mirror" read. It is only *when* this type of thing continues for a period of time and the child does not seem to be able to read correctly after patient prompting *that* one should seek professional help. It is estimated *that* as many as six million children may suffer from this difficulty. *When* their problem is recognized, they can be helped with special teaching techniques and a great deal of patience. *When* it is not recognized, they often suffer terribly in school because of constant frustration and failure.

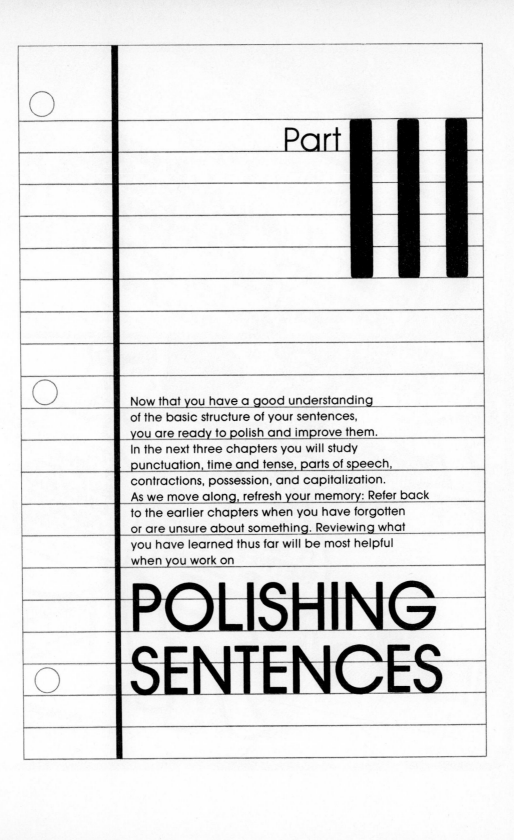

Part III

Now that you have a good understanding
of the basic structure of your sentences,
you are ready to polish and improve them.
In the next three chapters you will study
punctuation, time and tense, parts of speech,
contractions, possession, and capitalization.
As we move along, refresh your memory: Refer back
to the earlier chapters when you have forgotten
or are unsure about something. Reviewing what
you have learned thus far will be most helpful
when you work on

POLISHING SENTENCES

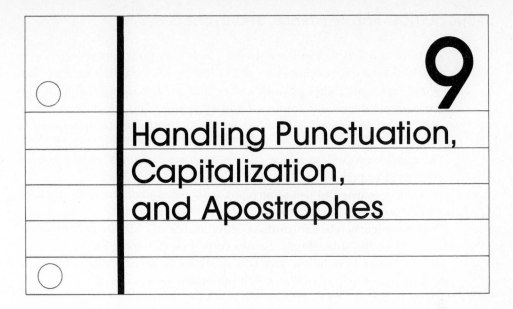

Handling Punctuation, Capitalization, and Apostrophes

Punctuation is an integral part of written language. It helps the writer to group ideas in a meaningful manner, to emphasize important points, and to differentiate between questions and statements. It represents in written form what intonation, pauses, and volume do in speech. While a speaker, for example, indicates a question by a rising tone at the end of a sentence, a writer represents it with a question mark. A speaker may signal subordinate ideas by pauses, while a writer signals them by commas.

The tendency in modern publishing is to establish maximum clarity in sentence structure and to use as little punctuation as possible. It is just as incorrect to overpunctuate as to underpunctuate. *Punctuation marks should never be inserted without a good reason.*

COMPREHENSION CHECK 1

1. Three of the functions of punctuation are to _____.
2. Punctuation represents in written form what _____, _____, and _____ do in speech.
3. What is a key factor in your handling of many punctuation problems?
4. The tendency in modern publishing is to establish maximum clarity in _____ and to use as _____ punctuation as possible.
5. It is just as incorrect to _____ as to _____.
6. _____ should never be inserted without a good reason.

PUNCTUATION AND SENTENCE STRUCTURE (A Review)

You have already worked extensively with end punctuation—periods, question marks, and exclamation points. Remember that if you place any of these end marks after phrases rather than sentences, you commit the error of *fragment writing* (Chapters 7 and 8). If you don't use the end punctuation after sentences, you write *run-ons* or *comma splices* (Chapters 6 and 8).

You have learned to place commas between clauses of compound sentences (Chapter 6).

You have learned to use semicolons with certain conjunctions in compound sentences (Chapter 6).

You have learned to use commas between subordinate clauses and main clauses when the subordinate clauses come first (Chapter 7).

In the pages that follow you will study some aspects of punctuation previously covered, as well as much important new material.

END PUNCTUATION

The Period

1. Periods mark the ends of sentences that are statements. These are called *declarative* sentences. They do not include questions or exclamations.

> New York is one of the most densely populated cities in the world.
> Frank is insane.
> Kathy wants to have five children.

2. Periods are used in dialogue for statements which may or may not be complete sentences.

> "Hello, Jennie."
> "Hi, Slink."
> "Nice day."
> "Yeah."

3. Periods are used in abbreviations.

> Dr. Paul D. Daniels
> S.O.S.
> two a.m.
> U.S. Post Office

Sometimes the periods are left out of abbreviations that have become well known: UN, GOP, USSR. Consult your dictionary for the correct usage and be consistent in how you handle such abbreviations.

The Question Mark

Question marks are used at the ends of direct questions. These are called *interrogative* sentences.

> Who are you?
> Where is the can opener?
> What did George Washington whisper to Martha?
> How can the project succeed?
> The President asked his advisors, "What will be history's judgment of our actions?"

Note the use of both question mark and period in the following sentence:

> "What will be history's judgment of our actions?" the President asked his advisors.

Sometimes a question is worded like a statement:

> Her uncle is really dead?
> You will be here on time tomorrow?
> It is still raining?

The Exclamation Point

Exclamation points are used after utterances that express strong feelings or that bear a sense of urgency. Sentences that end with exclamation points are called *exclamatory* sentences.

> Ughh! How she repels me!
> Ouch! You hurt me!
> Oh, what a beautiful day it is!
> You are a rotten scoundrel!
> Don't move!
> "Apologize immediately!" screamed Mr. Horly.

Ughh, ouch, and *oh* are called *interjections.* They are not considered as grammatical parts of any sentence.

QUOTATION MARKS

Quotation marks are used in three principal ways:

1. To set off direct quotations
2. To indicate certain titles
3. To show that words or phrases are used in a special way

Setting off Direct Quotations

Quotation marks signal the reader that the exact words of a writer or speaker are being copied. Note the placement of the quotation marks and the commas and periods in the following examples:

> "You go your way, and I'll go mine," said Claude.
> "You go your way," said Claude, "and I'll go mine."
> Claude said, "You go your way, and I'll go mine."

Setting off Titles

Short stories, poems, chapter titles, magazine articles, and acts of plays are usually set in quotation marks. Titles of books, plays, and names of magazines and newspapers are underlined. (In print these are italicized.)

> My favorite poem in Edmund Skryczinski's *Light and Fluffy* is "Tension."
> "How to Eat Eggs Intelligently" is a chapter in the new book on nutrition, *Diet or Die,* by Constance Gerdy.

Setting off Special Words

Quotation marks are used to indicate sarcasm or derision, to show that words are slangy or colloquial, or to discuss a specific word as a word.

> That march through the alligator-infested swamp was a real "picnic" all right.
> Florence "loves" Clyde so much that they'll be divorced next month.
> That woman "jus' ain't got no class" no matter how hard she tries.
> "Stink" is not a nice-sounding word.

Quotations within Quotations

Single quotation marks are used to indicate quotations within quotations.

> Barbara whispered to Ellen, "Jerry said, 'I love you,' to me today."

ELLIPSES

When copying parts of a quotation, use ellipses. Ellipses indicate intended omissions of words from quoted material. Ellipses are usually shown by three periods if the deleted material is within a sentence and four periods if it comes at the end of a sentence.

> Every day we recited together, ''I pledge allegiance to the flag . . . and to the Republic for which it stands. . . .''
> The words I like best in ''The Battle Hymn of the Republic'' are: ''. . . where the grapes of wrath are stored. . . . His truth is marching on.''

ASSIGNMENT 1: End Punctuation, Quotation Marks, Abbreviations

1. Periods mark the ends of sentences that are _____. They are not _____ or _____.
2. Write three unrelated declarative sentences.
3. Write four lines of informal dialogue.
4. Correct the punctuation where necessary:

   USO   nine pm.
   G B Shaw   Baltimore and Ohio R R
   Rev Carl B Struthers   St. Vincent's Hospital
   He got his BA and went to work for the BBC.
   Howard U is located in Washington, DC.
   She attended Mt Vernon Junior College.

5. Copy a short paragraph from this book in which you use ellipses correctly. Indicate the page number of your source.
6. Write a question that is worded like a statement.
7. Write a sentence which includes a question in quotation marks.
8. Write three interjections.
9. Write an exclamatory quotation within a sentence.
10. Write a sentence in which you discuss a word.

Punctuate the following sentences:

11. Come home now said John.
12. John said Come home now.
13. Come home said John now.
14. Total Destruction, a book by Melvin Stick, says, The world will last exactly six more years.
15. High Hopes is my favorite chapter in Total Destruction
16. Total Destruction was published in Washington D C
17. Flower Petals by Delmore Pund is my favorite poem said Louise
18. Fail is a word I detest.

19. If that's art, I'm a bank robber.
20. He's a sad sack if ever there was one.

INTERNAL PUNCTUATION

The principal tools of internal punctuation are the colon, the semicolon, and the comma. Of the three the comma is, by far, the most common and the most confusing. In studying this section, concentrate first on the colon and semicolon, which you should be able to master quickly and easily. With these under your belt, the comma will be easier to handle.

The Colon

The colon is often called the mark of anticipation because it announces to the reader that he should look for something. That something may be a series of directions, a list, or a quotation.

1. Colons are usually used after the term ''as follows'' or when ''as follows'' is implied.

> Pay careful attention to these directions:
>   Handle the dynamite gingerly.
>   Light the fuses carefully.
>   Run rapidly!

> Here are a few subjects for you to write about: ''The Dreams of High School Students,'' ''On Annoying Professors,'' and ''Cheating Can Be Stopped.''

2. Colons are used to introduce long quotations.

> In the *Dhammapada,* a book of Buddhist sayings, one will find this quotation: ''A man should first direct himself in the way he should go. Only then should he instruct others; a wise man will do so and not grow weary.''

3. Colons are used after the salutations of business letters.

> Dear Sirs:
> Gentlemen:
> Dear Ms. Wallingford:

The Semicolon

The semicolon represents a greater pause than a comma and a lesser pause than a period. The semicolon is used in three ways:

1. As indicated in Chapter 6, the semicolon is used in compound sentences before certain conjunctions.[1]

; accordingly	; however	; then
; consequently	; moreover	; therefore
; furthermore	; nevertheless	; thus
; hence	; otherwise	

Remember that the semicolons and the conjunctions are used together in this way only when they bridge two main clauses.

2. A semicolon may be used between two main clauses instead of a period (see p. 95). When you are in doubt, it is safer to use the period.

3. Semicolons are used in series of words, phrases, or clauses that become too complicated for commas alone to handle with clarity. This will be discussed again later in the chapter.

> Members of the band included Harold Epstein, clarinetist; Tony Zaluppo, tuba player; Angelo Smetano, drummer; and Luella Turnop, trumpeter.

COMPREHENSION CHECK 2

1. The three principal tools of internal punctuation are _____.
2. The colon is called the mark of _____.
3. List the three conditions under which the colon is used.
4. List the three situations in which semicolons are used.
5. List the eleven coordinate conjunctions that are used with semicolons.

Insert the proper internal punctuation in paragraphs 6 and 7 below. Only colons and semicolons are needed.

6. A partial list of baseball players and their respective positions is as follows Melvin Pew, first base Harlow Ellison, second base John Holly, third base Clement Ordl, short stop and Simon Klein, catcher.
7. We were invited to the Inaugural Ball last year accordingly, we had to buy new clothes for both my wife and me. This affected our clothing bill quite a bit because she ordered these items from the stores indicated a mink stole, $2,000, Gunter's Fur Shoppe a satin formal, $250, Hunter's Department Store a calfskin purse, $72.00, Lee's Leather Goods.

---

[1] Modern usage often allows for a period preceding these words and their use as transitional or introductory words of new sentences. For example: *Thus, the deed was successfully accomplished. However, they did arrive on time.* It is not acceptable to use only a comma or no punctuation in this situation, as the result would be a comma splice or a run-on.

Punctuate the paragraphs below, inserting colons and semicolons where necessary.

Guests at the Inaugural Ball included the following dignitaries Cyril Gobney, Ambassador from Australia Lady Frances Putnam, Proconsul from Great Britain Taylor Goodwin, Governor of Massachusetts and Ludwig Belicose, Ambassador from Lithuania.

Members of the Board of Directors are as follows Seth Morgan, chairman Todd Dewhurst, secretary Molly Kleinman, treasurer and Dorothy Steadfast, sergeant-at-arms.

The Comma

Commas represent in writing what short pauses represent in speech. They are used more often than any other punctuation mark because speech is so full of short pauses. The pauses help the speaker to group his words into meaningful units, to emphasize certain ideas, and to separate some words, phrases, and clauses from the rest of the sentence.

1. Commas in series.

a. *Commas with words, phrases, clauses.* To separate words, phrases, and clauses in a series is one of the simplest and most common functions of the comma.

> I bought peanuts, popcorn, ice cream, and jelly beans.
> We ran into the house, up the stairs, through the bedroom, and onto the back porch.
> Many of the men fought for their country, many died for their country, but most would have preferred to have lived in peace.

b. *Commas with semicolons in series.* When a series becomes too complicated for commas alone to clarify the meaning, semicolons can be of great help.

> Jerry lives at 1225 East 105 Street, Detroit, Michigan; Ken lives at 12206 Kenworthy Road, Akron, Ohio; and Bert lives at 1406 Budd Street, Los Angeles, California.

c. *Commas with adjectives in a series.* Since not all adjectives carry out quite the same function in a sentence, they are not always separated by commas in the same way. Those that are considered *coordinate* are separated by commas. Adjectives that are considered *non-coordinate* are not separated by commas.

Coordinate adjectives in a series can be interchanged without changing the meaning of the sentence, and they can be separated by *and*.

> The dog's coat was wet, muddy, and bloody.
> The look on his face was serene, thoughtful, and bemused.
> The snobbish, arrogant lieutenant was promoted.

Non-coordinate adjectives do not take *and* between them, and changing their order changes the meaning of the sentence.

> The thief entered the *musty second-story pawn* shop.
> He bought a *battered Ford pickup* truck.
> Horace Grove was the *handsome black bank* manager.

PRACTICE 1

Part A. Correct these sentences by adding commas. Two sentences are correct.

1. At the meeting were Buddhists Hindus and Moslems.
2. He gave her the money to buy some eggs at the corner store.
3. She kissed him on the nose on both eyes and on the left ear.
4. They fed the chubby chortling and dimpled Spanish baby.
5. She bought a secondhand Chrysler convertible.
6. They came to the party they bothered everyone and they refused to leave.
7. He bought nuts beans pickles apples and fish.

Part B. Correct the sentences below by adding commas and semicolons.

The team consisted of Tony Batista 12201 Blank Road Steve Mentor 1802 Snell Street Pete Totle 2291 Kemp Avenue and Bill Smick 707 Cleet Street.

The girls listed their addresses as follows: Mary Glass 1616 Bell Street Madison Wisconsin Jean Tease 1813 Todd Road Akron Ohio and Minnie Weed 601 Memp Avenue Friendship New York.

ASSIGNMENT 3: Commas that Separate Series

Write one of each of the following types of sentences:

1. Words in a series
2. Phrases in a series
3. Clauses in a series
4. A series using commas and a semicolon
5. A series using adjectives

2. Commas that follow introductory clauses and long phrases. In your study of sentence structure, you learned that a subordinate clause introducing a complex sentence is separated from the main clause by a comma. This rule also applies to long introductory phrases.

> Before he arrived in the U.S., Professor Cohen learned English thoroughly.
> Since she wanted to be an astronaut, Mary concentrated on science and math.
> After many years of travel in the Amazon jungles, George Stone returned home.
> In preparation for her final test in analytic geometry, Lena Harris spent 36 hours in almost constant study.

3. Commas that separate "intruders." Words that are outside the usual structure of the sentence are set off by commas.

a. *Nouns of address.* You may remember that these words are often incorrectly considered subjects of sentences (see Chapter 3).

> Fido, come here.
> Shine on, harvest moon.
> You, Frank, are an opinionated ass.

b. *Mild interjections.* These are interjections that are not strong enough to warrant the use of exclamation points.

> My, what a lovely place you have.
> Dear me, I didn't expect you so early.
> Well, what did you expect?

c. *Mild parenthetical expressions.* These are words added to or inserted in the basic sentence pattern.

> He, on the other hand, decided to go.
> You are, in effect, breaking the law.
> They did not, as a matter of fact, come near here.

d. *No, yes, perhaps.* These words, too, are usually set off.

> Yes, Thelma did arrive early.
> No, we cannot possibly agree.
> He will join us tomorrow, perhaps.

e. *Commas that separate words used out of their usual order.*

Usual:	The clever and resourceful detective quickly discovered the clues.
Not usual:	The detective, clever and resourceful, quickly discovered the clues.
Usual:	The once swift and clear brook was completely dry.
Not usual:	The brook, once swift and clear, was completely dry.

PRACTICE 2

Place commas where needed.

1. Why don't you talk to me more civilly George?
2. You are as a matter of fact breaking the law.
3. In general dogs are more faithful than cats.
4. The lake ill-smelling and filthy turned his stomach.
5. Well I told you so.
6. You will do it Steve whether you want to or not.
7. Oh I didn't know that.
8. Fred keen-eyed and alert caught the thief.
9. They will needless to say be glad to see you.
10. Some campers careless and inconsiderate had left their garbage in full view.

ASSIGNMENT 4: Further Practice with Commas

Place commas where needed.

1. You Gerome are incompetent and stupid.
2. Oh let's go with them.
3. The old man after all is absent minded.
4. The desert hot as the center of Hell lay ahead of them.
5. Yes we'll come to the celebration.
6. Igor grunting and whining found the body.
7. After waiting at the dock for many hours he finally saw the ship.
8. She on the other hand is very kind.
9. When the tide comes in this evening we can launch the boat.
10. Well at least we tried.

4. Commas that separate non-restrictive appositives.   The easiest way to understand what is meant by appositives is to look at examples.

Restrictive:	His friend Steve lives in Boston.
Non-restrictive:	Steve, his friend, lives in Boston.

In these sentences the words *Steve* and *his friend* are said to be in apposition, which means standing side by side. Appositives are restrictive if they must remain together in order to make a definite identification. If you dropped *Steve* from the first sentence, there would be no way of identifying the appositive, *his friend.* Appositives are called non-restrictive if they merely provide additional information which is not essential for positive identification. In the second sentence you could drop *his friend* and still know who was meant. Non-restrictive appositives are set off by commas. No commas are used with restrictive appositives.

| Restrictive: | He was discussing Lionel Smith the banker, not Lionel Smith the actor. |
| Non-restrictive: | Lionel Smith, the actor, met Ken Dodd, the painter. |

5. Commas that separate non-restrictive clauses. Like appositives, subordinate clauses can be restrictive or non-restrictive depending on whether they are vital to the meaning of the main clause or add new information. Restrictive clauses do not require commas; non-restrictive clauses do.

| Restrictive: | People who like sports are our best customers. Do not go until you have read all the directions. It was a report which he desperately needed. |
| Non-restrictive: | Boston, which is the site of the famous Tea Party, is a very old city. He gave the money to Leonard Sedder, who is my father-in-law. You are all invited to come, although the weather might be fairly cool. |

PRACTICE 3

Add commas where necessary.

1. Jean Dawson president of the sewing club was badly injured.
2. The girl who lived here was married last week.
3. People who lie should be punished.
4. The Essex Company which is located in a beautiful wooded area is known for its fine products.
5. The Essex Company which produces steel is not connected with the Essex Company which produces chemicals.
6. The team that practices hardest is not always the winner.
7. Steve Brody my best friend is in Florida.
8. His brother Melvin left town.

9. Mrs. Eliajal Walleer the first woman to drive an Army tank was cited for bravery.
✔ 10. St. Louis my hometown is an interesting city.

6. Commas used to insure clarity. In the most general sense, this is the primary use of all commas—to prevent misreading of a sentence. A comma should be used at any point in a sentence where words running together might be ambiguous or convey the wrong meaning. Other comma rules also apply to the examples below, but these particular sentences best demonstrate how commas can improve clarity.[1]

When the plane flies over the children will cheer.
When the plane flies over, the children will cheer.

To Lulu Belle told her innermost secrets.
To Lulu, Belle told her innermost secrets.

Scurrying below the people looked like ants.
Scurrying below, the people looked like ants.

However, they tried hard to win.
However hard they tried, they could not win.

PRACTICE 4

Add commas where needed.

1. After I shot it was Leonard's turn.
2. The diners were ashamed for the hungry child could see them.
3. The thief gave the money to the cop and the detective arrested the cop immediately.
4. If they gave up the tree would be removed.
✔ 5. He worked hard for his mother had no money.

ASSIGNMENT 5: Commas Used to Clarify

Add commas where necessary to make the meaning clear.

1. While the dog ran around the truck drove away.
2. Before they drowned the sharks attacked.
3. Whoever wins the country will survive. (Show that the *country* will survive.)
4. The hungry student did everything but dishwashing and a little house painting helped, too.

[1] A college professor once gave a class the following sentence to punctuate: "Woman without her man is nothing." Most of the men wrote: "Woman, without her man, is nothing." And the women wrote: "Woman! Without her, man is nothing."

7. Other common uses of the comma.

a. *In dates.* Commas are used to separate the day of the month from the year.

March 2, 1918
July 26, 1923

b. *In addresses.* Commas are used to separate the parts of an address: house number and street name, city or town, state, country.

12201 Burcheye Road, Fayette, Nebraska, U.S.A.
16 Neff Road, St. Louis, Missouri

c. *In correspondence.* Commas are used in the salutations of friendly letters and in the complimentary closings of both business and social correspondence.

Dear Mary,   Sincerely yours,
Dear Uncle Talbot,   Very truly yours,

d. *In direct quotations.* Commas are used to separate words of direct quotations from the rest of the sentence.

Clarence said, "Give my love to Luella," and his blush spread like catsup.
"I don't like her," replied Esmeralda, "but it's your life."

When end punctuation is used within the quotation marks, the commas are unnecessary.

"I hate her!" screamed Ella.
"Why should you, of all people, hate her?" shouted Rock.

REMINDER: Don't forget the use of commas between the main clauses of compound sentences and after subordinate clauses that begin complex sentences.

The angry crew refused to follow the captain's orders, and he finally had to change them.
After they had ridden fiercely for many days, the men reached home safely.

The Dash

The principal uses of the dash are to set off a series using commas, to emphasize a point, and to set off a disconnected expression.

1. To set off a series using commas:

> Some of the city's service departments—water, heat, sanitation, and safety—are vitally in need of funds.
> The men in question—Harold Keene, Jim Peterson, and Gerald Greene—deserve awards.

2. To emphasize a point:

> Thousands of young men were killed and many more were permanently injured in the Vietnamese War—the longest war in our history.
> Many people in this country suffer from malnutrition—in this, the richest country in the world.

3. To set off a disconnected or parenthetical remark:

> His idea—one which just suddenly popped into his head—seems like a very sound approach.
> The automobile—he had always dreamed of owning a fleet of them—lay in ruins at the bottom of the cliff.

Parentheses

The principal uses of parentheses are to inject a disconnected idea into a sentence (similar to the third use of the dash listed above), to enclose letters or numbers in a series, and to list sources of statements.

1. To set off a disconnected idea:

> The second lieutenant and the major (Robert could never understand why they had been commissioned) never saw action at the front.
> Before arriving at the station, the old train (someone said that it was a relic of frontier days) caught fire.

2. To enclose letters or numbers in a series:[1]

> The fact that the school imposed such severe discipline taught him: (1) to avoid taking any chances, (2) to be almost compulsively neat

---

[1] This technique is used when the writer wishes to emphasize the number or order of his items.

and clean, and (3) to be suspicious of any kind of informality or lack of order.

3. To list sources of statements:

Several historians have demonstrated conclusively that the war could have been averted. (Cass and Cass, *History of War,* p. 202.)

APOSTROPHES

The apostrophe has three uses which are often confused: to make contractions, to help show possession, and to help indicate plurality in letters and numbers.

Contractions

English speech often combines two words into one. *Is not* becomes *isn't,* and *I am* becomes *I'm.* In very formal writing, contractions are avoided, but in writing for general purposes they are acceptable, and at times desirable.

When a contraction is written, the apostrophe is placed at the point where a letter or letters have been omitted:

does not	doesn't	you are	you're
you have	you've	they are	they're
I will	I'll	that is	that's
it is	it's	will not	won't
are not	aren't	do not	don't

An apostrophe and *s* can be used to add *is* or *has* to any singular noun, but such noun contractions should be avoided except in direct quotations:

The bartender said, "Mr. Cahill's gone to New Haven." (but) Mr. Cahill *has been* my friend for years.

"The *newsboy's* here to collect," my son said. (but) Our *newsboy is* reliable.

In direct quotations, apostrophes are used to indicate almost any omission: "*He'd* come if he could." "We *don'* plant *'taters;* we *don'* plant cotton . . ." "*She's fixin' t'* quit."

Don't confuse noun contractions with the noun possessives that we will discuss next. The word *boy's* in *That is the boy's bicycle* does not, of course, translate into *boy is.* The context reveals the meaning.

PRACTICE 5

Place apostrophes where they belong.

1. Ill go to the bank with you when Im ready.
2. "Franks coming next week," said Sadie, "if hes got time."
3. Didnt the man say that the store isnt open on Tuesdays, and that it wont be open all summer?
4. Youre finished with the job, and youve earned your money.
✔ 5. Its time to call them and find out if theyre coming.

Possession

Possession is indicated in three ways:

1. By using possessive pronouns: *his, hers, mine, ours, its, yours,* and *theirs.* No apostrophes are used in these words.
2. By adding an apostrophe or apostrophe and *s* to nouns.
3. By using the preposition *of.*

Handling Possessive Nouns: Two Steps

Using apostrophes to show possession in nouns is a two-step process. First, you have to recognize a word as a possessive; then you have to decide where to place the apostrophe.

1. How to Recognize the Possessive Noun

In the sentences below, note the relationship between the possessive noun and the noun that follows:

> The mayor's home was robbed.
> Most customers like that store's produce.

Possessive nouns answer the question *whose?* They can be replaced by possessive pronouns: *his* home, *its* produce.

Most sentences containing possessive nouns can be rewritten by using the preposition *of:* The home *of* the mayor was robbed. Most customers like the produce *of* that store.

2. Where the Apostrophe Goes

All possessive nouns have an apostrophe at the end, and all possessive nouns have an *s* at the end, but which comes first?

Mistake-Proof Rules for Placing Apostrophes

1. If the possessive noun is singular, add an apostrophe and an *s.*

A boy came to the door. The *boy's* eyes were wet with tears.

A fox and a skunk have been bothering my chickens. The *fox's* visits are especially devastating.

The bus is cheaper than a taxi, but the *bus's* schedule is not very convenient. (It is, however, acceptable to omit the last *s* in these multi-*s* situations: *James'* car, *Jesus'* teachings.)

2. If the possessive noun is plural **and** ends with *s,* put the apostrophe **after** the *s.*

Three boys and a girl came to the door. The *boys'* hands were dirty.

Some foxes and a skunk have visited my yard. The *foxes'* visit was not appreciated.

3. If the possessive noun is a plural that does not end in *s,* put the apostrophe **before** the *s.*

The policemen and the sanitation workers asked for a raise. The *policemen's* request was denied.

Geese and storks fly over my house. The *geese's* honking disturbs my sleep.

4. In compound words the apostrophes are placed at the end of the last word: Commander-in-Chief's problems, father-in-law's carbuncle, Secretary-of-State's mother.

PRACTICE 6

Part A. Underline the possessive nouns. Label them S if they are singular and Pl if they are plural. Remember that all possessive nouns have apostrophes.

1. The Cleveland Indians played three games against the Chicago White Sox. The Sox's pitching was inconsistent.
2. The judge spoke to both attorneys. He found fault with the prosecuting attorney's use of precedent.
3. The three teams played extra games. The two losing teams' managers were fired.
4. The woman joined the Women Lawyers' Guild. That women's organization needs more members.
5. My aunts and my uncles made pies. I like my aunts' pies best.

Part B. Place apostrophes where they belong.

1. Twelve girls took their bicycles to camp. One girls bicycle was stolen.
2. The lady entered the ladies washroom. She found a ladys purse there.
3. Foreigners come here often. The foreigners visas are kept in my safe.

4. The Puerto Ricans are welcome. The Puerto Ricans French wife has just arrived.
5. The buildings are newly built, but three buildings sprinkler systems are defective.

ASSIGNMENT 6: Noun Possessives

Part A. For each sentence below, write another sentence that uses the possessive form of the underlined noun. Label your possessive S if it is singular and Pl if it is plural.

EXAMPLE

The underline{waiter} and the busboy were both from China. The *waiter's* English was very good.

1. My brother and my father both got shirts for their birthdays.
2. Janet and Shirley both have apartments near the park.
3. Both the policemen and the firemen got raises.
4. Houston and Dallas have professional football teams.
5. The Japanese and Chinese both have ancient cultures.

Part B. Write sentences using the following words.

1. believers	5. animal	9. friends	13. woman
2. believers'	6. animal's	10. friends'	14. women
3. believer	7. animals'	11. friend's	15. woman's
4. believer's	8. animals	12. friend	16. women's

Possessive Forms without Ownership

Some words express the idea or sense of ownership when, in fact, there is none:

> He did a good *day's* work.
> The *ocean's* depths revealed many secrets.
> *Today's* young people are healthier than their parents.
> He asked for six *months'* pay in advance.

Although no real ownership is involved in the above examples, notice that, like other possessive words, they can be rewritten with the use of *of:* *The depths of the ocean revealed many secrets. The young people of today . . .*

Plurality

If you have to make the plural of a letter or a number, use the apostrophe before the *s:*

There are three *e's* in receive.
How many Indianapolis *500's* had he raced in?

CAPITALIZATION

Capital letters help indicate the difference between the general and the specific. Words that give general names to things are called *common nouns;* these are not capitalized. Words that give specific names are called *proper nouns;* these are capitalized. Study the lists below.

GENERAL TERMS (common nouns)	SPECIFIC TERMS (proper nouns)
school	Branham High School
college	Cuyahoga Community College
state	Ohio, California, Georgia, Alabama
nation, continent	the United States, India, Nigeria, Asia
woman	Mrs. Blossom Smig, Senator Mary Ross
man	Tarzan, George Smith, Mr. Jones
priest, nun, minister, rabbi	Father Thomson, Sister Josephine, Reverend Jenkins, Rabbi Gorman
doctor	Doctor Eberhardt
city	Chicago, Buffalo, Atlanta
month	July, August, September
sister	Sis
mother	Ma, Mom
father	Dad, Pa
dog, cat	Lassie, Whiskers
company	the Gulch Oil Company
cigarettes	Choker Specials
candy	Yummy Goo Bars
tires	General Goodwear Tires
legislative body	the Senate, the House of Representatives, the Iowa State Legislature
court	the Supreme Court, Municipal Court, the Court of Appeals
building	the Empire State Building, the Chrysler Building
historic period	the Middle Ages, the Renaissance
language	French, English, Italian, Spanish
history course	History 102, Russian History 222
Spanish course	Spanish 301

GENERAL TERMS (common nouns)	SPECIFIC TERMS (proper nouns)
department	the Sociology Department, the Department of Urban Affairs
president	President Hoover
king	King Louis IV

Capitalization in Titles

Capitalize the first word, the last word, and every important word of the titles of books, plays, poems, magazines, short stories, articles, and the chapters of books. The words that are not capitalized are the articles: *a, an, the;* two conjunctions: *and, or;* and short prepositions: *in, on, at, of, to, by, with, for, from.*

The titles of magazines, books, newspapers, movies, and plays are set in italics when printed but underlined when typed or written in longhand.

The Caine Mutiny	*The Writing Clinic*
For Whom the Bell Tolls	*International Wildlife*
Principles of Grammar	*The Boston Globe*

The titles of short stories, poems, articles, and titles of chapters in books are placed in quotation marks.

"Aspects of Animal Communication: The Bees and Porpoises"
"Towards a Theory of Protest"
"The Pit and the Pendulum"

Other Capitalization Rules

Capitalize the first letter of the first word of every sentence.
Capitalize the personal pronoun *I.*
Capitalize specific geographical sections but not compass directions:

He traveled northward for many days.
He lived in the South.
The children came from East Birmingham.
We will head east for two days and then turn south.

Capitalize words used as names:

Mother said that Father is angry.
"I'm coming, Sister."
He gave the book to his mother.

Do not capitalize *the* unless it is a specific part of a name or title:

> He has lived in the United States for many years.
> She chairs the Urban Affairs Committee.
> His clothing store is called The Price Is Right.
> She stopped at The Hague enroute to Amsterdam.

Capitalize months and days of the week, but do not capitalize the seasons:

July	Monday	spring
August	Tuesday	winter

Capitalize nationalities, religions, names of languages, and racial groups (except, usually, color words):

Italian	Protestant	black
Russian	Catholic	Negro
American	Hindu	Caucasian
Mexican-American	Jewish	white

Capitalize special titles:

President of the United States	Governor of Maine
Ambassador to New Zealand	Colonel Zlott

Capitalize adjectives formed from capitalized nouns:

American customs	French toast	Freudian slip
Swiss cheese	Venetian blind	Dutch oven

PRACTICE 7

Capitalize all words that should be capitalized.

1. emily and letitia traveled north to seattle, washington, after living for many years in the east.
2. he worked at the stanton building in july and august.
3. the children read *a tale of two cities* in woodworth elementary school today.
4. stanley longstreet, the new minister, liked to call his mother "ma."
5. reverend mc allister visited the president in the california white house.
6. my brother took courses in business, spanish, and sociology. His teacher in sociology 202 is a reformed alcoholic.
7. the old man lived on limpwillow road in southern alabama during the civil war.

8. during her trip to europe she visited the duke of edinborough, stayed at hastingden castle, and fell into lake tahootie.
9. the article, ''don't eat too much turtle soup,'' was published in the may issue of *town and country magazine.*
10. over and over again emily screamed, ''i don't believe you, henry. You are a member of the ku klux klan.''

what you have learned in chapter 9

In addition to reviewing the use of punctuation as related to sentence structure, this chapter has demonstrated how to treat series of words, phrases, and clauses, how to group words together or separate certain ideas from others, how to emphasize or question, and how to handle restrictive and non-restrictive phrases and clauses. It has shown how to punctuate abbreviations, addresses, dates, salutations, and other special situations. It has also demonstrated how to use the apostrophe in contractions, possession, and in the plurals of letters and numbers. Finally, it has provided the rules of capitalization.

Punctuation should help the reader to read your words as you intend them to be read. Use it carefully and sparingly.

C—Key 1

(1) group ideas meaningfully, emphasize important points, differentiate between questions and statements   (2) intonation, pauses, volume   (3) understanding of sentence structure   (4) sentence structure, little   (5) overpunctuate, underpunctuate   (6) punctuation marks

C—Key 2

(1) colon, semicolon, comma   (2) anticipation   (3) after the term ''as follows'' or when it is implied, to introduce long quotations, after the salutation of business letters   (4) before certain coordinate conjunctions, between two main clauses, to separate series too complicated for commas alone   (5) accordingly, consequently, nevertheless, hence, however, therefore, then, thus, otherwise, moreover, furthermore   (6) A partial list of baseball players and their respective positions is as follows: Melvin Pew, first base; Harlow Ellison, second base; John Holly, third base; Clement Ordl, short stop; and Simon Klein, catcher.   (7) We were invited to the Inaugural Ball last year; accordingly, we had to buy . . . . This affected . . . from the stores indicated: a mink stole, $2,000, Gunter's Fur Shoppe; a satin formal, $250, Hunter's Department Store; a calfskin purse, $72.00, Lee's Leather Goods.

P—Key 1

A. (1) Buddhists, Hindus,   (2) correct   (3) nose, eyes,   (4) chubby, chortling,   (5) correct   (6) party, everyone,   (7) nuts, beans, pickles, apples,

B. The team consisted of Tony Batista, 12201 Blank Road; Steve Mentor, 1802 Snell Street; Pete Totle, 2291 Kemp Avenue; and Bill Smick, 707 Cleet Street.

The girls listed their addresses as follows: Mary Glass, 1616 Bell Street, Madison, Wisconsin; Jean Tease, 1813 Todd Road, Akron, Ohio; and Minnie Weed, 601 Memp Avenue, Friendship, New York.

P—Key 2

(1) civilly,   (2) are, fact,   (3) general,   (4) lake, filthy,   (5) Well,   (6) it, Steve,   (7) Oh,   (8) Fred, alert,   (9) will, say,   (10) campers, inconsiderate.

P—Key 3

(1) Dawson, club,   (2) correct   (3) correct   (4) Company, area,   (5) correct   (6) correct   (7) Brody, friend,   (8) correct   (9) Walleer, tank, (10) Louis, hometown,

P—Key 4

(1) shot,   (2) ashamed,   (3) cop,   (4) up,   (5) hard,

P—Key 5

(1) I'll, I'm   (2) Frank's, he's   (3) Didn't, isn't, won't   (4) You're, you've   (5) It's, they're

P—Key 6

A.   (1) S, Sox's   (2) S, attorney's   (3) Pl, teams'   (4) Pl, Lawyers'; Pl, women's   (5) Pl, aunts'

B.   (1) One girl's bicycle was stolen.   (2) The lady entered the ladies' washroom. She found a lady's purse there.   (3) The foreigners' visas are kept in my safe.   (4) The Puerto Rican's French wife has just arrived.   (5) The buildings are newly built, but three buildings' sprinkler systems are defective.

P—Key 7

(1) Emily, Letitia, Seattle, Washington, East   (2) He, Stanton Building, July, August   (3) The, A Tale, Two Cities, Woodworth Elementary School   (4) Stanley Longstreet, Ma   (5) Reverend McAllister, President, California White House   (6) My, Spanish, Sociology 202   (7) The, Limpwillow Road, Alabama, Civil War   (8) During, Europe, Duke of Edinborough, Hastingden Castle, Lake Tahootie   (9) The, "Don't Eat Turtle Soup," May, Town, Country Magazine   (10) Over, Emily, I, Henry, Ku Klux Klan

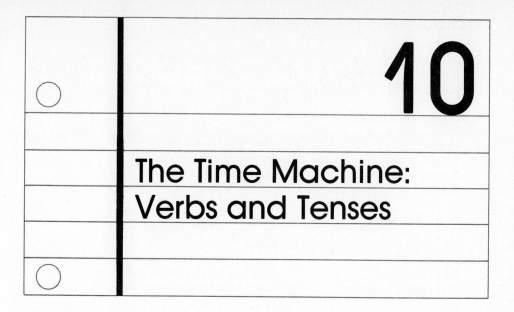

10

The Time Machine: Verbs and Tenses

TIME SIGNALS

The English language provides a finely calibrated set of signals for describing the time of events in a very precise manner. It does this with specific "time" words and phrases and by using various forms of verbs and/or verb phrases. The most evident kinds of time signals are words, such as the following, which state the time in specific terms:

now	July 26, 1923
immediately	at noon today
tomorrow at 6 p.m.	22 B.C.

The writer sets the exact time with specific time designations such as the examples above; then he keeps the time consistent throughout the paragraph by control over the verb.

The basic tenses (times) are *past, present,* and *future.* There is also a wide range of other tenses which help the writer specify the time in various ways. She can indicate whether an action is in progress at the moment, whether it has been continuing over a period of time, and whether one action in the past happened before another action in the past.

TRACKING "KISS" THROUGH TIME

The table below will give you an idea of the many shades of meaning that are made possible by the various tenses. Study the table carefully. Note how the verbs and verb phrases are used to depict time in various ways.

PRESENT TENSES

Present	I kiss her whenever I leave.
Present perfect	I have kissed her every day.
Present progressive	I am kissing her right now.
Present perfect progressive	I have been kissing her ever since I arrived.

PAST TENSES

Past	We kissed.
Past perfect	We had kissed just once before her mother arrived.
Past progressive	We were kissing when they walked in.
Past perfect progressive	We had been kissing for several minutes before the bell rang.

FUTURE TENSES

Future	He will kiss her (tonight or never).
Future perfect	He will have kissed her by 3 p.m. tomorrow.
Future progressive	He will be kissing her tomorrow morning.
Future perfect progressive	He will have been kissing her for three hours by noon.

NOTE: You will find that some of the tenses within the same general classification tend to overlap. For example, the difference is very slight between "We kissed just before mother arrived" (and) "We had kissed just before mother arrived." The time words "just before" make the situation clear. Time words often make it possible to avoid using the more complicated tenses. *What is important is that you be consistent and clear in your use of tenses.*

As you work with tense, don't forget that verbs must agree with their subjects in number and person (see Chapter 5).

Tracing Time through Two Paragraphs

To make you aware of how important the time system is, note the numerous time words and tense words (verbs) in the paragraphs below:

The explorers' supplies *did* not *reach* them *until long after* they *had arrived* at the base camp. Mud, rock slides, and swollen rivers *had impeded* the progress of supply trucks *when* they *had attempted* to reach the stranded men. *When* the supplies *reached* the camp, there *was* great rejoicing and the explorers and the truck drivers *shared* a sumptuous meal.

The teenagers of Clifton Beach *will hold* their *Annual* Beach Ball on *Tuesday, February 2* at *nine p.m.* Since the weather *will be* extremely cold *at that time,* the ball *will be held* in the beach house on Canal Street. The Beach Ball *was* originally *scheduled* for *August 26,* but there *was* an oil leak from an offshore pumping station *at that time,* and it *contaminated* the beach for the balance of the season. This *will be* the *first time* in the history of Clifton Beach that a beach party *will be held* in *mid-winter.*

COMPREHENSION CHECK 1

1. Write three words or phrases (not verbs) which indicate time.
2. _____ work with time words and phrases to maintain a consistent time pattern throughout a paragraph.
3. The _____ must help set the _____ and must also agree with the subject both in _____ and _____.
4. The three basic tenses are _____, _____, and _____.
5. The auxiliary _____ signals future action.
✔ 6. Progressive tenses can be identified by the _____ ending.

Your Tour through Time

As indicated at the beginning of this chapter, writers usually set the initial time of their sentences by using time words; then they adjust their verbs to fit that time by changing the form of the verbs and by using auxiliaries.

There are two types of verbs, *regular* and *irregular.* Both have three principal parts: *present, past,* and *past participle.*

Regular verbs are easy to learn because their tenses are formed in a regular, consistent manner. Irregular verbs, however, vary widely in their manner of tense formation, and they must be memorized. In the pages that follow, you will work your way through all twelve tenses of both types of verbs. You already know much about them, but doing the exercises carefully will reinforce what you know and help correct any weaknesses in your handling of tense. It should give you a feeling for tense as well as a better understanding of it.

REGULAR VERBS: PRINCIPAL PARTS

The principal parts of regular verbs are formed as follows:

Present. This part is formed from the infinitive by dropping *to.* It is the base form as found in the dictionary.

Past. Add *d* or *ed* to the base form to create the past tense: *laugh, laughed; live, lived; lie, lied.*

Past Participle. This part is identical with the past tense, so it presents no problem. The regular verb *pluck,* for example, adds *ed* for both the past tense and past participle. *Plucked* combines with auxiliaries to form all the perfect tenses: *have* or *has plucked, will have plucked, had plucked,* etc.

The Present Tenses of Regular Verbs

Present

The present tense is used in commands, suggestions, and to indicate habitual action or continuing ability. (See p. 202 for other uses of the present tense and further explanation.)

Command:	*Deliver* this message immediately, Private Gross.
Suggestion:	*Discourage* them from coming if you can.
Habitual action:	She *sews* well. He *paints* beautifully.

Present Perfect [*have / has* ⌇⌇⌇ *d / ed*]

The present perfect tense is used to indicate a past action with a continuing present effect. This tense is formed by a combination of *have* or *has* plus the *ed* form of the verb.

We *have loved* each other for a long time.
They *have declined* our offer, but we will try again.
She *has devoured* her steak raw and is still hungry.

Present Progressive [*am / are / is* ⌇⌇⌇ *ing*]

This tense indicates that something is taking place now and may continue to occur for a while. It requires a *be* auxiliary plus the *ing* form of the verb. Remember that the *ing* alone doesn't do the job. *Ing* deactivates the verb (see p. 52).

I *am* driv*ing* carefully.
In her petition she *is* demand*ing* equal pay for equal work.
The defendants *are* deny*ing* the allegations.
He *is* breath*ing* his last breath.

Present Perfect Progressive [*have / has been* ⌇⌇⌇ *ing*]

This tense indicates an action that has been occurring in the past and continues to occur. It is formed by a combination of *have been* or *has been* and the *ing* form of the verb.

In my opinion, they *have been* support*ing* the wrong candidate all along.
It *has been* rain*ing* steadily for weeks.
People *have been* visit*ing* here for years.
I *have been* tak*ing* a bath every time you have called.

ASSIGNMENT 1: The Present Tenses, Regular Verbs

Write sentences using the five verbs listed below the example. Underline subjects once and verbs twice.

EXAMPLE: dice

Present: His mother dices the carrots.
Present perfect: She has diced the carrots many times.
Present progressive: She is dicing the carrots now.
Present perfect progressive: She has been dicing carrots all day.

1. fish   2. chop   3. chew   4. glue   5. argue

The Past Tenses of Regular Verbs

Past   [∿∿ *d/ed*]

The past tense is formed by adding *d* or *ed* to the present tense of the verb.

He stumbl*ed* into the house.
They present*ed* him with the medal.

Past Perfect   [*had* ∿∿ *d/ed*]

The past perfect tense goes one step further back into time than the past tense. To form it you use *had* plus the *ed* form of the verb. It is often used in the same sentence with the past tense to show that one past action occurred before the other.

He *had* jump*ed* before his parachute opened.
You arrived long after they *had* depart*ed*.
They *had* already order*ed* dinner before we joined them.

Past Progressive   [*was/were* ∿∿ *ing*]

This tense describes an action in the past that continued for a period of time. It is formed with *was* or *were* plus the *ing* form of the verb.

He *was* drill*ing* the well.
They *were* slic*ing* the bread.
The Earth *was* turn*ing* on its axis.

Past Perfect Progressive   [*had been* ∿∿ *ing*]

The past perfect progressive tense describes an action that continued for a period of time in the past before something else occurred. To form it you use *had been* and the *ing* form of the verb.

They *had been* rac*ing* all day when we found them.
The birds *had been* chatter*ing* in the treetops when the storm engulfed them.
We *had been* travel*ing* all day but had arrived late.

ASSIGNMENT 2: The Past Tenses, Regular Verbs

Write sentences using the five verbs listed below the example. Underline subjects once and verbs twice.

EXAMPLE: start

Past: He started the car every morning.
Past perfect: He had started the motor.
Past progressive: She was starting her singing lessons.
Past perfect progressive: They had been starting out early for many years until his heart attack occurred.

1. greet   2. place   3. state   4. scream   5. blame

The Future Tenses of Regular Verbs

Future   [*will* ∿∿]

This tense signals action that is to take place in the future at a time which may or may not be specified. It is formed by *will* plus a verb in the present tense.

I *will walk* alone today.
The people *will laugh* at us.
The teachers *will demand* smaller classes.

Future Perfect   [*will have* ∿∿ *ed*]

The future perfect tense indicates an action which is carried from a given time (past, present, or future) to a specific time in the future. It is formed by a combination of *will have* plus the *ed* form of the verb.

He has suffered for many years. He *will have suffered* long enough by the time his pardon is granted.

The turtles have begun to cover their eggs in the sand. They *will have covered* all of them before the tide rises.

They will start studying now. They *will have studied* for twenty hours by tomorrow afternoon.

Future Progressive   [*will be* ∿∿ *ing*]

This tense indicates a future continuing action. It is formed by *will be* plus the *ing* form of the verb.

I *will be* row*ing* there tomorrow while you are driving.
The Senate *will be* discuss*ing* one bill while the House *will be* debat*ing* a different one.

Future Perfect Progressive   [*will have been* ∿∿ *ing*]

This tense indicates a continuing action that starts in the past, present, or future and that may or may not end in the future. It is formed by combining *will have been* plus the *ing* form of the verb.

They *will have been* climb*ing* for 24 hours by tomorrow afternoon.
The council *will have been* debat*ing* for two whole weeks by 5 p.m.
By nightfall the girls *will have been* talk*ing* for six hours.

ASSIGNMENT 3: The Future Tenses, Regular Verbs

Write sentences using the five verbs listed below the example. Underline subjects once and verbs twice.

EXAMPLE: pick

Future: We will pick apples today.
Future perfect: They will have picked all of the apples by noon.
Future progressive: The men will be picking cotton tomorrow.
Future perfect progressive: By midnight she will have been picking nuts for 18 hours.

1. trim   2. pluck   3. shovel   4. sneeze   5. pitch

Summary: Formation of Tenses, Regular Verbs

PRESENT TENSE

The present tense (base form) is formed by dropping *to* from the infinitive.

to vary → vary
to rate → rate
to pit ⟶ pit

PAST TENSE

The past tense is formed by adding *d* or *ed* to the present tense of the verb.[1]	vary $\longrightarrow$ vari*ed* rate $\longrightarrow$ rat*ed* pit $\longrightarrow$ pit*ted*

FUTURE TENSE

The future tense is formed by using *will* before the present tense of the verb.	will vary will rate will pit

PERFECT TENSES

The perfect tenses are formed by using *have, has, had,* or *will have* with the *ed* form of the verb.	pres. perf. past perf. fut. perf.	have (has) varied had rated will have pitted

PROGRESSIVE TENSES

The progressive tenses are formed by using a *be* auxiliary (*am, are, is, was, were, will be*) with the *ing* form of the verb.	pres. prog. past prog. fut. prog.	am (are, is) varying was (were) rating will be pitting

PERFECT PROGRESSIVE TENSES

These tenses use *have, has,* or *had* with *been* plus the *ing* verb form.	pres. perf. prog. past perf. prog. fut. perf. prog.	have (has) been varying had been rating will have been pitting

IRREGULAR VERBS

Irregular verbs differ from regular verbs in several ways. You probably know most of the principal parts of the irregulars. Concentrate on those you don't know. When you are unsure, get in the habit of referring to a list like the one below or to a dictionary.

Irregular verbs, like regular verbs, have three principal parts:

Present. With the exception of the verb *to be* (*am, is*), the base form of the present is formed by dropping the preposition *to* from the infinitive. For progressive tenses, add *ing* to this part and make necessary spelling changes (see column two in the following list).

Past. Unlike regular verbs which add *d* or *ed* in the past tense, irregular verbs change in ways that cannot be predicted.[2]

---

[1] Note: *y* changes to *i;* final consonant is sometimes doubled.

[2] Some verbs are identical in all three parts. See, for example, *bid* and *burst.*

Past Participle.   The past participle is used with *have, has,* or *had* in the present, past, and future perfect tenses. In the present perfect tense, *have* or *has* is used with the past participle: He *has chosen.* They *have flown.* In the future perfect, *will* and *have* are used: He *will have chosen.* They *will have flown.* In the past perfect, *had* is used with the past participle: He *had chosen.* They *had flown.* (For a further discussion of the function of the participle, see p. 190.)

Principal Parts of Irregular Verbs

PRESENT	PRESENT PARTICIPLE[1]	PAST	PAST PARTICIPLE
arise	*arising*	*arose*	*arisen*
awake	*awaking*	awoke	awaked
be (am, is, are)	*being*	was (were)	been
beat		beat	beaten, beat
become	*becoming*	became	become
begin	*beginning*	began	begun
bend		bent	bent
bet	*betting*	bet	bet
bid (*offer*)	*bidding*	bid	bid
bite	*biting*	bit	bitten
blow		blew	blown
break		broke	broken
bring		brought	brought
breed		bred	bred
build		built	built
burst		burst	burst
buy		bought	bought
catch		caught	caught
choose	*choosing*	chose	chosen
cling		clung	clung
come	*coming*	came	come
cost		cost	cost
creep		crept	crept
deal		dealt	dealt
dig	*digging*	dug	dug
dive	*diving*	dove, dived	dived
do		did	done
draw		drew	drawn
drink		drank	drunk
drive	*driving*	drove	driven
eat		ate	eaten
fall		fell	fallen
feed		fed	fed (*cont.*)

[1] All present participles add *ing.* Those listed in this column demonstrate the use of double consonants and the substitution of *i* for *e*.

PRESENT	PRESENT PARTICIPLE	PAST	PAST PARTICIPLE
feel		felt	felt
fight		fought	fought
find		found	found
flee		fled	fled
fling		flung	flung
fly		flew	flown
forbid	*forbidding*	forbad(e)	forbidden
forget	*forgetting*	forgot	forgotten
freeze	*freezing*	froze	frozen
give	*giving*	gave	given
go		went	gone
grind		ground	ground
grow		grew	grown
hang (*a person*)		hanged, hung	hanged, hung
hang (*a thing*)		hung	hung
hide	*hiding*	hid	hidden
hold		held	held
keep		kept	kept
know		knew	known
lay (*put or place*)		laid	laid
lead		led	led
leave	*leaving*	left	left
lend		lent	lent
lie (*recline*)	*lying*	lay	lain
light		lighted, lit	lighted, lit
lose	*losing*	lost	lost
make	*making*	made	made
mean		meant	meant
pay		paid	paid
put	*putting*	put	put
quit	*quitting*	quit	quit
read		read	read
rid	*ridding*	rid	rid
ride	*riding*	rode	ridden
ring		rang	rung
rise	*rising*	rose	risen
run	*running*	ran	run
say		said	said
see		saw	seen
sell		sold	sold
send		sent	sent
set	*setting*	set	set
shake	*shaking*	shook	shaken
shine (*glow*)	*shining*	shone, shined	shone, shined
shoot		shot	shot
show		showed	shown, showed

PRESENT	PRESENT PARTICIPLE	PAST	PAST PARTICIPLE
shrink		shrank	shrunk
sing		sang	sung
sink		sank	sunk
sit	*sitting*	sat	sat
slay		slew	slain
speak		spoke	spoken
spend		spent	spent
spin	*spinning*	spun	spun
spring		sprang	sprung
stand		stood	stood
steal		stole	stolen
sting		stung	stung
stink		stank	stunk
stride	*striding*	strode	stridden
strike	*striking*	struck	struck
strive	*striving*	strove	striven
swear		swore	sworn
swim	*swimming*	swam	swum
swing		swung	swung
take	*taking*	took	taken
teach		taught	taught
tear		tore	torn
tell		told	told
think		thought	thought
throw		threw	thrown
wake	*waking*	woke, waked	waked, woken
wear		wore	worn
wring		wrung	wrung
write	*writing*	wrote	written

Tracking "Sing" and "Drive" through Time

The sentences below should help you more clearly visualize how the irregular verbs are used in the twelve tenses.

Present tense:	sing	drive
Past tense:	sang	drove
Future tense:	will sing	will drive
Past participle:	sung	driven

PRESENT	They *sing* while they *drive*.
Pres. perf.	We *have sung* for years.
	He *has driven* for years.
Pres. prog.	I *am singing* because I'm happy.
	She *is driving* recklessly today.

| Pres. perf. prog. | You *have been singing* since this morning. |
| | It *has been driving* me insane. |

| PAST | They *sang* while they *drove*. |

| Past perf. | They *had sung* for hours before we got there. |
| | My brother *had driven* for hours before he was located. |

| Past prog. | The chorus *was singing* when the neighbors complained. |
| | He *was driving* slowly when he was apprehended. |

| Past perf. prog. | The group *had been singing* loudly before the ceiling fell. |
| | His uncle *had been driving* there every day before the road was closed. |

| FUTURE | They *will sing* while they (will) *drive*. |

| Future perf. | John *will have sung* many songs by noon tomorrow. |
| | They *will have driven* many miles by noon tomorrow. |

| Future prog. | Lulu *will be singing* many times next week. |
| | Mike *will be driving* all day tomorrow. |

| Fut. perf. prog. | They *will have been singing* for weeks by Easter. |
| | She *will have been driving* for ten years by next August. |

PARTICIPLES PLAY IMPORTANT PARTS

Because of the important parts that participles play in the sentence, the following summary of their functions may be helpful.

The Present Participle

The present participle is the *ing* form of the verb. Used with auxiliaries, it forms the various progressive tenses that are discussed in this chapter. Without auxiliaries it can be used as a noun or an adjective.

When the present participle is used as an adjective, it is usually called a *participle;* when it is used as a noun, it is called a *gerund*.

The Past Participle

The term *past participle* may be confusing to some students because it is used to form the present and future perfect tenses as well as the past tense. In the present perfect and future perfect tenses, however, there is usually a sense of some past action.

The past participle in regular verbs is identical to the past tense of the verb.

The past participle works with *have* and *has* to form the present perfect, with *had* to form the past perfect, and with *will have* to form the future perfect tenses.

The past participle alone can be used as an adjective.

For more on participles, see "When a 'Verb' Is Not a Verb" in Chapter 3 and the sections on "switched" and "*inged*" verbs in this chapter.

ASSIGNMENT 4: The Present Tenses, Irregular Verbs

Write sentences using the five verbs listed below the example. Underline your subjects once and your verbs twice. In doing these irregular verb exercises, do not hesitate to check the irregular verb list for the proper forms of the past tense and the past participle of various verbs.

EXAMPLE: take

> Present: I take aspirins every four hours.
> Present perfect: The dog has taken the cat's ball.
> Present progressive: We are taking the bus home.
> Present perfect progressive: We have been taking soil from here for years.

1. shake 2. break 3. hang 4. grind 5. blow

ASSIGNMENT 5: The Past Tenses, Irregular Verbs

Write sentences using the five verbs listed below the example. Underline your subjects once and your verbs twice.

EXAMPLE: write

> Past: I wrote six letters yesterday.
> Past perfect: He had written six letters.
> Past progressive: The student was writing letters all day.
> Past perfect progressive: People had been writing to him for many years before his execution.

1. tear 2. swim 3. stand 4. slide 5. run

ASSIGNMENT 6: The Future Tenses, Irregular Verbs

Write sentences using the five verbs listed below the example. Underline your subjects once and your verbs twice.

EXAMPLE: teach

> Future: I will teach every weekday.
> Future perfect: She will have taught for ten years by next June.
> Future progressive: Her mother-in-law will also be teaching.

Future perfect progressive: <u>Henry</u> <u>will</u> <u>have</u> <u>been</u> <u>teaching</u> for ten years by 1986.

1. steal   2. catch   3. think   4. bend   5. bite

COMPARISON OF REGULAR AND IRREGULAR VERBS

	REGULAR	*IRREGULAR*	*COMMENT*
PRESENT	talk(s) dance(s) deny (denies)	sing(s) run(s) do (does)	No difference
Present Perfect	have | talked *or* | danced has | denied	have | sung *or* | run has | done	Regular uses *ed* form Irregular uses 3rd principal part
Present Progressive	am | talking are | dancing is | denying	am | singing are | running is | doing	No difference
Present Perfect Progressive	have been | talking *or* | dancing has been | denying	have been | singing *or* | running has been | doing	No difference
PAST	talked danced denied	sang ran did	Regular uses *ed* form Irregular uses 2nd principal part
Past Perfect	| talked had | danced | denied	| sung had | run | done	Regular uses *ed* form Irregular uses 3rd principal part
Past Progressive	was | talking *or* | dancing were | denying	was | singing *or* | running were | doing	No difference
Past Perfect Progressive	| talking had been | dancing | denying	| singing had been | running | doing	No difference
FUTURE	| talk will | dance | deny	| sing will | run | do	No difference
Future Perfect	| talked will have | danced | denied	| sung will have | run | done	Regular uses *ed* form Irregular uses 3rd principal part
Future Progressive	| talking will be | dancing | denying	| singing will be | running | doing	No difference

	REGULAR		IRREGULAR		COMMENT
Future Perfect Progressive	will have been	talking dancing denying	will have been	singing running doing	No difference

ACTIVE VOICE AND PASSIVE VOICE

With a knowledge of regular and irregular verbs behind you, you may profit from a brief look at the verb from another point of view: the active and passive voices.

In the active voice the subject-verb relationship is such that the subject *does* the acting, the possessing, the feeling. In the passive voice the subject *receives* the action of the verb.

Active voice is more forceful and direct than passive voice, but situations do arise fairly often in which the passive voice is more appropriate. Compare the uses of the two voices in the sentences below. Note how the passive voice changes tenses as readily as the active voice. Note that in most of the sentences the active voice is more direct and succinct than the passive voice.

PASSIVE	ACTIVE
You are requested by Mr. Jones to deliver this box.	Mr. Jones requests you to deliver this box.
He is denied his rights by the new law.	The new law denies him his rights.
I was seen by several witnesses.	Several witnesses saw me.
You were detained by the police.	The police detained you.
I will be followed by many people.	Many people will follow me.
You will be greeted by the Queen.	The Queen will greet you.

PRACTICE 1

Rewrite the following sentences to change them from passive voice to active voice. Do not change the tense or the meaning. (You may have to add a subject in some cases.) Be sure to watch your verb endings, especially the *s's* and *ed's*.

1. We are cautioned not to go. (Note the *ed* ending of the main verb even though the present tense is used.)
2. You are expected to attend the party.
3. They were invited to the Anniversary Ball by the President.
4. We were carried to the ambulance by the medics.
5. She was informed of the accident by the police.

PRACTICE 2

Write the following sentences in the passive voice. Underline subjects and verbs as usual.

EXAMPLE: Shelly trusts you. You are trusted by Shelly.
His mother believed in him. He is believed in by his mother.

1. Oklahoma welcomes tourists.
2. Clarence loves Irma.
3. The government taxes the middle class more than the rich.
4. France invaded Germany.
5. The gardener gave her the roses.

ASSIGNMENT 7: Changing Passive Voice to Active Voice

Rewrite the following paragraph in the active voice. Underline subjects and verbs as usual.

Most headaches are caused by simple nerve and muscle tension, according to many doctors. Headaches are suffered mostly by people who worry a great deal. To avoid headaches people should be relieved of their children, their mortgages, and their secret love affairs. Aspirin can be given to those who need additional help.

MOODS

Verbs are classified into three moods: *indicative, imperative,* and *subjunctive.*
You have been working with the first two types throughout this course. The *indicative* is used to make a statement or ask a question: *The sun is hot. How are you?* The *imperative* is the "*you* understood" form: *Go home. Please bring me a fig.*
The subjunctive mood is far less common, but it deserves some mention. It is used to discuss a wish or a condition contrary to fact. Note the unusual use of the verbs in two of the most common subjunctive types, *were* and *be.*

The Subjunctive "Were"

Were is used as a subjunctive primarily to express wishes or hopes and to make statements contrary to fact when the writer knows that they are contrary to fact.

WISHES

I wish I were there now.
He wishes that there were some other way of doing the job.

STATEMENTS CONTRARY TO FACT

These statements are usually expressed in a subordinate clause introduced by *if*.

If I were king, you would be my queen.
If the general were here, he would signal a retreat.
If she were you, she would have committed suicide.

The Subjunctive "Be"

Be is sometimes used as a subjunctive when one wishes to express a command or a desire. It is usually found in subordinate clauses introduced by *that*.

He stipulated that all firearms be registered.
They asked that the buildings be torn down.
It is the President's wish that Sergeant Tawny be given the Medal of Honor.

TROUBLE-SHOOTING IN THE TIME MACHINE

In this section we will examine some of the problems that students often have with tenses.

Problem 1: You may forget to write the *ed* endings which signal the past and perfect tenses because they are scarcely heard in spoken language. (Try saying *walked, talked, searched.*) This is a serious error in writing because you are not making a clear distinction between your past and present tenses.

Solution: Become aware of what tenses you are using when you write. Remember that the past tense of all regular verbs (and the majority of verbs are regular) ends in *d* or *ed*.

Problem 2: You do not know the principal parts of the irregular verbs.

Solution: Quiz yourself on the list of irregular verbs. Cover all but the first column and write the past and participle forms on a sheet of paper. Don't stop working at it until you achieve between 90 and 100 percent correct. Since you will forget some of them, get in the habit of checking this list or a dictionary when you are unsure.

Problem 3: You may misspell the verb forms.

Solution: Pay attention to the spelling rules that apply when adding *ed* or *ing,* such as doubling of consonant: *tag—tagged, swat—swatted, begin—beginning;* or changing *y* to *i: hurry—hurried, carry—carried.* If you are unsure, check the dictionary.

Problem 4: You may fail to use auxiliaries when writing the perfect or progressive tenses. In other words, you use the participle as a verb but don't add the auxiliaries.

Solution: This can be corrected by adding an auxiliary to the participle to make it a verb, or by leaving the participle alone and adding a new verb.

Incorrect:	The fat old chicken dressed and plucked for market. (*There is no verb in this sentence. The chicken didn't dress and pluck itself.*)
Correct:	The fat old <u>chicken</u> <u>was</u> <u>dressed</u> and <u>plucked</u> for market. The fat old <u>chicken,</u> dressed and plucked for market, <u>looked</u> good enough to eat raw.
Incorrect:	The boy's jalopy stolen from the used car lot.
Correct:	The boy's <u>jalopy</u> <u>has</u> <u>been</u> <u>stolen</u> from the used car lot. The boy's <u>jalopy,</u> stolen from the used car lot, <u>was</u> <u>found</u> in an hour.
Incorrect:	It sunk. They done. She begun. We drunk. I sung. I brung. I busted.
Correct:	It has (had) sunk. They have (had) done. She has (had) begun. We have (had) drunk. I have (had) sung. I have (had) brought. I have (had) broken.

COMPREHENSION CHECK 2

1. _____ verbs are far more numerous than _____ _____.
2. Once you learn the _____ verbs, you know that the rest are _____.
3. The past tense and the past participle of _____ verbs end in *ed* or *d*.
4. Some students omit the *ed* endings when they write because they do not _____ them.
5. The best cure for misspelling verb forms when you add *ed* or *ing* is to pay attention to spelling rules regarding _____ consonants and changing _____.
6. Write the *ing* form and the past tense for each of the following verbs: tag, beg, disturb, call, spot, love, approach, deny, hurry, carry, ferry, vary.

Correct the following sentences by adding an auxiliary. Use past tense only.

7. The large cumbersome package delivered very late.
8. In the morning the pretty girls soaked by the pouring rain.
9. After arriving on the plane from Ethiopia, the envoy tired and disappointed.
✔ 10. Some of the brown and white pigeons frightened by the shot.

PRACTICE 3

Correct each of the following incorrect constructions and complete the sentences. Do not change the form of the verb. Add a suitable auxiliary.

EXAMPLE: (I eaten) I have eaten there many times.

1. I sung
2. He thrown
3. I swum
4. They eaten
5. She begun
6. I drunk
✔ 7. Sam and Tom taken

Clarifying Some Confusing Verbs

Three pairs of common verbs often cause a great deal of confusion because they are so similar: *rise—raise, sit—set,* and *lie—lay.* Let's try to clarify them. We will not go into all possible meanings; only the troublesome ones will be dealt with.

Rise *versus* Raise

PRESENT	PAST	PAST PARTICIPLE
rise	rose	risen
raise	raised	raised

Rise is an irregular verb. It usually refers to a steady or customary upward movement done (actually or in a sense) by itself. For example: The sun *rises.* The people *rise* to applaud the President. Dust *rises* from the pavement. Fog *rises* from the meadow. Your fever *rose* yesterday. You have *risen* from bed against the doctor's orders. The farmer *rose* at 4 a.m.

Raise is a regular verb. It usually means "to cause to rise, move to a higher level, lift, elevate." The raising is done by a force outside that which is raised. For example: The boy *raised* and lowered the flag. The crocodile *raised* its huge head. (But it *rose* from the mud in one rapid motion.) The crane *raised* the car from the bottom of the river. The girl *raised* her hand. Senator Crabbe *raised* many objections.

Sit *versus* Set

PRESENT	PAST	PAST PARTICIPLE
sit	sat	sat
set	set	set

Sit is an irregular verb usually meaning to be seated or come to a resting position:

Our cat *sits* on the fence. The judge *has been sitting* in his chambers for a long time. Let's *sit* down and talk.

Set usually means to put or place:

I *set* the table. I *set* the hot pot on the cot. He *sets* the tomato plants in long, even rows.

Lie *versus* Lay

PRESENT	PAST	PAST PARTICIPLE	
lie, lying	I lied.	I have lied.	(to tell a falsehood)
lie, lying	I lay.	He has lain.	(to recline)
lay, laying	I laid.	We have laid.	(to put, place, arrange, etc.)

EXAMPLES

After laying down his weapon, the soldier lay down to sleep.
He was lying there when the moose lay down beside him.
We lied to each other.
Will you lie down and rest?
They have lain in bed all day.
Who laid out my clothing?

If you continue to have difficulty with the proper use of these verbs, always check yourself, using this book or a dictionary. When you cannot do so (during an exam, for example) it might be advisable to substitute a synonym that you are sure of: "*Put* (instead of *lay*) your weapon down." "They have *been* (instead of *lain*) in bed all day."

ASSIGNMENT 8

Write a sentence using each of the following words correctly. You may use any tense.

1. rise
2. sit

3. set
4. lie (recline)
5. lay (put)
6. lie (tell a falsehood)
7. raise

Inged Verbs Revisited

In Chapter 3 you learned that *ing*ed verbs are "frozen" unless auxiliaries are added to activate them. Unless an *ing*ed verb is activated by adding an auxiliary or unless another verb is added to make a sentence, you have written a fragment.

Incorrect:	The rugged sailor sailing far out to sea.
Corrected by adding auxiliary:	The rugged sailor is sailing far out to sea.
Corrected by adding new verb:	The rugged sailor, sailing far out to sea, is slightly intoxicated.
Incorrect:	The two lovers roaming through the wooded back acres of the farm.
Corrected by adding auxiliary:	The two lovers were roaming through the wooded back acres of the farm.
Corrected by adding new verb:	The two lovers roaming through the wooded back acres of the farm were secretly married yesterday.

"Switched" Verbs Revisited

Participles alone cannot be used as verbs. Unless the past participle is activated by adding *have, has,* or *had,* a form of *be,* or another verb to make a sentence, you are writing a fragment.

Incorrect:	The sensitive young doctor disturbed by the rumors.
Corrected by adding auxiliary:	The sensitive young doctor has been disturbed by the rumors.

Corrected by adding new verb:	The sensitive young <u>doctor</u>, disturbed by the rumors, <u><u>left</u></u> town.
Incorrect:	During the game the children frozen by the icy blasts.
Corrected by adding auxiliary:	During the game the <u>children</u> <u><u>were frozen</u></u> by the icy blasts.
Corrected by adding new verb:	During the game the <u>children</u>, frozen by the icy blasts, <u><u>huddled</u></u> together.

ASSIGNMENT 9

Complete each of the sentences below in two ways and punctuate correctly. In your first sentence add an auxiliary; in your second sentence add a verb and other necessary words.

EXAMPLE: The twelve angry senators on the Agricultural Committee, worrying and fretting,
    a. The twelve angry senators on the Agricultural Committee *were* worrying and fretting.
    b. The twelve angry senators on the Agricultural Committee, worrying and fretting, *decided to investigate the danger of crop dusting.*

1. In spite of the rain, large beetle-like insects covered with mud
2. Nearly every varsity member of the girls' swimming team tired but victorious
3. The sinking freighter in the Gulf of Mexico almost completely destroyed by fire
4. The new sociology professor frightened by the noisy class
5. Before the night baseball game, the wind sweeping across the field
6. The mysterious and legendary creature known as the Loch Ness monster
7. In planning to descend into the angry volcano, the men, fully realizing the danger
8. The fraternity men and women excited about the possibility of having an open door policy in the women's dormitories
9. The kindly benefactor of the county orphanage seen only occasionally by the children
10. The little girl unable to swim

ASSIGNMENT 10

Part A. Write sentences using the verbs below in the tenses indicated. Refer to the appropriate sections in this chapter for help.

1. run (*past*)
2. go (*present*)
3. sail (*past perfect*)
4. begin (*past*)
5. think (*present progressive*)
6. do (*future*)
7. deny (*past progressive*)
8. deliver (*present perfect*)
9. bring (*future*)
10. learn (*past progressive*)
11. give (*future*)
12. fish (*present progressive*)
13. admit (*past perfect*)
14. burst (*past*)
15. kidnap (*future perfect*)
16. speak (*present*)
17. saw (*past perfect*)
18. take (*present*)
19. work (*future perfect*)
20. cry (*past perfect*)

Part B. Using whichever tense you prefer, write a ten-sentence paragraph in which you maintain that tense throughout. Underline your verbs.

USING THE TIME MACHINE

In the first section of this chapter we were largely concerned with the mechanism of the time machine. You learned the parts and how to use them. That took you a long way toward mastering the machine. In this section we will, of course, continue to be concerned about the mechanics, but we will focus primarily on using the time signals logically and consistently.

Whenever you write a sentence, you are dealing with at least one time period. In many sentences you work with more than one period, and in paragraphs and themes you may find it necessary to switch back and forth between time periods.

Tense Shifts in Sentences

The Past and Perfect Tenses.   When dealing with time changes from past to present, one does not often run into difficulty. For example, one readily says, "I went to the dentist yesterday, and I am going there again today," or "I played chess last week, and I am playing again tonight." But when students are dealing with the past tense, and the logic of their statements goes back one time period further, they often forget to use the past perfect tense.

Incorrect: I arrived in June, but Noah was already there and left.

Correct: I arrived in June, but Noah *had* already *been* there and *had* left.

A Series of Tenses. Consistency of tense is an important part of tense writing. One should establish a particular tense and maintain it unless there is a good reason for changing it. When one writes about a series of actions which happen at the same time, there is no reason to change the tense.

Incorrect: She starts to scream at me, she throws pots and pans and dishes at me, and then she changed her mind and kissed me.

Correct: She started to scream at me, she threw pots and pans and dishes at me, and then she changed her mind and kissed me.

(or)

She starts to scream at me, she throws pots and pans and dishes at me, and then she changes her mind and kisses me.

Uses of the Present Tense

There are four special variations in the use of the present tense.

1. Universal Present Tense. If a statement was true at a particular time in the past and continues to be true today, we often write that statement in the present tense (called the *universal present*) even though a past tense may introduce it.

Acceptable: The learned astronomer proved that the earth *revolved* around the sun.

Preferred: The learned astronomer proved that the earth *revolves* around the sun.

2. Habitual Present. The habitual present indicates a continuing ability, custom, or habitual action.

The car *runs* well.   The dog *howls* at the moon.
He *learns* rapidly.   French cooks *make* good onion soup.
They *play* regularly.   We always *salute* the flag.

3. Historic Present. In order to describe a past action more vividly, writers occasionally use the present tense. They make this clear to the reader by paragraphing the section separately.

The queen *descends,* trembling, from the throne. Her usually impenetrable eyes *show* the faintest signs of inward terror. "I love you, Essex," she *says,* "but your head must be removed."

4. Present "Future." Sometimes the present and present progressive tenses are used to express future action. Note that in these situations the time word is very close to the verb.

We *leave* tomorrow.   We *are leaving* tomorrow.
The judge *arrives* on Sunday.   The judge *is arriving* on Sunday.
The people *vote* next week.   The people *are voting* next week.

COMPREHENSION CHECK 3

1. An important part of tense writing is to maintain _____.
2. When one is writing of a series of actions that happen at the same time, there is no reason to change the _____ of the verbs.
3. What are the three basic tenses?
4. What are the four variations in the use of the present tense?
5. When something that occurred in the past is described in the present tense, the tense is called the _____.
6. The statement, "He speaks well," is an example of the _____ present tense.
7. "My aunt leaves tomorrow" is an example of the present _____.
8. If a statement was true in the past and continues to be true today, we often write the statement in the _____.

PRACTICE 4

Make whatever corrections are necessary. Do not change the meaning of any sentence.

1. Paul ate his supper and is soon asleep.
2. The thieves break into the bank, steal the money, and made a complete getaway.
3. Before he came to this country, he made his fortune in France.
4. No one was told that he arrived in Portugal the day before.
5. The teacher told them that H_2O was the formula for water.
6. Marvin dives into the lake, swims to the terrified child, grabs her under the chin, and towed her to shore.
7. Columbus helped prove that the earth was round.
8. The doctor decided to operate after he definitely diagnosed appendicitis.
9. They bathed and dressed in clean clothes before they get in the car and drive away.
10. Benjamin Franklin discovered that lightning discharged electricity.

Tense Shifts in Paragraphs

By now you probably realize how important time is in your paragraphs and how many words and phrases are affected by the time signal system. Paragraphs, of course, show this much more clearly than individual sentences. Four brief rules should help you keep your time mechanism in good working order.

1. Set your time clearly.
2. Do not change the time without good reason.
3. Keep your tenses consistent within each time period.
4. When you change the time, be sure that your change is clear.

The following paragraphs are marked to indicate each time change. Study them carefully so that you can mark other paragraphs in similar fashion.

1. This paragraph shifts tenses back and forth easily and clearly.

The teenagers who dominated a large part	PAST
of the American scene in the 1960's have	PRESENT PERFECT
grown up. As young adults they will have a	FUTURE
significant influence on the nation's economy	
in the 1970's. There are 25 million young	PRESENT
adults (20–29) in the U.S. today. By 1980	
they will total about 40 million. Economists	FUTURE
now predict that the loud squawling of babies,	PRESENT
crying for bottles and balloons, will soon	FUTURE
smother the demand for Beatle-type bands.	

2. When you write biographical material such as you find in the following paragraph, it is fairly easy to control your time system so that it moves logically from past to present or present to past.

When I was a child, my paternal	PAST
grandfather sometimes beat me with the	
hockey stick with which he had won the	
International Hockey Championship in 1882.	
He had started life as a chicken farmer in	
northwestern Vermont, but the chicken	
ague, a disease spread by certain careless	PAST PERFECT
Eastern chickens, had killed off several	
consecutive flocks. He had grown so sick of	
living on hard-boiled, scrambled, and poached	
eggs that he had left his wife and seventeen	
remaining chickens and had set out to make	

his living as a professional hockey player.
Aside from those beatings, my grandfather
was usually kind and good to me, and when
it came time to send me off to a city high
school, he pawned all of his hockey medals to
help pay the way. Grandpa died in 1942. I
have since tried to attend hockey games out
of respect for the old fellow, but whenever a
player swings a stick I seem to feel it in my
nether parts. I have never found out what
happened to my grandmother and her
seventeen chickens.

PAST

PRESENT PERFECT

PRESENT
PRESENT PERFECT
PAST

PRACTICE 5

Analyze the time systems of the following paragraphs. Underline verbs and label
the tenses. Check the first before going on to the second.

1. My sister was about ten and I nearly six
when she brought home her first toad. She
had found the toad on the sand near a pond that
ran behind the school. The toad was a very quiet
fellow who looked a little like some pictures I
had seen of Winston Churchill—puffy-joweled,
plump-bellied. He was quite dry, not slippery like
a frog, and when you looked closely you could see
the many subtle colors that helped him blend with
rocks and sand and leaves and twigs. He allowed
us to pick him up, and he would hop about in the
palms of our hands, wetting us only occasionally.
Our friends and even some older relatives and
teachers said that we would get warts, but we
never did. Even today I find people who shudder
when I mention toads, but I think that they are
quite beautiful.

2. Air travel has come a long way from Kitty
Hawk. One of the newer jet airliners seats
about 500 people and is divided into six sections.
Seating is arranged so that movies can be shown
in each section, and each is decorated in different
color combinations. There are three galleys,
14 lavatories, and closet space for clothing and
handbags is available in the giant ship.
In the first class section there is a spiral
staircase that leads to a lounge on the flight

deck. The Wright brothers' plane did not fly more than the length of a football field. Now people are flying in planes that are almost that long.

FINAL TEST

This is to see how well you can put together all you have learned about time and tense. Select any two of the following assignments and write a paragraph as directed. You may use reference books in preparing your topics.

1. Describe an activity that occurred in the recent past and compare it with something that occurred in the more distant past. For example, you might compare two ball games, two picnics, two Christmas or birthday celebrations or family visits.
2. Tell about a historical event. Compare it with a similar but more recent occurrence.
3. Discuss the development of an invention such as the telephone or the light bulb. Compare it with the development of the computer or one of the moon rockets.
4. Tell about the experiences of three generations of a family (yours or someone else's). Start with the present, work back to the past and past perfect, and return to the present. Be sure to have a good reason for every change of tense.

what you have learned in chapter 10

Chapter 10 has focused on *tense* and *time words* and how to handle *regular* and *irregular verbs* in the various tenses. It has helped you form all tenses from the three principal parts of any verb. It has reviewed "switched" verbs and *ing*ed verbs, and discussed various special problems related to tense. It has also demonstrated the tense shifts in sentences and in paragraphs.

Remember that when you write, you must clearly establish the time for your reader and handle your tenses consistently so as not to confuse him. Never shift your tenses without good reason.

C—Key 1

(1) You should have used "time signals" like the examples in paragraph 1 of this chapter. (2) Verbs (3) verbs, time, number, person (4) present, past, future (5) will (6) ing

P—Key 1

(1) They caution us not to go. (2) They expect you to attend the party. (3) The President invited them to the Anniversary Ball. (4) The medics carried us to the ambulance. (5) The police informed her of the accident.

P—Key 2

(1) <u>Tourists</u> <u>are</u> <u>welcomed</u> by Oklahoma. (2) <u>Irma</u> <u>is</u> <u>loved</u> by Clarence. (3) The <u>middle</u> <u>class</u> <u>is</u> <u>taxed</u> more than the rich by the government. (4) <u>Germany</u> <u>was</u> <u>invaded</u> by France. (5) <u>She</u> <u>was</u> <u>given</u> the roses by the gardener.

C—Key 2

(1) regular, irregular verbs (2) irregular, regular (3) regular (4) hear (5) doubling, *y* to *i* (6) tagging, tagged; begging, begged; disturbing, disturbed; calling, called; spotting, spotted; loving, loved; approaching, approached; denying, denied; hurrying, hurried; carrying, carried; ferrying, ferried; varying, varied (7) package *was* delivered (8) girls *were* soaked (9) envoy *was* tired (10) pigeons *were* frightened

P—Key 3

(1) have, had (2) has, had (3) have, had (4) have, had (5) has, had (6) have, had (7) have, had

C—Key 3

(1) consistency (2) tense (3) present / past / future (4) universal / historic / habitual / future (5) historic present (6) habitual (7) future (8) universal present

P—Key 4

1. Paul *ate* his supper and *was* soon asleep. (Paul eats . . . is)
2. The thieves *break* into the bank, *steal* the money, and *make* a complete getaway. (The thieves *broke* . . . *stole* . . . *made*)
3. Before he came to this country, he *had made* his fortune in France.
4. No one was told that he *had arrived* in Portugal the day before.
5. The teacher told them that H_2O *is* the formula for water.
6. Marvin *dived* (*dove*) into the lake, *swam* to the terrified child, *grabbed* her under the chin, and *towed* her to shore. (Marvin *dives* . . . *swims* . . . *grabs* . . . *tows*)
7. Columbus helped prove that the earth *is* round.
8. The doctor decided to operate after he *had* definitely *diagnosed* appendicitis.
9. They *had bathed* and *dressed* in clean clothes before they *got* in the car and *drove* away.
10. Benjamin Franklin discovered that lightning *discharges* electricity.

1. My sister was about ten and I nearly six
when she brought home her first toad. She
had found the toad on the sand near a pond that
ran behind the school. The toad was a very quiet
fellow who looked a little like some pictures I
had seen of Winston Churchill—puffy-joweled,
plump-bellied. He was quite dry, not slippery like
a frog, and when you looked closely you could see
the many subtle colors that helped him blend with
rocks and sand and leaves and twigs. He allowed
us to pick him up, and he would hop about in the
palms of our hands, wetting us only occasionally.
Our friends and even some older relatives and
teachers said that we would get warts, but we
never did. Even today I find people who shudder
when I mention toads, but I think that they are
quite beautiful.

} PAST
   and
   PAST PERFECT

} PAST

} PRESENT

2. Air travel has come a long way from Kitty
Hawk. One of the newer jet airliners seats
about 500 people and is divided into six sections.
Seating is arranged so that movies can be shown
in each section, and each is decorated in different
color combinations. There are three galleys,
14 lavatories, and closet space for clothing and
handbags is available in the giant ship.
In the first class section there is a spiral
staircase that leads to a lounge on the flight
deck. The Wright brothers' plane did not fly
more than the length of a football field. Now
people are flying in planes that are almost that
long.

PRESENT PERFECT

} PRESENT

PAST

} PRESENT PROG.
   PRESENT

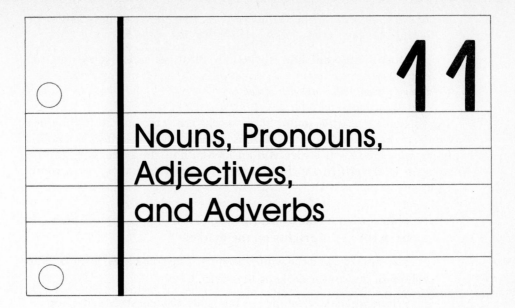

Nouns, Pronouns, Adjectives, and Adverbs

You have learned the fundamentals of sentence construction by studying three parts of the sentence: subjects, verbs, and conjunctions. You have learned to polish the "interiors" of sentences by working with agreement of subject and verb (where you also became acquainted with prepositions), and by studying the time system. You have learned how to guide the flow of ideas with punctuation.

This chapter continues the polishing process by examining closely the use and misuse of three kinds of words that sometimes cause difficulty—pronouns, adjectives, and adverbs.

But first, because an understanding of pronouns and adjectives depends upon an acquaintance with nouns, you will study briefly the characteristics of nouns.

NOUNS

You are already familiar with nouns as subjects of sentences and clauses. You have also seen them used as objects of prepositions. In Chapter 5 we studied their singular and plural forms, and in Chapter 9, their possessive forms.

How can nouns be identified?

1. Nouns can be described by adjectives: a yellow *submarine*, the golden *rule*, the great, white *hope*, the straight and narrow *path*.

2. Most nouns can be numbered; that is, they can be singular or plural: *car, cars; pickle, pickles; nationality, nationalities.*

3. Most nouns can show possession, and that which is possessed is also a noun: the *dog's* bone, my *aunt's* gift, *children's* toys, *man's* fate, *Henry's* talent, *life's* disappointments.

As you learned earlier in this book, words are verbs only if they *function* as verbs in sentences. So, too, a word is a noun only if it *functions* as a noun. The examples below will give you an idea of how the same word can be employed as a <u>verb</u> (underlined twice), an *adjective* (italics), or a **noun** (boldface).

1. They <u>uprighted</u> the overturned car. He bought an *upright* piano. It is one of the best **uprights** on the market.

2. The sun <u>yellowed</u> the white curtains. The *yellow* bowl is mine. The **yellow** of the sunset darkens to orange.

3. I <u>hope</u> we make it on time. That is her *hope* chest. My one **hope** is that she remain.

PRACTICE 1

Underline the nouns in the following sentences.

1. She trained the dog to stay away from the train.
2. His face purpled with anger when he saw his son's purple shirt. The purple in his father's face frightened the boy.
3. The cow was cowed by the cowbell.
4. The photographer developed the pictures with the new developing fluid while we awaited developments.

✔ 5. That farm was farmed by a different farmer.

ASSIGNMENT 1

Write five sentences that you might use in a letter to an appliance manufacturer about a defective toaster. Underline the nouns.

PRONOUNS

Pronouns are words that substitute for nouns.[1] Without pronouns writing is repetitious and longwinded. For example:

---

[1] To be exact, the pronoun takes the place of not just the noun in a sentence, but also the modifiers and articles that are clustered around it: *The blue and green flower pot is very ugly. It should be discarded. It* refers to *the ugly blue and green flower pot.*

"The crew and officers are going through!" The Commander's voice was like thin ice breaking. The Commander wore the Commander's full-dress uniform with the heavily braided white cap pulled down rakishly over one cold gray eye. "The crew and the officers can't make it, sir. The weather is spoiling for a hurricane, if the Commander asks Lieutenant Berg." "The Commander is not asking Lieutenant Berg, Lieutenant Berg," said the Commander. "Throw on the power lights. Rev the ship up to 8,500. The crew and the officers are going through!"

The paragraph as originally written—with pronouns:

"*We*'re going through!" The Commander's voice was like thin ice breaking. *He* wore his full-dress uniform with the heavily braided white cap pulled down rakishly over one cold gray eye. "*We* can't make *it,* sir. *it*'s spoiling for a hurricane, if *you* ask *me.*" "*I*'m not asking *you,* Lieutenant Berg," said the Commander. "Throw on the power lights! Rev *her* up to 8,500! *We*'re going through!" [From "The Secret Life of Walter Mitty" by James Thurber]

The italicized words in the paragraph above are called personal pronouns. They are among the most commonly used words in the language. They are, as the above paragraphs illustrate, not only handy, but essential in any kind of speaking or writing. Usually personal pronouns are easy to use, but sometimes they give headaches even to experienced writers. In this section you will study the way pronouns change, and look at the most common headache-causing situations created by personal as well as other types of pronouns.

If you've ever wondered whether to say *I* or *me, we* or *us, he* or *him;* if *who* and *whom* have bothered you; if you tend to say *you* when you mean *I;* and if words like *everyone* and *somebody* throw you off the track, you'll get some help from the discussion that follows.

Personal Pronouns

The following practice will demonstrate how pronouns change form. The list of personal pronouns below is more complete than that which you used in Chapter 5, where only those related to subject-verb agreement were used.

I	we	you	she	he	it	they
me	us	your	her	him	its	them
my	our	yours	hers	his		their
mine	ours					theirs

PRACTICE 2

In each blank, insert a correct pronoun from the list. Use some of these words more than once.

1. The counselor advised me. He said that if _____ didn't do _____ math homework, Professor Bickel would flunk _____, and the fault would be _____, not the professor's.

2. The teacher warned my brother and me. He said that if _____ didn't learn _____ lines the drama coach would replace _____. He said some actors had difficult lines, but _____ were easy.

3. The other passenger on the bus wanted you to turn off the radio. He said that if _____ didn't turn off _____ radio he would ask the driver to kick _____ off. He said the choice was _____.

4. The priest met with you and your fiancé. He said that when _____ had settled on _____ plans for the wedding he would marry _____. He said that his ideas about the ceremony were similar to _____.

5. Your mother warned your little brother. She said if _____ didn't clean _____ room she wouldn't let _____ watch TV. The choice was _____.

6. The doctor admonished your sister. He said that if _____ didn't take _____ medicine, it obviously couldn't do _____ any good. He said a lot of medicines tasted worse than _____.

7. Professor Lopez has a potted plant in his office. _____ started to lose _____ leaves.

8. The track coach warned your brother and your sister. He said _____ would have to improve _____ times before he would let _____ run in the state meet. Several other runners had times better than _____.

What determines your choice of pronouns in Practice 2? It is governed by four factors: *person, number, gender,* and *case.* You have already studied person and number in Chapter 5. In this section we'll review them and also study gender and case.

As you study the ways that pronouns change, you will also practice choosing the correct form. While trying to solve your pronoun problems in these exercises and in your other writing, keep in mind two considerations:

1. There is usually more than one correct way to say what you want to say.

2. Often a good solution is to rewrite the sentence to avoid a troublesome word or phrase.

COMPREHENSION CHECK 1

1. List three ways of identifying nouns.
2. Pronouns are words that _____ for nouns.
3. The pronouns used in Practice 1 are called _____ pronouns.
✔ 4. Identify the four factors that determine your choice of pronouns.

PERSON

First person pronouns refer to the person or persons who are speaking or writing. See the answers to 1 and 2 in Practice 2 for examples.

Second person pronouns refer to the person or persons spoken or written to. See the answers to 3 and 4 in Practice 2.

Third person pronouns refer to anyone or anything else besides the speaker or the person spoken to. See the answers to 5–8 in Practice 2.

PRACTICE 3

✔ List the 23 pronouns used in Practice 2. Group them according to *person*. You will have 8 first person pronouns, 3 second person pronouns, and 12 third person pronouns.

Problems with Person: About whom are you talking?

The most common person problem is that writers sometimes use second person (*you*) when they should use first or third person (*I* or *he/she*).

> When you go into a strange place, you often feel that everyone is looking at you. You feel a tingling in your left toe, and you break out in a rash. Your tie seems out of kilter, your sleeves seem too long or too short, and you seem to say all the wrong things.

If the paragraph above is about the writer, first person should be used: *When I go into a strange place, I often . . . .* If it is about a particular person or group, third person is best: *When he goes into a strange place, he often . . . .*

There is a legitimate use of *you* to mean people in general, especially in compositions that give instructions:

Correct: When you go to your first job interview, you may feel tense and unsure of yourself. To avoid this, you should dress carefully for the occasion and plan what you will say to the interviewer.

Third person can be used in the above paragraph, but it may seem somewhat strained:

Correct, but not as good: When a person goes to his first job interview, he may feel tense and unsure of himself. To avoid this, he should dress carefully for the occasion and plan what he will say to the interviewer.

Don't change *persons* in mid-paragraph.

Incorrect: When one goes to his first job interview, he may feel tense and unsure of himself. To avoid this, you should dress carefully for the occasion and plan what you will say to the interviewer.

ASSIGNMENT 2

Rewrite each passage, solving any person problems. Remember that there is more than one way to solve most problems.

1. (*A letter to a newspaper from an old man*)   Today a lot of young married people are fortunate to be on welfare and don't have to worry about the high cost of living. Why should you work when you can get everything free? But what about us old people? You work most of your life, pay taxes, and then get a Social Security check that is hardly enough to survive on.

2. (*Advice from a physical education expert*)   Should a person visit a doctor before he starts exercising? I think it is an excellent idea. When you see your doctor, tell him that you plan to start a vigorous exercise program, and ask him if there are any limitations.

3. (*Advice from a nutrition expert*)   Dieters should try to get over the notion that the meal is over only when your plate is clean.

4. (*A strong opinion*)   You don't have to be intelligent to be a doctor. They just had the connections to get into medical school and the money for tuition.

5. (*A letter of complaint*)   I have found the city buses unsatisfactory this winter. In the morning, the buses are filled by the time you get to my stop. Some buses don't even stop for you. When a rider finally gets on a bus, of course, there are no seats for you.

NUMBER

The difference between the pronouns *I, me,* and *my,* on the one hand, and *we, us,* and *our,* on the other, is a difference of *number. I* is singular (one person). *We* is plural (two or more people). Similarly, *she* is one person, and *they* refers to two or more people. In first and third person, there is one set of pronouns that are singular and another group that are plural. Second person pronouns, however, are the same in singular and plural.

PRACTICE 4

Classify the 23 personal pronouns used in Practice 2 according to *number.* You should have 15 singular and 11 plural pronouns. Three of the pronouns can be used twice and should appear on both lists.

Problems with Number: How many are you talking about?

Pronouns must have *antecedents* (the nouns for which they are substituting) and they must agree with their antecedents in number and gender. (Gender refers to masculine, feminine, and neuter.)

If the antecedent is plural, the pronoun must be plural:

The cars were badly rusted. They had to be junked.

If the antecedent is singular, the pronoun must be singular:

The girl was so beautiful that she made the old men gasp.

Incorrect:

PLURAL · SING.

Can homework *assignments* help a *first-grader* or does *it* do *them*

SINGULAR · PLURAL

harm?

The pronouns do not match their antecedents in number.

Correct:

PLURAL · PLURAL

Can homework *assignments* help a *first-grader* or do *they* do *him*

SINGULAR · SING.

harm?

Sometimes a better sentence will result from changing the number of the nouns.

Correct:

SINGULAR   SING.

Can *homework* help *first-graders* or does *it* do *them* harm?

PLURAL   PLURAL

How Many Is "Everyone"?

Remember that the following words are considered singular and require singular pronouns: *each, anyone, everyone, everybody, anybody, someone, somebody, either, neither, one.*

Correct:

> When it started to rain, almost *everyone* in the park donned *his* raincoat.

Incorrect:

> When it started to rain, almost *everyone* in the park donned *their* raincoats.[1]

Good alternative:

> When it started to rain, *most* of the people donned *their* raincoats.

Collective Nouns

When using a collective noun (*team, orchestra, crowd*), differentiate between referring to the group as a unit (singular) and referring to individuals in the group (plural).

> The *band* traveled to *its* destination.
> (*Band* is considered a single unit here; therefore the singular pronoun *its* is used.)

> The *band* tuned *their* instruments one at a time.
> (Here we refer to the various members of the band; therefore the plural pronoun *their* is used.)

To simplify the singular-plural problem when using collective nouns, use the words *member* or *members* when you intend that meaning.

---

[1] The use of *their* with words like *everyone* and *everybody* is gaining acceptance.

Every band *member* tuned *her* own instrument.

Each club *member* was proud of *his* donation to charity.

Members of the P.T.A. raised *their* voices to ask a wide range of questions.

PRACTICE 5

Underline the correct pronoun in the parentheses.

1. Everyone in the room kept (his, their) hat on.
2. Has anyone here brought (his, their) car?
3. Each of the plans has (its, their) advantages.
4. Everybody brought (her, their) husband.
5. Everyone who comes with us must guard (his, their) belongings carefully.
6. Everybody who brings (her, their) husband gets a prize. (She, They) will also be given a free dinner.
7. The first group which arrives at the airport will be greeted by a special committee. (It, They) will be given the city's royal welcome.
8. Members of the committee are working at (their, his) own homes. (They, It) will meet on Monday. The committee will make (its, their) report on Monday.

ASSIGNMENT 3

Write a correct version of each of the following faulty passages.

1. Mr. Able, a school counselor, often phones a parent at night because they can't be reached during the day.
2. Once in a while an ex-student will come by and say, "Thanks for prodding me," and report that they are in college.
3. The person who exercises is more productive on their job.
4. Everyone tried to do their job as effectively as they could.
5. Either John or Lisa will read their report.
6. Someone wrote a good composition, but they forgot to put their name on it.

GENDER

Gender involves only eight of the personal pronouns—those that are third person and singular: *she, her, hers; he, him, his; it, its.*

Most students handle *he, she,* and *it* without trouble. Remember, however, that the English language has been slanted toward the male animal, so when writing about the human race as a whole, you must usually use the masculine gender or make a conscious effort to get around it.

Man has a long history of conflict. His history is a chronicle of wars and conquests. From the time of the caveman, he has sought to conquer much more often than he has sought to compromise.

Because such statements seem to exclude women, the following revision is preferable:

Humanity has a long history of conflict. It is a chronicle of wars and conquests. From the time of the cave dwellers, people have sought to conquer more often than they have sought to compromise.

Most writers today still tend to use *he, his,* and *him* in referring to people in general: "A good student does *his* homework regularly." Some are using feminine pronouns in the same general sense: "A good student does *her* homework regularly." The use of masculine and feminine, connected either with a slash (/) or with *or,* is awkward and should be avoided.

Awkward: A good student does *his* or *her* homework before *he* or *she* turns on *his* or *her* television.

There are several ways to avoid the clumsiness of *he or she:*

1. Rewrite the sentence using plural nouns and pronouns.
2. Rewrite, using second person instead of third person.
3. Eliminate the pronouns.

Correct: Good students do their homework before they turn on the television.
Correct: You should do your homework before you turn on your television.
Correct: A good student does homework before watching television.

Neuter Pronouns

It and *its* refer to things. Animals whose sex is not easily identifiable are *it.* "My dog Duchess cornered a rabbit, but she didn't kill *it.*" The dog's gender (*she*) is known; the rabbit's probably is not.

A group of people is usually referred to as *it:* "The Chess Club is growing rapidly. Several of my friends have joined *it.*"

Another use of *it* is as a sentence starter (an expletive): *It is fun to learn a new language. It's a beautiful day.*

CASE

Case signals the relationship of a word to other words in a sentence. In some languages a word may have five different forms that indicate five different functions in a sentence. In English nouns have only two cases: *regular* and *possessive,* while pronouns have three: *subjective* (nominative), *possessive,* and *objective.* Since most problems with pronouns occur in the subjective and objective cases, we will review the possessive briefly, and then study the subjective and objective cases.

The Possessive Case

As indicated by their name, possessive pronouns substitute for nouns and show possession. Some always modify nouns: *my, our, your, her, their.* Others operate alone: *mine, yours, ours, hers, theirs.* Two pronouns can be used either way: *his, its.*

That is *my* house. *Mine* is across the street.
It is *our* garden. The garden is *ours.*
That is *your* potato patch. *Yours* is filled with bugs.
Her business is booming. The business is *hers.*
His car was stolen. It was *his. His* is better than *yours.*
The oak tree lost *its* leaves early. The maple lost *its* later.
That is *their* money. It is *theirs.*

The problems that usually occur with possessive pronouns are in spelling: *its* is confused with the contraction *it's, your* is confused with *you're,* and *their* is confused with *they're.* For clarification see the discussion of apostrophes in Chapter 9.

The Subjective and Objective Cases

SUBJECT PRONOUNS: I, we, you, he, she, they, it
OBJECT PRONOUNS: me, us, you, him, her, them, it

The difference between *he* and *him* is one of case. Both *he* and *him* are third person, singular, and masculine pronouns, but they are used in different ways. Except for a few special situations, the subject pronouns are used when they substitute for the noun subjects of sentences and clauses, and the object pronouns are used at all other times. The pronouns *it* and *you* do not change.

Lolita gave the ball to Pedro.
She gave *it* to *him.* She gave *him* the ball.

Frank kissed Betty on the cheek.
He kissed *her* on the cheek.

Carlos rented the car to Jamal.
He rented *it* to *him*.

People like animals.
They like *them*.

The exception to the above rule (that most pronouns that are not subjects are objects) occurs when the verb of the sentence is any form of *be* (*am, are, is, was, were, have been, has been, had been, will be,* etc.). In such situations the subjective form of the pronoun is used:

It is *I*. The winner was *she*. It was *I* who ate the egg roll.
It was *she* who had been winning the races.

If the above constructions sound too formal, change them:

It's Henry. I am here. She was the winner. I ate the egg roll. She had been winning the races.

Similarly, when you use *than* and *as* in comparisons, beware of subjects after the verb:

Correct: She is smarter than *he*.
          You are almost as beautiful as *I*.

These sentences become less stilted if we add an auxiliary after the subject at the end of the sentence:

Better: She is smarter than *he is*.
          You are almost as beautiful as *I am*.

There are comparison situations that call for objects, not subjects:

The teacher praised John more than (he praised) *her*.
My friend was more jealous of Frieda than (she was of) *me*.

I or Me?

The choice between *I* and *me* becomes a problem when the pronoun is coupled with other subjects or objects:

_____ went to the rally.

There is never a doubt that only the subject pronouns—*I, she, he, we, you,* or *they*—fill the above blank. But if the sentence has two or more subjects, some writers are thrown off:

The band leader, the coach, and _____ went to the rally.

The correct choices are still the same:

The band leader, the coach, and I (*not* me) went.
The band leader, the coach, and she (*not* her) went.
The band leader, the coach, and he (*not* him) went.
The band leader, the coach, and they (*not* them) went.

Similarly, when one pronoun is an object rather than a subject, the choice is usually obvious:

The congressman sent (me, her, him, us, them) a letter.

Any of the choices is correct. But when two or more words are in the object position, some students get confused:

The congressman sent Mario and _____ a letter.

Your choices should be the same as before—object pronouns:

The congressman sent Mario and me (*not* I) a letter.
The congressman sent Mario and her (*not* she) a letter.

Helpful Hint: When a series of words which includes a pronoun causes you to question whether to use the subject or object form, read *only* the pronoun with the rest of the sentence. This helps to make the pronoun's function in the sentence clearer. You would not, for example, say, "Me go there very day," so you would *not* say "Molly, Jerry, and me go there every day."

We or Us

We and *us* are sometimes followed by a noun that explains who *we* or *us* is:

We students went to see the dean last week.
The dean met with us students.

If the choice is confusing, try the sentence without the noun: "We went to see the dean" is correct, so "we students" is correct.

PRACTICE 6

Choose the correct pronoun in the parentheses.

1. Gwendolyn, Rosemarie, and (I, me, us) went to the dance early.
2. The hunters—Jake, Irving, and (I, me)—were caught in a storm.
3. Our family doctor, the radiologist, and (I, me) agreed that she needed the treatments.
4. Bunny, Cordell, and (he, him) never got there.
5. They gave all of (we, us) students the wrong information.
6. The company sent the crate of coconuts to Ed, Egbert, and (she, her).
7. Are you older than (he, him)?
8. (We, Us) teachers were also evaluated.
9. The house belongs to the bank and (I, me).
10. I wanted to give everyone, but especially (she, her), a gift.

Who, Whose, and Whom

Who, whose, and *whom* are pronouns used in questions and in certain kinds of complex sentences (see Chapter 7):

Who ate the pie? *Whose* pie was it? For *whom* were you saving it?

Who is used in subject positions. You can substitute other subject pronouns (*I, he, she, we,* or *they*) and make sense.

Whose is possessive. It is followed by a noun.

Whom is used in object positions. If you can substitute *me, him, her, us,* or *them,* then you should use *whom.* As in the ''It is she'' situation (see page 220), the ''correct'' form may sound too formal for your audience.

Correct: You'll never guess whom I met at the store.
Acceptable: You'll never guess who I met at the store.

Who in object positions is acceptable—except after prepositions:

Acceptable: Who did you send the letter to?
Correct: To whom (*not* who) did you send the letter?

PRACTICE 7

Fill each blank with *who, whose,* or *whom.*

1. The people with _____ I live are friendly in a quiet way.
2. Light beer is obviously designed for people _____ don't like beer.

3. The woman _____ tools I borrowed is a long-time friend.
4. They met all the baseball players except those _____ had been injured in the fight.

Unclear Pronoun Reference

In sentences where more than one noun precedes the pronoun, you must make absolutely clear which noun you are referring to. Consider the following sentence:

Because the youth group at the church is very active, I joined it.

Did you join the youth group or the church? Your reader may not be sure because of unclear reference. Rewrite the sentence:

I joined the church because its youth group is very active.
The church which I joined has a very active youth group.
I joined the very active youth group at the church.

In the sentences below, can you be sure who has become balder and whether the toy or the flower pot is broken?

Frank told Jasper that he had become balder.
The child hurled the toy at the flower pot and broke it.

Note the lack of clarity in the following sentence from a student's paper:

My father and mother didn't want us to see the movies because they were too sexy and full of obscene ideas.

The first of the following statements is probably what the student intended to say, but both statements are possible interpretations:

My father and mother didn't want us to see the movies because the movies were too sexy and full of obscene ideas.
(or)
My father and mother didn't want us to see the movies because my parents were too sexy and full of obscene ideas.

This and *that* and their plural forms, *these* and *those,* are sometimes used as pronouns, and sometimes their reference is unclear:

That is a good idea.
These are the best for our purpose.

The reader doesn't know what the good idea is unless she has read the preceding sentence. She doesn't know what things are best for our purpose.

> Dr. Jay Tarkinson, the noted geologist, shortly before his party was caught in an avalanche, received word that his wife in Paris had sued for divorce. *This* set the expedition's progress back many months.

What set the expedition's progress back? The best way to clarify the statement is to repeat the antecedent: *The avalanche set the expedition back . . .*

ASSIGNMENT 4

Change the pronouns to nouns whenever the meaning is not clear. You may have to make a choice between two possible meanings. Either can be correct, but the meaning must be *clear*.

EXAMPLE: Tom visited his dead captain's widow, and Ted took his guard duty. This was a nice gesture.
CORRECTED: Tom visited his dead captain's widow, and Ted took Tom's guard duty. The visit was a nice gesture.

1. Frank told Jasper that he had become balder.
2. The child hurled the toy at the flower pot and broke it.
3. Luella told Lucinda that she had given Susie the wrong advice.
4. The job description said, "Wanted: male flute player and female singer." I applied for it.
5. In answer to your letter, I did not come down to the Bureau of Internal Revenue as you requested last week because I was married on the day that I was supposed to see you. I am sorry that I did this.
6. The operation was successful although the surgeon left a sponge in the patient's stomach. This pleased the patient no end.
7. While my uncle and brother-in-law were hunting, he was taken ill.
8. Some of the ladies at the Congregational Church invited Mrs. Spongle and Mrs. Cuttle to the box lunch picnic. Mrs. Cuttle could not come at all, but Mrs. Spongle managed to get there, although she was a little late. The ladies decided that she was "uppity."

ADJECTIVES AND ADVERBS

As with nouns and verbs, you can recognize adjectives and adverbs according to their use in a sentence:

> 1. An adjective modifies a noun or pronoun. (*Modify* means to limit, describe, or indicate degree.)
> 2. An adverb modifies a verb, an adjective, or another adverb.

Sentences that do not have adjectives or adverbs are dry and colorless, sometimes intentionally so:

> He took out his knife, opened it and stuck it in the log. Then he pulled up the sack, reached into it and brought out one of the trout.   [From "Big Two-Hearted River" by Ernest Hemingway]

Except for one adverb, *then,* Hemingway has written two sentences virtually without modifiers.

When a writer chooses to use adjectives and adverbs, he adds qualities to the experience:

> On the smoking skillet he poured smoothly the buckwheat batter. (From the same story by Hemingway)

Here *smoking* is used as an adjective, modifying the noun *skillet. Smoothly* is an adverb, modifying the verb *poured.*

The Three Adjective Positions

1. Adjectives come before the nouns they modify.

The *paunchy* detective tried to follow the *lithe* youth over the

rickety fence.

Her *gray, sunstrained* eyes stared straight ahead.

2. Adjectives also come after *be* and sensory verbs.[1]

The child is *sensible.*

The music sounds *beautiful.*

The senator looked *sloppy* and *undignified.*

When the adjective is in this position, it is as important as the subject and the verb; without the adjective, the sentence is not complete. The adjective which follows *be* or a sensory verb modifies the subject of the sentence. It is called a *predicate adjective.*

---

[1] The sensory verbs (as noted in Chapter 3) and *look, appear, smell, taste, feel,* and *sound.* Adjectives may also follow the verbs *seem, become, remain, grow,* and *get.*

3. Adjectives sometimes follow the nouns they modify, usually as part of a phrase.

My mother, *lovely* in her new dress, sang for the Monday Tea Club.

Alexander, *showing* signs of fatigue, worked less efficiently.

PRACTICE 8

Underline the adjectives in the following sentences and draw arrows to the nouns or pronouns that they modify.

1. He grew scared.
2. A curious pride bubbled in his throat.
3. The weather has not given me a friendly welcome.
4. The wind seems cruel.
5. The restless child, bored by the long sermon, started to make spitballs.

ASSIGNMENT 5

Add at least two adjectives to each of the following sentences or incomplete sentences. Circle the adjectives you add.

EXAMPLE: The man needed a meal.   The *weary* man needed a *hot* meal.

1. He was wearing a shirt and pants.
2. The oatmeal was
3. The spaghetti and meatballs tasted
4. The African children were given food.
5. Her dress is

ADVERBS: Functions and Positions

Adverbs are less predictable than adjectives. While adjectives modify only nouns and pronouns, adverbs modify three kinds of words: verbs, adjectives, and other adverbs. Adverbs are also less predictable in their positions; many adverbs can be used in different places in a sentence, often without changing the meaning.

1. The adverbs which modify verbs tell *how, when,* or *where* the action of the verb takes place.

a. At the beginning of the sentence:

Sometimes he talks to himself.

b. In the middle of the sentence:

She *carefully* weighed her decision.

c. At the end of the sentence:

They slept *outdoors*.

2. Adverbs which modify adjectives and other adverbs usually come before the words they modify:

She was *tremendously* strong.

The *very* long meeting was a success.

An exception is *enough,* an adverb which follows the word it modifies.

They don't pay me soon *enough*.

PRACTICE 9

Underline the adverbs. Draw arrows from the adverbs to the words they modify.

1. She is hardly aware of her departed lover.
2. My mother opposed the notion strongly.
3. She was very quiet.
4. He was deeply touched.
5. He rattled out of town and along the highway through a wonderfully rich stretch of country.
6. Pepe smiled sheepishly.

ASSIGNMENT 6

Use the adverbs from the following list in five of your own sentences (one or more adverbs to a sentence). Draw arrows from the adverbs to the words they modify.

unusually	slowly	sadly
strangely	quietly	joyfully
beautifully	carefully	frequently

Don't Use Adjectives Where Adverbs Belong

Incorrect:
    I slept *good* last night.
    He drives *careful*.
    He argues *unfair*.
    Your wife drives as *good* as mine.

She is a *real* fast swimmer.
He sings *terrible*.

All of the sentences above have adjectives where adverbs belong.

Correct:

I slept *well* last night.   (The adverb *well* modifies the verb.)

I had a *good* sleep last night. (The adjective *good* modifies the noun *sleep*.)

PRACTICE 10

Label the italicized word ADJ or ADV, and draw an arrow from the adjective or adverb to the word it modifies.

1. He drives *carefully*.
2. He is a *careful* driver.
3. He argues *unfairly*.
4. His argument is *unfair*.
5. Your wife drives as *well* as mine.
6. Your wife is as *good* a driver as mine.
7. She is a really *fast* swimmer.
8. She is a *real* athlete.
9. He sings *terribly*.
10. His singing is *terrible*.

   In order to choose between words like *good* and *well, real* and *really,* and *poor* and *poorly,* you need two pieces of information:

   1. Decide whether your sentence requires an adjective modifier or an adverb. Adjectives modify nouns and pronouns. Adverbs modify verbs, adjectives, and other adverbs.
   2. Know which words are correctly used as adjectives, and which are used as adverbs. The dictionary is a good source for this information. Here are some examples:

ADJECTIVES	ADVERBS
good	well
well (healthy)	healthily
real	really, very
poor	poorly
awful	awfully

ADJECTIVES	ADVERBS
horrible	horribly
bad	badly
correct	correctly
considerable	considerably
hurried	hurriedly
malicious	maliciously
curious	curiously
terrible	terribly

Although most adverbs end in *ly,* there are many that don't. Some words are correctly used as both adjectives and adverbs: *fast, slow, hard, deep, late, early, high, low, right.* Don't be misled, furthermore, by the *ly* words that are adjectives but not adverbs: *friendly, lovely, kindly, mannerly, likely, timely.*

Don't Use Adverbs Where Adjectives Belong

The modifier that comes after a verb is usually an adverb:

He sings *beautifully.*
He writes *clearly.*

But the sensory and *be* verbs are correctly followed by adjectives, not adverbs:

She looks *beautiful* (not *beautifully*).
The food tastes *bad* (not *badly*).
He must have been feeling *brave* (not *bravely*).

PRACTICE 11

Label the italicized word ADJ if it is an adjective and ADV if it is an adverb. Draw an arrow from the adjective or adverb to the word modified.

1. The cookies don't taste *sweet* enough.
2. The birds were singing *sweetly.*
3. The fruit will get *sweet* later this summer.
4. The judge looked *angrily* at the defendant.
5. The judge looked *angry.*
6. They tasted the casserole *cautiously.*
7. The casserole tasted *bitter.*
8. The child reacted *bitterly* to her punishment.

PRACTICE 12

Underline the correct word in the parentheses.

1. The answer sounded (correct, correctly).
2. She adapted (quick, quickly) to any situation.
3. He measured the floor (exactly, exact).
4. You must send the monthly payment (regular, regularly).
 5. The gas smelled (dangerous, dangerously).

ASSIGNMENT 7

Fill in the blanks with adjectives or adverbs that make sense and are grammatically correct.

1. I was _____ surprised to find a skunk in the kitchen.
2. He walked around the room _____.
3. He hadn't been feeling _____.
4. The test seemed _____.
5. Without her glasses she can't see _____.
6. Without her glasses she doesn't look _____.
7. He thinks that she is a _____ attractive woman.

Past Participles Used as Adjectives

In Chapters 3 and 10 you were reminded that words usually used as verbs can sometimes be used as adjectives. The trick is to remember to use the *past participle* of the verb, not the simple present or past form.

Incorrect:	My counselor was *surprise* when he saw my grades.
	Any *concern* citizen is welcome.
	The *froze* food was inedible.
	The *stole* car was located.
Correct:	My counselor was surpris**ed** when he saw my grades.
	Any concern**ed** citizen is welcome.
	The froz**en** food was inedible.
	The stol**en** car was located.

PRACTICE 13

Put two lines under the verbs and write ADJ above the "verbs" used as adjectives.

1. The storm surprised us.
2. We were surprised that he didn't come.
3. Elephants had trampled the brush.
4. The hut was trampled by the rhinoceros.

ASSIGNMENT 8

The following sentences end with the past participle forms of verbs used as adjectives. For each sentence, write another sentence using the same word as an adjective to modify a noun.

EXAMPLE: The old house seems *abandoned*.
               The *abandoned* old house belongs to my uncle.

1. The meat smells spoiled.
2. The audience was bored.
3. Clarence's wound became infected.
4. Chef Blortz's sauce tasted burned.
5. Her blouse felt starched.

Comparisons with Adjectives and Adverbs

Some students are unsure about when to add *er* and *est* to adjectives and adverbs.

Comparing Short Adjectives and Adverbs.   Most short adjectives and adverbs (almost all those with one syllable and some with two) add *er* when comparing two things and *est* when comparing three or more things. The *er* form is called the **comparative** degree; the *est* form is the **superlative.**

She is *nicer* than he is. Her daughter is the *nicest* one in the family.
Nobody drives *faster* than Zeke. Zeke is the *fastest* driver in the club.

Comparing Longer Adjectives and Adverbs.   Many two-syllable modifiers and all those with three or more syllables use the words *more* and *most* instead of adding *er* and *est*.

Your floral display is *more* beautiful than mine, but Steve's is the *most* beautiful of all.
Ken is *more* agile than Larry, but Ray is the *most* agile boy in the class.

Irregular Adjectives and Adverbs

The following adjectives and adverbs have irregular comparative and superlative forms:

bad	worse	worst
good	better	best
well	better	best
little (quantity, not size)	less	least

much	more	most
many	more	most
far	farther/further	farthest/furthest

ASSIGNMENT 9

Change each sentence so that the adjective or adverb is a *comparative* form. Add words to the sentence to complete the comparison.

EXAMPLE: My driving instructor talks slowly.
          My driving instructor talks *more* slowly than Aunt Hilda does.

1. I used to drive fast.
2. These are sweet cookies.
3. Cleopatra was a powerful ruler.
4. Angela is an intelligent person.
5. My brakes don't work well.

ASSIGNMENT 10

Rewrite each sentence so that the adjective or adverb is a *superlative* form. Add words to the sentence if necessary.

EXAMPLE: The engine of this car is quiet.
          The engine of this car is the *quietest* engine I've ever had.

1. Glenda's brother is intelligent.
2. We took a long drive.
3. Cal is wiser than Morris.
4. Mrs. Tozzle is despondent.
5. The Orioles have a good team this year.

what you have learned in chapter 11

You have broadened your understanding of nouns and have studied pronouns, adjectives, and adverbs in depth. To sharpen your understanding of the function of pronouns, you have worked with person, number, gender, case, and unclear reference. You have learned the positions of adjectives and adverbs and how to make comparisons.

This concludes the section on "polishing sentences." Demonstrate your mastery of this material as you write paragraphs and short themes.

P—Key 1

(1) dog, train (2) face, anger, son's, shirt, purple, father's face, boy (3) cow, cowbell (4) photographer, pictures, fluid, developments (5) farm, farmer

P—Key 2

(1) I, my, me, mine   (2) we, our, us, ours   (3) you, your, you, yours
(4) you, your, you, yours   (5) he, his, him, his   (6) she, her, her, hers
(7) It, its   (8) they, their, them, theirs

C—Key 1

(1) Nouns are modified by adjectives; nouns can be singular or plural; nouns can show possession.   (2) substitute   (3) personal   (4) person, number, gender, and case

P—Key 3

First Person: I, me, my, mine, we, us, our, ours
Second Person: you, your, yours
Third Person: she, her, hers, he, him, his, it, its, they, them, their, theirs

P—Key 4

Singular: I, me, my, mine, you, your, yours, she, her, hers, he, him, his, it, its
Plural: we, us, our, ours, you, your, yours, they, them, their, theirs

P—Key 5

(1) his   (2) his   (3) its   (4) her   (5) his   (6) her, She   (7) It   (8) their, They, its

P—Key 6

(1) I   (2) I   (3) I   (4) he   (5) us   (6) her   (7) he   (8) We   (9) me   (10) her

P—Key 7

(1) whom   (2) who   (3) whose   (4) who

P—Key 8

(1) He . . . *scared*   (2) *curious* pride   (3) *friendly* welcome

(4) wind . . . *cruel*   (5) *restless* child, *bored* . . . *long* sermon

P—Key 9

(1) *hardly* aware   (2) opposed . . . *strongly*   (3) *very* quiet

(4) *deeply* touched   (5) *wonderfully* rich   (6) smiled *sheepishly*

P—Key 10

(1) drives *carefully* (ADV)   (2) *careful* (ADJ) driver

(3) argues *unfairly* (ADV)   (4) argument . . . *unfair* (ADJ)

(5) drives *well* (ADV)   (6) *good* (ADJ) driver   (7) *fast* (ADJ) swimmer

(8) *real* (ADJ) athlete   (9) sings *terribly* (ADV)

(10) singing . . . *terrible* (ADJ)

P—Key 11

(1) cookies . . . *sweet* (ADJ)   (2) were singing *sweetly* (ADV)

(3) fruit . . . *sweet* (ADJ)   (4) looked *angrily* (ADV)

(5) judge . . . *angry* (ADJ)   (6) tasted . . . *cautiously* (ADV)

(7) casserole . . . *bitter* (ADJ)   (8) reacted *bitterly* (ADV)

P—Key 12

(1) correct   (2) quickly   (3) exactly   (4) regularly   (5) dangerous

P—Key 13

(1) surprised   (2) were surprised—ADJ didn't come   (3) had trampled
(4) was trampled—ADJ

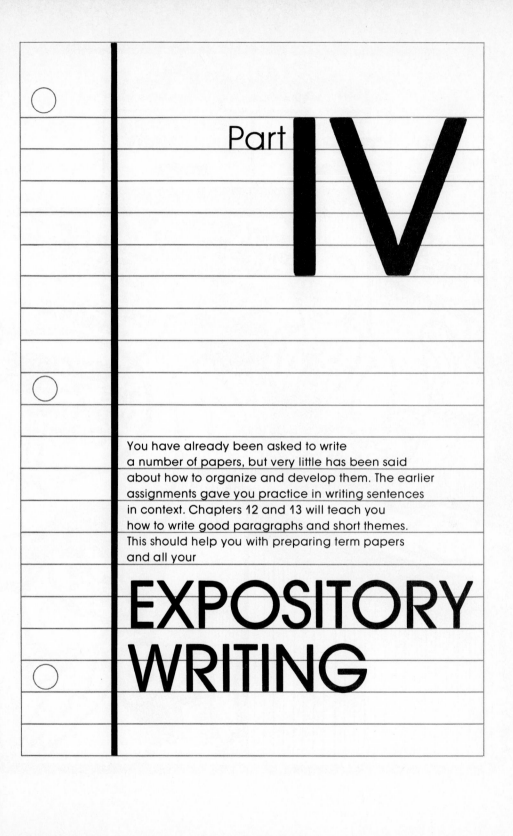

Part **IV**

You have already been asked to write
a number of papers, but very little has been said
about how to organize and develop them. The earlier
assignments gave you practice in writing sentences
in context. Chapters 12 and 13 will teach you
how to write good paragraphs and short themes.
This should help you with preparing term papers
and all your

EXPOSITORY WRITING

Writing Paragraphs

You can best improve your writing (a) by doing a lot of it; (b) by having your writing evaluated by an expert, your instructor; (c) by learning to evaluate your own writing; and (d) by doing more writing. Studying well-written paragraphs will also help. Many examples are in this chapter, and a special group of student-written paragraphs are at its end.

ASSIGNMENT 1

paragraph one: description

Follow these directions: (1) Read the *descriptive* paragraph below carefully. (2) Select one of the sentences that follows the paragraph and write that sentence on a separate sheet of paper. (3) Add four or five descriptive sentences of your own to support the sentence you selected. (4) Leave space to add a final sentence.

The lost dog seemed barely alive. Her skin was so taut against her body that it seemed as if the ribs might break through. Her tongue hung loosely from her mouth, and her eyes had a weary, haunted look about them. She seemed too tired and listless to lick at the plate of milk I had set before her. Her tail, once the liveliest part of her body, hung limply, sadly down, like a thin, wet rope. She was hunger and hopelessness on four skinny legs.

a. The campsite was littered with trash.
b. The wild horse was full of anger and frustration.

c. The hot city street was jammed with stinking cars.

d. The old car was definitely ready for the junk yard.

paragraph two: examples

The paragraph below has been developed by *examples*. Follow the same directions as in paragraph 1 above, but write two or three *examples* instead of descriptions.

People trained in CPR (cardio-pulmonary resuscitation) have saved many lives. Judge John Sirica, for example, had a heart attack while giving a speech. The famous trial judge of Watergate fame had no heart beat and was "legally dead" for four minutes. Luckily, a marshall knew mouth-to-mouth breathing and chest compression (CPR). He revived the judge and kept him alive until an ambulance arrived. At a California beach, a lifeguard brought a drowning woman to shore. When she failed to respond to mouth-to-mouth breathing, he applied chest compression. She was breathing when the medics arrived. In New Jersey a girl who had learned CPR at school saved her father's life. He had collapsed in the kitchen. His breathing and heart had stopped. While the teenager gave her father CPR, her mother phoned for help. Thus, many hearts that doctors have called "too good to die" have been saved by lay people who took the 6 to 12-hour course in CPR from the Red Cross or other agencies.

a. Some of my instructors have been really concerned about me.

b. Some of my instructors have been hard to take.

c. My course in first aid has come in very handy over the years.

d. Summer jobs can provide valuable experience.

e. My cooking ability (or mechanical aptitude) has been useful to me on a number of occasions.

paragraph three: persuasion

The paragraph below has been developed by persuasion (reasons). Follow the same directions as in paragraph 1 above, but add *reasons* instead of descriptions.

Students over 16 who do not wish to attend high school should not be required to do so. By the age of 16 most students are either "sold" on the value of school or they do not see much sense in it. If a student doesn't care for school, he isn't likely to learn much, and he will probably be resentful and disruptive. Because of this, much of the teachers' time is spent on disrupters instead of on those who want to learn. This situation tends to make a school a disciplinary institution rather than a place for learning. For these reasons, we should open the doors and "set free" those who don't value education.

a. Dress codes should (should not) be required at all elementary and secondary schools.
b. All car occupants should (should not) be required by law to wear seat belts.
c. People who have more than enough to eat have (do not have) an obligation to contribute to those who cannot feed themselves.

Write Conclusions

When you have written your three paragraphs, read each over separately and try to add a final sentence to each. The concluding sentence should summarize the paragraph, repeat the first sentence in different words, or heighten the meaning of the paragraph, *but it should not begin a new subject.* If you have already written concluding sentences, check to see if they meet these requirements and make changes if necessary.

Specific Check Points

Before submitting your assignment, evaluate each of your three paragraphs with the help of the specific check points below. Then follow the general check points that apply to all paragraphs.

Paragraph 1 (Description). Be sure that your campsite is *littered with trash,* that your horse is *wild, angry* and *frustrated,* that your *city* street is *hot,* or that your car is *old.* All of your supporting sentences must describe your initial statement.

Paragraph 2 (Examples). Have you given specific examples of *concerned* or *hard-to-take* instructors, of *honest* mechanics, of *valuable* or *boring* summer jobs? Are the examples all different? Does each support the first statement of your paragraph?

Paragraph 3 (Persuasion). Don't take both sides or an in-between position. That would require a different first sentence. All of the reasons must be different, but each must support the first sentence. Be sure that they don't just say the same thing in different words.

General Check Points

All paragraphs (and themes) should be checked against these six points:

1. My concluding sentence summarizes the paragraph, repeats the topic sentence with different words, or in some way heightens the meaning. It doesn't start a new subject.
2. Punctuation has been checked.
3. Sentences are complete. Each contains at least one subject-verb core and presents a complete idea.

4. Subjects agree with verbs and pronouns agree with antecedents.

5. Plurals end in *s* and *es; ed* is used, when necessary, to form the past tense.

6. All questionable words have been checked in the dictionary, especially the "easy" ones like *their, there,* and *its, it's.*

Now compare your paragraphs with the three sample paragraphs on pp. 237–238. The content is, of course, different, but the form should be the same. If your work compares favorably, it's ready to give to your instructor.

What You Have Accomplished

If you have done what you were asked to do in Assignment 1, you have just written three well organized expository paragraphs, developed, in turn, by description, example, and persuasion (reasons). Each paragraph has a *topic sentence* (the sentence you selected), a *body* (the four or five supporting sentences you wrote), and a *conclusion* (the final sentence you added).

Definitions of Terms

Below are brief definitions of some of the terms used in this chapter. Study them. Most of the terms will be discussed in greater detail later in this chapter.

> **expository writing (exposition):** a type of writing used to expose or explain as clearly as possible. Expository writing is usually written with a definite introduction, body, and conclusion. This kind of writing is used in business letters, scientific reports, textbooks, and college themes and term papers. It is the only type of writing this textbook teaches.
>
> **expository paragraph:** a group of sentences unified around a single idea and having a definite introduction, body, and conclusion.
>
> **paragraph:** a group of sentences unified around a single idea.
>
> **topic sentence:** a sentence that expresses the main idea of a paragraph. In this chapter the topic sentence will be used as the introductory sentence.
>
> **body:** sentences which support the idea set forth in the topic sentence.
>
> **concluding sentence:** sentence which summarizes the paragraph or in some way heightens its meaning.

1. What is the only type of writing that this textbook teaches?
2. Expository writing is used to _____ or _____.
3. List three of the major uses for this type of writing.
4. Define the following terms: paragraph, expository paragraph, topic sentence, body, conclusion.

THE EXPOSITORY PARAGRAPH

This chapter will take you step-by-step through the complete process of expository paragraph writing in the following order:

1. Outlining the whole paragraph
2. Writing the topic sentence
3. Planning the order of ideas
4. Developing the body

OUTLINING THE WHOLE PARAGRAPH

The human mind can more easily grasp ideas that are presented in a planned, logical form than those which are confused and disjointed. For this reason, one of the most essential aspects of good writing is that it be well organized. Outlining is the most effective way of looking at the whole paragraph before developing it in detail. Expository writing follows the form that you have already begun to work with:

Introduction (or topic sentence)
Body
Conclusion

The outlines below will help you see the basic organizational patterns of the three paragraphs used as examples in Assignment 1. Check each outline against its corresponding paragraph.

Outline of Paragraph One

INTRODUCTION
(Topic sentence)   The lost dog seemed barely alive.

BODY
1. Skin
2. Tongue
3. Eyes
4. Tiredness
5. Tail

| CONCLUSION | She was hunger and hopelessness on four skinny legs. |

Outline of Paragraph Two

INTRODUCTION	People trained in CPR have saved many lives.
BODY	1. Judge Sirica saved by marshall. 2. Drowning woman saved by lifeguard. 3. Father saved by teenage daughter.
CONCLUSION	Many hearts have been saved by lay people who took the course in CPR from the Red Cross or other agencies.

Outline of Paragraph Three

INTRODUCTION	Students aged 16 and above who do not wish to attend high school should not be required to do so.
BODY	1. By 16, either "sold" or not "sold" 2. Uninterested student unlikely to learn 3. "Unsold" may get disruptive, take too much teacher time 4. Forces discipline, spoils learning situation
CONCLUSION	Open the doors and "free" those who don't value education.

PRACTICE 1

Using the outlines above as models, outline the following paragraphs.

1. Development by Description

The house seemed almost beyond repair. It leaned decidedly to one side. Each gust of wind made it groan and bend. Most of the windows were broken, only a few threadbare shingles remained in patches on the roof, and there was no paint in evidence anywhere. The chimney, even with its cracked and missing bricks, looked relatively solid as it sat dejectedly amid the ruins. So far the house had been collapsing piece by piece; a sudden storm might well finish the job.

2. Development by Example

My cousin Henry looks at everything with an optimistic eye. When his car skidded into a bridge abutment, Henry said, "Lucky I wasn't killed. I need a new car anyhow." When he lost his job, he said, "It's about time I had a vacation." When his wife ran off with another man, it seemed as if that would be too much even for Henry. But after a few days of looking glum, he pulled himself together with a shrug of his shoulders and the comment, "Well, without a car or job, it's better to be a bachelor." The optimism that bubbled in Henry had surfaced again.

3. Development by Persuasion

Sex education should be taught in schools by carefully trained educators. Many parents are either too shy or too uninformed to do a good job. Children who don't learn from school or parents usually get their sex education from lavatory walls or gutter talk. Sex education is not strictly a private problem, because it deals with social relationships and social diseases that affect the entire community. This is not to say that home and church will stop playing whatever role they wish to play. Children will learn about sex in one way or another, and school is one place that they can learn in a wholesome way.

✔ CHECK YOUR OUTLINES AGAINST THE KEY.

Outlining Is a Helpful Tool

Many students hate to outline. The reason might be that outlining forces you to think ahead, to plan, to analyze what you're doing, and that's much more difficult than writing "off the top of your head" or "shooting the breeze."

Writing, however, is *not* the same as talking. Writing is much more formal, its rules are stricter, and worse, once the words are down on paper they don't disappear in thin air like spoken words do.

The purpose of the outline is to help you see where you're going before you get there, and to save you time and frustration. It makes more sense to write a few dozen words before expending your time on a few hundred or a thousand. In writing short paragraphs an outline is not always necessary, but it helps you be aware of the structure of the paragraph so that you can control the presentation of your ideas and begin to get a feeling for the outlining process.

Longer Outlines

As your writing gets longer and more complicated, good outlining becomes increasingly important. In addition to diagraming the organization of a paragraph or theme, an outline shows the relative values of the various parts. For example, in the model paragraph about the dog, the body of the paragraph is divided into approximately five parts, each contributing about one-fifth of the description. In longer paragraphs and themes each of the parts might have sub-parts. Then you add letters and numbers and your outline might look like this:

Introduction

I.
  A.
    1.
    2.
    3.
  B.
    1.
    2.
  C.
II.
  A.
    1.
    2.
  B.
    1.
    2.
    3.
    4.

Conclusion

NOTE: Introductions and conclusions are not numbered because they relate to the *whole* idea, not to any single part.

In this chapter you are being introduced to a formal method of outlining. Your instructor may or may not require you to use this method. In Chapter 13 on theme writing you will find a less formal method.

The outline should not be considered a rigid form to which you must adhere, but a flexible tool to help you plan your work. Often, for example, you can't write your topic sentence until you have planned the body. Just as often you have to change the body after you have written the topic sentence, and other changes may occur to you while you are writing. Sometimes you think of your ending before you start your outline. Sometimes it may not occur to you until you are working on the final draft.

Regardless, the outline starts the thinking process. It helps you to plan ahead and also to look back—to help you keep your work well organized, logical, and clear.

WRITING THE TOPIC SENTENCE

All sentences in a well written paragraph are important—or they shouldn't be there. From a writing point of view, however, the topic sentence is the most important. It helps the writer focus on his subject and limit its scope.

It is often part of the introduction of a paragraph and many times it serves as the entire introduction.

You have already developed paragraphs by description, example, and persuasion. You have not, however, written your own topic sentences. In this section you will first study how the content of the paragraph decides the topic sentence and vice versa. Next, you will be asked to find topic sentences in various paragraphs, to select the topic sentence in a group of sentences, and finally, to write some yourself.

How Paragraph Content Decides the Topic Sentence

The Stateroom, the Ocean Liner, the Carpet, and the Grain of Sand. Watch how the topic shifts in the five paragraphs below. (Don't confuse *topic* with *topic sentence.* A topic is like a label: the luxuriousness of the stateroom, the grandeur of the *Roman Candle.* The topic sentence expresses the main idea of the paragraph.)

The luxuriousness of the stateroom is the topic. That's what all the other sentences describe.

(1) The stateroom of the *Roman Candle,* a huge, ocean-going liner, is extremely luxurious. It contains a thick-piled carpet of rich, white wool, which is a perfect setting for the ultra-modern, form-fitting furniture and the satin-covered twin beds with double-deep mattresses. There is a small bar at the far end of the room, a view from two sides through the extra-large portholes, and a profusion of mirrors along the other walls.

The grandeur of the *Roman Candle* is the topic. The stateroom discussed in paragraph 1 is a detail.

(2) The *Roman Candle,* a huge ocean-going liner, carries 1,500 passengers and crew in a grand manner. There are three swimming pools, seven bars, two night clubs, and a small gymnasium. The staterooms are luxurious. The food, served five times a day, is prepared by master chefs from Italy, France, and Switzerland.

H. Blotzwilder's magnificent fleet is the topic. The *Roman Candle* is one of three examples.

(3) Hugo Blotzwilder owns a magnificent fleet of passenger ships. The *French Pheasant* is the oldest of his line, but its original wood-panelled cabin's fine Danish furniture is still in good condition. The *Green Turtle* is a medium-sized vessel that has seen many years of service, but it is still very seaworthy and has recently been completely refitted and redecorated with the finest of materials. The *Roman Candle,* a huge ocean-going liner, is the most luxurious. The food, the decor, and the

service are all keyed to satisfy the wealthiest passengers in the world.

The uniqueness of the carpet is the topic. The *Roman Candle* merely helps identify the carpet.	(4) The thick-piled carpet in the luxurious stateroom of the *Roman Candle* is the only carpet of its type. The wool was bleached in Afghanistan by a special process that eliminates shrinkage and prevents moth damage. The intricate design in the borders of the carpet is an original pattern conceived by a Turkish artisan, who destroyed the pattern after the carpet was made.
The strange luminosity of the grain of sand is the topic. The carpet, Blotzwilder's fleet, and the *Roman Candle* are incidental.	(5) A grain of sand found in the wool of the carpet in the stateroom of the *Roman Candle,* a luxury liner in Hugo Blotzwilder's fleet, is strangely luminous at night. In daytime it appears to be nothing more than an ordinary, whitish-colored grain of sand. In the dark, however, it glows with a greenish light far out of proportion to its size. Scientists have, as yet, not discovered the reason for this luminosity.

The five paragraphs above demonstrate that a sentence is a topic sentence only when the other sentences in the paragraph support it. A topic in one paragraph may be just a detail or an example in another paragraph.

PRACTICE 2

Study the two paragraphs below. After each, briefly explain its weakness.

1. The thick-piled carpet in the luxurious stateroom of the *Roman Candle* is the only carpet of its type. The captain who purchased the carpet in Turkey was slain by Bedouin tribesmen in Afghanistan, and his body was never recovered. He left behind several wives who had never heard of each other until the reading of the captain's will. Each of the wives was bequeathed an exact copy of the carpet.

2. A grain of sand found in the wool of the carpet in the stateroom of the *Roman Candle,* a luxury liner, is strangely luminous at night. The grain of sand comes from a beach on the Baltic Sea and has the appearance of most other grains of sand. It is hard, whitish, and, of course, very tiny. No similar grains of sand have been found in the carpet. The grain of sand was almost lost, but a cleaning woman found it and gave it to the bursar.

✔ *TURN TO THE KEY.   CHECK AND CORRECT YOUR ANSWERS.*

PRACTICE 3

Underline the topic sentences in the paragraphs below. Be careful. The topic sentence is not always the first sentence.

EXAMPLE

The cattle were dying by the thousands. Grass had become dried blades of straw. Small fires started spontaneously. *The worst drought in many years had hit the Kansas Plains.* Farmers were going bankrupt. Rivers had become thin streams.

NOTE: The fourth sentence in the example (shown in italics) is the topic sentence because all of the other sentences describe effects of the drought. It is the only sentence that "covers" all the other sentences.

Is this mostly about rocks, about fish, or about dried river beds?

1. (*a*) Rocks that people hadn't ever seen before were jutting up from muddy riverbeds. (*b*) Fish struggled to find the deepest pools. (*c*) Dead water snakes lay drying in the sun. (*d*) Rivers had become thin streams or had dried completely.

Is this mostly about the Union, the Confederates, or about both?

Ask your own questions from this point on.

2. (*a*) During the Civil War both the Union and the Confederates had certain advantages. (*b*) The Union had more people from whom to raise an army. (*c*) The Confederates were more united. The Union had a strong industrial base. (*d*) The Confederates had good supplies of food and animals. (*e*) The Union had much longer lines of communication and transport to contend with. (*f*) The South was fighting on its home territory.

3. (*a*) Chicano children face language problems in school. (*b*) The parents face both language problems and prejudices at work. (*c*) Mexican-Americans, in their struggle for survival, encounter many difficulties. (*d*) Many can find work only as stoop laborers in the lettuce fields and vineyards. (*e*) The transient life adds to their burdens, making it almost impossible for them to improve their status in life.

4. (*a*) Some college students find it easier to cheat than to study. (*b*) Some think that it's sort of a game. (*c*) Others find it necessary for survival. (*d*) Few consider that cheating is, in the long run, self-defeating. (*e*) Such responses indicate that college students have different attitudes toward cheating.

5. (*a*) His eyes gleamed with happiness. (*b*) His face shone with the sunshine it had absorbed for three months. (*c*) Matt looked like a completely different person on his return from the island. (*d*) There was a certain robustness about him, a sureness and confidence that hadn't been there before. (*e*) Matt's gestures were quick. (*f*) His stride was long and purposeful.

✔ CHECK YOUR WORK.

PRACTICE 4

Read each paragraph below carefully; then circle the letter next to the sentence that best expresses its main idea. The topic sentence you select should be broad enough to include the ideas in all the sentences it introduces, but not so broad that it can include much else. Remember that each of the supporting sentences represents only a part of the idea of the topic sentence.

1. The average amount spent per pupil in the United States was $532. In Connecticut $637 per pupil was spent. Alabama spent $355 per pupil and Mississippi spent $317.

   a. Mississippi spends less on education than any other state in the United States.
   b. There is a big difference in the amount spent per pupil in various states.
   c. More money should be spent on education in the United States.

2. Clinics of every kind are needed in many rural areas in the U.S. as well as in the inner cities. Conducting prenatal classes for women and training teachers in child development would help produce healthier babies and children. Health education could help prevent sickness and contain the spread of communicable diseases.

   a. There is a great need for better medical care in the U.S.
   b. Rural areas need better food and prenatal care for women.
   c. Health care everywhere should be improved.

3. Some retired people derive most of their satisfaction from visiting their children. Others enjoy fishing, camping, and traveling about the country. A gradually increasing percentage attend college to get degrees or to take courses that interest them. Many develop hobbies such as painting, stamp collecting, or ceramic work.

   a. All retired people develop special interests.
   b. Retired people enjoy going back to school.
   c. Many retired people develop various activities to keep themselves busy.

4. The body begins to prey upon itself, using up its fats, muscles, and tissues for fuel. The liver, kidneys, and other organs stop functioning properly. The brain is affected by shortages of carbohydrates and other necessary foods. The starving person's ability to work grows less each day. The victim often becomes confused and unaware of what is happening.

   a. Starving people cannot work effectively.
   b. Starvation is widespread throughout the world.
   c. The body and mind of a starving person are gradually affected by the lack of food.

5. Before going into the water at a strange beach, ask about possible dangers. Make sure that small children play far enough from the water so that a sudden wave won't pull them in. Be especially careful about rocky areas. Don't go swimming alone.

   a. Swimming can be very dangerous.
   b. Here are some tips to help you and your family keep from drowning at the beach.
   c. Don't swim in strange areas.

 *TURN TO THE KEY.*

PLANNING THE ORDER OF IDEAS

In some paragraphs and themes the order in which you place your ideas makes little or no difference. In others the order is very important. Four basic types of order are:

1. *Spatial.* Used in descriptions of persons, places, things, and processes, this kind of order helps the reader picture the situation in his mind as he reads. The description usually takes the reader from the general to the particular, helping the person visualize the object as a whole first and then describing the parts in an orderly fashion: from top to bottom, left to right, north to south, clockwise, etc.

2. *Chronological.* When time is an important factor, you must give your reader an orderly sense of backward or forward movement. First, you make clear what your starting point in time is: present, past, or future; then, by using time words and tense, you move backward or forward in time.

3. *Logical.* Logic is an ingredient in all types of order, but its primary use is in themes dealing with reasoning. In arguing for or against something, you must often present your ideas in a step-by-step

fashion, each step laying the groundwork for the next. The writer must decide whether to place the topic sentence first, last, or somewhere in between. In most cases, a topic sentence is found at the beginning, and this text encourages students to start their paragraphs with topic sentences and their themes with thesis statements.

4. *Emphatic* and *Dramatic*. You must often decide whether your most important point will be more effective if placed first or last. Similarly, when you wish to get an emotional response, you must carefully plan the order of your ideas.

Consider the order of the ideas carefully as you read the paragraphs in the next section, and as you write your own papers.

DEVELOPING THE BODY

The body of the paragraph carries out the promise of the topic sentence. Among the many ways of doing this are through *description, example, persuasion, comparison/contrast, process, enumeration, analogy, classification,* and *division.* Since you have already written paragraphs using description, examples, and persuasion, we will concentrate on development by classification, process, and comparison/contrast.

Development by Classification

To classify is to analyze a subject, grouping its parts according to a single standard. Secretaries file letters according to subject matter or the names of the senders or recipients. Movie producers classify movies according to the amount of sex and violence depicted. Similarly, doctors classify patients by their symptoms, and hospitals assign them to wards in like manner.

Study the two classification paragraphs and outlines below; then answer the questions for discussion and do Assignment 3.

CLASSIFICATION OUTLINE 1

Although pickles all come from the cucumber family, their "personalities" derive from the two general types of brines they are soaked in, sweet and sour.

I. Sweet pickle
   A. Description
   B. Other vegetables served with
   C. Main dishes served with
   D. Close "relations"

II. Dill pickle
   A. Description
   B. Main dishes served with

Never the stars of the show, these bit players perform fine supporting roles in "matinee" lunches and full course dinner "performances."

THE PARAGRAPH

The "Personalities" of the Pickle

Although pickles all come from the cucumber family, their "personalities" are derived from the two general types of brines they are
soaked in, sweet and sour. The sweet pickle is usually the smallest,
darkened by the rich, spicy brine that gives it a certain zesty taste.
Served with other side dish specialties, such as green onions, olives,
and hot peppers, it is a welcome addition to a meal featuring roast
turkey, beef, lamb, or ham. Other sweet types depend more on their
physical treatment than on the brine, for some of them are ground
into relish and others, the larger ones, are made into crisp slices. The
dill pickle, usually a large cucumber, is the "tough guy" of the
crowd. Soaked for weeks in a brine of vinegar, salt, dill, and other
spices, it gives welcome contrast to the flavor of hamburger, corned
beef, cheese, or other sandwiches, spurring the appetite to another
bite of pickle and another hunk of sandwich. It, too, has close
relatives in the slice and relish fields, noted most for their ability to
slide easily between two pieces of bread or onto a hamburger bun.
Never the stars of the show, these bit players perform fine supporting
roles in "matinee" lunches and full course dinner "performances."

CLASSIFICATION OUTLINE 2

Executioners in U.S. prisons can be classified in at least three
ways: the "It's Just Another Job" type, the "I Do It Right" type,
and the "It's God's Will" type.

   I. First type
      A. Does it mainly for money
      B. Thinks about it as little as possible
  II. Second type
      A. May have seen botched execution
      B. May be against capital punishment
      C. Thinks he can do it right
 III. Third type
      A. Thinks he is serving God and country
      B. Sometimes a religious zealot
      C. May look forward to job

Regardless of the feelings of the executioner, however, the end result is a state-decreed death.

THE PARAGRAPH

The Executioners

Executioners in U.S. prisons can be classified in at least three ways: the "It's Just Another Job" type, the "I Do It Right" type, and the "It's God's Will" type. The first type usually looks on the job as a way of getting a few extra dollars for his family. He feels that someone has to do the work, and he thinks about it as little as possible. The second type may have seen a poorly performed execution which needlessly extended the death agony of the victim. He may actually be against capital punishment, but he feels that, since he cannot stop the killing, he will do it right. The last one, the "It's God's Will" type, does it out of a sincere but sometimes extreme feeling that he is serving God and society. Sometimes a religious zealot, he may even look forward to the grisly work. Regardless of the feelings of the executioner, however, the end result is a state-decreed death.

for discussion

(1) Do the above paragraphs contain the three basic paragraph parts of expository paragraphs: introduction, body, and conclusion? (2) Which sentences are the topic sentences? (3) Is the order of ideas in either paragraph important? Why? Is the concluding sentence in *The Executioners* neutral in tone or slanted?

ASSIGNMENT 3

First write a classification outline; then, write a paragraph using one of the topic sentences below.

1. There are salespersons who help, salespersons who hide, and salespersons who harass.
2. There are _____ kinds of truck drivers: _____, _____, and _____. (Fill in the blanks.)
3. Some disc jockeys are _____, some are _____, and some are just plain obnoxious.

General Check Points (continued)[1]

7. My outline has been followed. Changes in paragraphs have been indicated in my outline and vice versa.
8. Changes in the paragraph have been checked against my topic

---

[1] For general check points 1–6, see pp. 239–240.

sentence to be sure that they support the topic sentence. (Sometimes the topic sentence must be changed.)

9. Any part of the paragraph that has been changed has been checked against all other parts of the paragraph to be sure that no contradictions or unnecessary repetition has been added.

Classification Check Points

1. Be sure each classification supports the topic but is different from the other classifications. They should not be repetitious or overlapping.

2. Be sure you have developed each classification as fully as possible by describing it and/or giving examples.

Development by Explaining a Process

In explaining a process one describes a series of actions performed in a fixed sequence to accomplish a task. *Historical* process writing tells how something was done in the past.

Often called "How to . . ." paragraphs, process paragraphs are sometimes accompanied by diagrams and are written in list form. We will limit this study, however, to the usual paragraph form. Two "How to" outlines and paragraphs follow. A student-written historical process is at the end of this chapter.

Describing a process well is a difficult job, and it can sometimes be a very important one. Its subject matter can range from "How the Coronation of Queen Elizabeth Was Performed" to "How to Tie Your Shoelace" to "How to Defuse an Underwater Mine in Three Minutes."

Process papers are difficult to write well. The writer is usually adept at doing what he is describing, and therefore may forget to include one or more steps in his explanation because he may do those steps subconsciously. If you have been frustrated by poorly written directions for assembling a child's toy or another product, you can understand the importance of carefully written process papers. If you were a deep sea diver who had to disconnect a live mine in three minutes, you would certainly want to have the most careful and precise directions.

Study the two process outlines and paragraphs below, then answer the questions for discussion and do Assignment 4.

PROCESS OUTLINE 1

Surveying a nonfiction book will help you study it more quickly and effectively.

    I. Title
   II. Author
  III. Copyright date

    IV. Preface
    V. Table of contents
    VI. Individual chapters
    VII. Back matter

Surveying a book is something like climbing a tree when you are lost in the forest. It helps you get your bearings so that you will have a better idea where you are going when you start hiking again.

THE PARAGRAPH

Surveying Nonfiction Books

Surveying a nonfiction book will help you study it more quickly and effectively. First, consider the title and keep it in mind to see how its intent is carried out. Second, consider who the author is. His background, experience, and views usually influence his writing. Next, look at the copyright date and decide whether the book is current enough for your purpose. Fourth, read the preface. It usually tells what the author thinks is most important about the book. Fifth, study the table of contents. It provides an outline of the major ideas offered in the book. Sixth, leaf through a chapter to see what kinds of study aids are provided. Boldface headings point up main ideas. Charts and pictures help you visualize important ideas. Questions and summaries at the ends of chapters are excellent study aids. Finally, be sure to check the back of the book for appendixes, bibliography, index, glossary, maps and charts, and answers to problems in the text. Surveying a book is something like climbing a tree when you are lost in the forest. It helps you get your bearings so that you will have a better idea where you are going when you start hiking again.

PROCESS OUTLINE 2

With the cost of food going higher and higher, many people are banding together to organize neighborhood food cooperatives.
    I. Get interested people together.
        A. Neighbors and friends
        B. Notices and ads
    II. Decide on scope of cooperative.
        A. Number of people to be included
        B. House or store?
    III. Other decisions
        A. Amount of money each member to be assessed
        B. Responsibilities of members
        C. Where to buy produce

A food cooperative may not solve all of its members' food problems, but it gives them a little greater control over an important aspect of their lives—the cost of food.

THE PARAGRAPH

How to Start a Food Co-op

With the cost of food going higher and higher, many people are banding together to organize neighborhood food cooperatives. The first step is for a group of interested people to get together. Usually, one or two people get the idea and start talking to neighbors and friends to see if there are enough interested people to make the effort worthwhile. Organizers can place notices on bulletin boards at churches, in nearby schools, at bowling alleys or other meeting places, and put an ad in the neighborhood newspaper. At the first meeting the group should decide on the scope of their cooperative. Do they want a small one or large one? Do they want to work out of someone's home or rent a small store? Should they hire some part-time help, or should they do all the work themselves? Are there legal problems to be considered? After these decisions are made, they can discuss how to finance the co-op, what the ongoing responsibilities of each member will be, and where to buy the goods and produce. A food cooperative may not solve all of its members' food problems, but it gives them a little greater control over an important aspect of their lives—the cost of food.

for discussion

Is order important in the two process paragraphs? Why? Do the topic sentences and conclusions carry out their functions properly?

ASSIGNMENT 4

Since you can't describe a process that you don't know anything about, decide on a process topic of your own choosing; then write an outline and a paragraph. Don't choose a process that is too complicated or one that is too simple. Here are a few suggestions: (1) How to Memorize a Set of Medical (or Other Technical) Terms, (2) How to Be Elected to Student Government, (3) How to Watch a Football Game, (4) How to Put on Makeup. Write in paragraph form. Read the process check points below before you start working.

Process Check Points

1. Carefully check the *order* of the directions. That is usually one of the most important factors. You can't put in the bolts until you have the holes aligned.

2. Re-read the directions to be sure you haven't omitted any. Remember that you are writing for people who may never have tried to do the job. Try to picture every step that you actually do. Be sure to review the general check points on pp. 239–240 and p. 252.

Development by Comparison/Contrast

Many things can be evaluated or understood best when they are compared and/or contrasted with other things. When you compare, look for similarities; when you contrast, look for differences.

Comparison/contrast papers can be organized in three ways:

1. *Alternating method:* Each aspect of a subject being examined is immediately followed by a study of its counterpart. For example, in comparing cars, you would pose the engine of the Duster against the engine of the Vega and the body of the Duster against the body of the Vega.
2. *Block method:* All aspects of one subject are discussed first, then all aspects of the other subject. Using this method, you would evaluate the headlights and bumpers of the Vega first, then the headlights and bumpers of the Duster.
3. A combination of the above methods.

The writer selects the method which she feels will most effectively illustrate the similarities and differences that she thinks important. Sometimes she must try writing the paper both (or all three) ways at least in outline form before she can decide.

Below are two examples. One paragraph uses both comparison and contrast; the other uses contrast alone. Each paper is written first in alternating form, then followed by an outline using the block method.

Alternating Comparison/Contrast 1

THE OUTLINE

In the minds of many male chauvinists, all men have certain inborn traits and all women have other inborn traits.

Grouping similarities together in one place makes it unnecessary to mention them separately later.

This organizational plan follows the alternating method.

I. Similarities
  A. Survival needs
  B. Physical likeness
II. Differences
  A. Physical traits
    1. Men are strong
    2. Women are soft and cuddly
  B. Intellectual traits
    1. Men are scientific and logical
    2. Women are unscientific and illogical
  C. Emotional traits
    1. Men are cool, stable
    2. Women are emotional and unstable

The chauvinist sees only what he wants to see, carefully ignoring the female truck driver and engineer as well as the male cake decorator and flower arranger.

THE PARAGRAPH

Here, the differences are paired with each other.

The Male Chauvinist Mind

In the minds of many male chauvinists, all men have certain inborn traits and all women have other inborn traits. The chauvinist will admit to similarities only in survival needs such as breathing, eating, and sleeping, and physical likenesses in such things as ears, eyes, and toenails. Otherwise, he firmly believes that all men are strong, while women are soft and cuddly. Men are naturally scientific-minded, and women are unscientific and illogical. Men are always cool in difficult situations, stable under pressure; women are emotional under stress and unstable when the going gets rough. The chauvinist sees only what he wants to see, carefully ignoring the female truck driver and engineer as well as the male cake decorator and flower arranger.

Block Comparison

THE OUTLINE

This outline indicates that all of the men's traits will be grouped in one or more sentences, and all the women's traits will be grouped separately.

Introduction: Same as above

   I. Similarities
     A. Survival needs
     B. Physical likeness
  II. Differences
     A. Men
       1. Strong
       2. Scientific, logical
       3. Cool, stable
     B. Women
       1. Soft and cuddly
       2. Unscientific, illogical
       3. Emotional, unstable

Conclusion: Same as above

for discussion

Is the block or the alternating method of organization more effective in showing differences? Would this necessarily apply in all situations?

Alternating Comparison/Contrast 2

THE OUTLINE

Sane, a national peace organization, questions the value of much of our military spending and lists civilian goods and services that could have been purchased for comparable amounts.

    I. Cost overrun on destroyers vs. Dallas' annual budget
    II. Cost overrun on tanks vs. Baltimore's annual education budget
    III. Cost of two four-star generals vs. deficit for hospital blood bank

Since the U.S. already has enough weaponry to wipe out the Soviet Union and other potential enemies many times over, *Sane* questions whether our real security lies in producing more weapons or in improving the lives of the American people.

THE PARAGRAPH

Bombs or Bread?

Costs for military spending compared directly with similar costs of civilian services. (Contrasts made within sentences and alternating sentences.)

Sane, a national peace organization, questions the value of much of our military spending and lists civilian goods and services that could have been purchased for comparable amounts. There was, for example, a cost overrun of $272.4 million for DD963 destroyers during one six-month period in 1973 as compared to $269 million spent for the total annual budget of the city of Dallas. In that same year there was another cost overrun in the period of six months, this one for $394.1 million spent on XM-1 tanks. Compare that amount to Baltimore's total annual education budget for the same year, $395 million. The cost to the taxpayer of two four-star Army generals for one year (quarters, salary, retirement, income tax adjustment, etc.) is $113,028. Funds needed to cover the deficit for the blood bank of the San Francisco General Hospital were $110,000. *Sane* declares that the U.S. already has enough weaponry to wipe out the Soviet Union and other potential enemies many times over, and it questions whether our real security lies in producing more weapons or in improving the lives of the American people.

Block Comparison

THE OUTLINE   Introduction: Same as above

First all military
expenditures are
listed, then all
civilian expenditures.

   I. Expenditures for military purposes
     A. Cost overrun for destroyers
     B. Cost overrun on tanks
     C. Cost of two four-star generals
  II. Comparable civilian expenditures
     A. Dallas annual budget
     B. Baltimore education budget
     C. Deficit of hospital blood bank

Conclusion: Same as above

ASSIGNMENT 5: Writing Comparison Papers

1. Write a paper using one of the block outlines above.
2. Compare any of the following: two politicians, two friends, two relatives, two cars, or two movies.

Comparison Check Points

1. In your introduction clearly point out what aspects of your subject are being compared.
2. Balance your paper so that the comparable features of the items being compared are treated in a reasonably even-handed manner.
3. Plan your organization carefully to achieve the effect you seek. Does an alternating pattern make clear the difference you want to emphasize, or is a block system more effective? Sometimes you can't be sure until you have finished your outline or even your rough draft.

STUDENT PARAGRAPHS

Development by Examples

My "Thrifty" Husband

"Thrift" is the middle name of my husband. When we go shopping, he never diverges from the grocery list he made at home—after having carefully studied the supermarket advertisements—even when I urge him to buy a most appealing bargain. To save gas and water he limits family baths to two per person per week, turns down the heat to 50 degrees even on the coldest nights, and makes me cook one-pot dinners. When guests come to our house, he limits our offerings to pretzels and potato chips unless they bring the drinks. Then he supplies the ice cubes. His favorite dining out place is at someone else's house. When going on a double date, we, naturally, travel in the other couple's car. Sometimes I go beyond calling Ken merely "thrifty." "Skinflint" fits better. And on cold, winter nights I get really honest and call him a low-grade, cheap tightwad.

Development by Description

The Ghetto Is My Home

The ghetto is very similar to a dump, but I like it there. The houses are ragged. The streets are full of chuck holes and debris. Rusty and dilapidated cars are parked in streets and driveways. And everywhere you turn you see rogues and bums just sitting and waiting for a chance to steal something. There aren't too many stores left to shop at anymore, because so many of them have been looted or burned. Those that are left have barred windows, and the merchandise is old and dusty. There are churches in store fronts on almost every block, and everywhere there are lots filled with junk. Sociologists say that ghetto people who get educated and make money leave as soon as they can. That's one reason it's a ghetto. When I leave—even for a short while—I miss the trash-filled alleys, the sweet aroma of the alcohol in the bars and joints, and even the rogues and bums. I intend to work in the wealthier areas of the city and spend my money in the ghetto. Otherwise I would be betraying myself and my neighbors. All the junk in the world couldn't turn me against my ghetto.

Development by Description

A Ten O'Clock Bus Ride

On my way to school the past few mornings I have noticed that the majority of the people riding the bus are old women. These hump-backed women, some more humped than others, with their long, sagging faces, wear long, heavy coats, funny knitted hats, and ankle-high plastic boots. They usually carry purses and a shopping bag or sack of some sort. The old women are all very talkative and very impatient. They always say, "Where's the bus?" or "This bus is never on time." If it's snowing, they wonder when it will stop, and if it's not snowing, they try to estimate when it will start. After a few minutes, the bus usually arrives. The old women approach it with very short steps, the size of the steps proportional to the amount of ice and snow. They start their ascent by grasping the railing on the door; then they proceed to climb, making sure that both feet are on the same step before going to the next. While struggling up the stairs, the women greet the driver and, in a joking manner, ask, "What took you so long?" Once aboard they sit in the first seat available because the motion of the bus makes it difficult for them to walk to the rear. As the bus gets closer to downtown, more and more old women get on, and soon the front of the bus is filled with their chatter. Soon we arrive downtown, and the old women depart in the same fashion in which they boarded, slowly, carefully, and very talkatively.

Development by Classification

What a Choice!

After careful analysis, I've classified my recent dates into three types: the possessive type, the "in-love-with-love" type, and the "boy-next-door" type. The possessive type is easy to recognize because he is usually seen about two feet away from his girlfriend, where he can be heard badgering her with questions about where she's been and when she got home. He drives past her house at all hours of the night to make sure that she's where he thinks she belongs. The "in-love-with-love" type overwhelms his girlfriend with flowers, candies, and candlelight dinner dates. He is full of overdone compliments, and he will even send her mother flowers on Mothers' Day. He is actually more in love with the *idea* of love than with the girl he is courting. The "boy-next-door" type is usually a knee-slapping, back-whacking, arm-punching guy, who treats his date like "one of the boys," and she has to pad herself well before going out with him. On the other hand, he is usually very warmhearted and provides a good shoulder to cry on. Which to choose? I'm looking for one with a little bit of each.

Development by Comparison/Contrast

City Water and Country Water

One of the differences between city and farm life is the water supply. In the city water is readily available from the tap—unless you forgot to pay the bill. On the farm where my grandfather lives, there is no water in the house. We have to take pails to a spring at the bottom of a nearby hill. The city water has chemicals, and sometimes you can taste the algae from the lake. The country water is sweet and clear. At home it's great to get up in the morning, turn on the faucet, and wash in warm water. On the farm we have to dress, get a pail of cold water from the spring, bring it back, and heat it on the stove. At home I use water without much thought. In the country simple things like doing dishes or taking a bath become complex, and we drive to town to do the wash at the laundromat. I won't even mention the differences between our modern bathroom at home and the outhouse on the farm. My experiences in both places help me appreciate the convenience of city water and the good, clean taste of farm water.

Development by Process

How I Won and Survived in Vegas

Almost everyone has the fantasy of winning a fortune by playing a slot machine. The stress of playing and the aftereffects of winning can lead to multiple distress, but I won and survived. To begin, I decided that ten dollars was all that I could afford to "kinda throw away." From the choices of glittering slot machines I selected the one with fruit combinations. In order to get the big $100, I had to get three of one kind in a row. I dropped in one silver dollar and up registered "cherry, cherry, apple." I had lost, but I still had nine dollars. I dropped in two dollars and up came "apple, apple, apple." I had won two dollars and broken even, so I decided to drop in three dollars to triple my chances. Calamity! Up came "grape, apple, cherry." Sweat began to ooze from my forehead and my palms. I had six dollars remaining, and I played four of them one by one with no success. Now, my heart was pumping wildly. I was down to two dollars, hadn't won a thing, and was ready for cardiopulmonary resuscitation. I shoved my second-last dollar into the machine and lost again. I was so nervous that I could hardly shove my last dollar in the slot. I took a breath and pulled the crank. The fruit spun wildly. The first column registered "cherry." The second column registered "cherry,"—and the third column, taking all eternity to stop, registered "CHERRY!" Lights flashed and bells rang. The coins clanged and banged as they issued from the belly of the machine. I had won $100! I was pale and shaky but still standing. I had won and survived!

what you have learned in chapter 12

You have learned how to write effective expository paragraphs by careful planning (outlining). You know that an expository paragraph contains an introduction, body, and conclusion, and that it is important to clearly establish your central idea with a good topic sentence. Further, you have learned to support your topic sentence with description, examples, classification, comparison/contrast, and persuasion. You can also describe a process. Finally, you have learned to write conclusions that help unify the paragraph.

In Chapter 13 you will apply this knowledge to the writing of short themes.

P—Key 1

(1) The house seemed almost beyond repair.

        A. Leaned
        B. Groaned and bent
        C. Windows, shingles, paint
        D. Chimney

So far the house had been collapsing piece by piece; a sudden storm might well finish the job.

(2) My cousin Henry looks at everything with an optimistic eye.

        A. Reaction to car skid
        B. Reaction to job loss
        C. Reaction to loss of wife
        D. General reaction (This could also have been used as a conclusion.)

The optimism that bubbled in Henry had surfaced again.

(3) Sex education should be taught in schools by carefully trained educators.

        A. Many parents don't teach it.
        B. Negative sources of information
        C. Social problem
        D. Contribution of church and home

Children will learn about sex in one way or another, and school is one place that they can learn in a wholesome way.

P—Key 2

(1) The second and third sentences discuss the captain and not the uniqueness of the carpet. The last sentence contradicts the first sentence. (2) The second to fourth sentences discuss the grain of sand but not the luminous quality.

P—Key 3

(1) d   (2) a   (3) c   (4) e   (5) c

P—Key 4

(1) b   (2) a   (3) c   (4) c   (5) b

Writing Short Themes

Since much of what you have just learned about paragraph writing also applies to theme writing, you should move through this chapter easily. It is divided into five parts:

1. Organization of the theme
2. The thesis statement
3. Methods of development
4. Seven-step writing formula
5. Student themes

ORGANIZATION OF THE THEME

An expository paragraph is comprised of sentences unified by a single idea and having a definite introduction, body, and conclusion.

An *expository theme* is comprised of a group of paragraphs unified by a single idea and having a definite introduction, body, and conclusion.

Thus, an expository paragraph is like a miniature theme. To write an expository theme you merely have to expand the paragraph form, accordion-like. This does not mean that you write a theme by first writing a paragraph, although that is one possible way. It does mean that you start with sufficient material to write a theme; then you develop a theme outline using the expository form: introduction, body, and conclusion.

INTRODUCTION: The introduction is a paragraph which contains the main idea of the theme. It usually includes a *thesis statement*. The thesis statement is to the theme what the topic sentence is to the paragraph; that is, the thesis statement provides the main idea of the theme.

BODY: The body is a series of paragraphs which fulfill the promise of the introduction.

CONCLUSION: The conclusion is a paragraph which summarizes the theme, restates the introduction in different words, or in some way heightens or dramatizes the main idea.

What Happens to the Paragraph?

In a theme, a paragraph may or may not retain its model form; that is, it may not always start with a topic sentence and end with a concluding sentence. Within a theme, a paragraph may carry out certain specialized functions. It can introduce, conclude, or support. In some cases it may begin or end with a transitional sentence that connects the paragraph with ideas from the preceding or following paragraphs. Modern journalists tend to write short paragraphs, and sometimes they paragraph a single sentence to emphasize a point.

Study the following outlines and themes to see how the same expository form that you have been using in the paragraph is applied to the theme.

Paragraph Outline 1 (Classification)

Although the exact cause of alcoholism is not known, researchers have focused on two general problem areas: psychological and physical. [1]
    I. Psychological
    II. Physical
One or both of the above factors may be the cause of alcoholism, but, thus far, no researcher has fully proved his case.

PARAGRAPH 1

What Causes Alcoholism?

Although the exact cause of alcoholism is not known, researchers have focused on at least two general problem areas: psychological and physical. Some psychologists believe that alcoholism may be caused by an ''alcoholic personality,'' a personality with many anxieties, fears, and guilt feelings. In the physical area, some researchers suspect vitamin deficiencies, some blame hormones, and a third group believes that a

---

[1] In this section the topic sentence (in paragraphs) and thesis statement (in themes) are shown in italics.

metabolic problem may cause the terrible craving for alcohol. One or both of the above factors may be the cause of alcoholism, but no researcher has, thus far, fully proved his case.

Now, see how the paragraph idea is expanded into a theme idea.

Theme Outline 1 (Classification)

Alcoholism, a disease that can be controlled but not cured, has been defined as a type of drug dependence that interferes with the drinker's health, his social relationships, and often with his job. It is a disease that affects an estimated 10,000,000 Americans. *Although the exact cause of this dread disease is not known, researchers are working in three general areas: psychological, physical, and sociological.*

    I. Psychological causes
       A. Tense, fearful, anxious people
       B. How dependency develops
    II. Physical causes
       A. Three sources
       B. Reverse situation is possible
    III. Sociological causes
       A. Negative social, cultural attitudes
       B. Positive social, cultural attitudes

Despite all the furor about the use of marijuana and other drugs in recent years, alcoholism remains the major drug problem in the United States. One or all of the above factors may be the cause of alcoholism, but no researcher has, thus far, fully proved his case.

THEME 1

Three Causes of Alcoholism

Alcoholism, a disease that can be controlled but not cured, has been defined as a type of drug dependence that interferes with the drinker's health, his social relationships, and often his job. It is a disease that affects approximately 10,000,000 Americans. *Although the exact cause of this dread disease is not known, researchers are working in at least three general areas: psychological, physical, and sociological.*

Many psychologists believe that there may be an "alcoholic personality." They believe that people who are tense, fearful, anxious, and perhaps guilt-ridden are logical candidates for the disease. They believe that the victim first uses alcohol to overcome his fears, anxieties, and guilt feelings, and that he gradually becomes dependent on the drug.

In the physical area researchers look for the influence of various foods and chemicals on the body as well as the results of defects in bodily organs. Some researchers suspect vitamin deficiencies, some blame hormones, and a third group believes that a metabolic problem may cause the terrible craving for alcohol. None of these theories has been fully proved, and it is possible that the reverse might be true: that it is the alcohol that causes the vitamin, hormonal, and metabolic problems.

Sociologists, on the other hand, believe that alcoholism may be rooted in social and cultural factors. Some family and cultural groups, for various sociological reasons, tend to extol the virtues of alcohol, to admire those who can "hold their liquor," to look with benevolent humor on those who get drunk, and even to be slightly suspicious of people who don't drink. For those who can tolerate alcohol, such group attitudes may not present problems, but for those with alcoholic tendencies this kind of group encouragement of drinking proves disastrous.

Despite all the furor about the use of marijuana and other drugs in recent years, alcoholism remains the major drug problem in the United States. One or all of the above factors may be the cause of alcoholism, but no researcher has, thus far, fully proved his case.

Two Types of Expansion

An idea can be expanded in *breadth* or in *depth.* In-breadth expansion is accomplished by adding major points, which usually necessitate a broadening of the thesis statement. In-depth expansion is accomplished by adding details, examples, reasons, or other insights. If these are apt and purposeful additions, not just padding or needless repetition, they usually add greater quality to the writing than new major points that are not fully developed. The decision about whether a theme should be broadened or deepened or both is usually dependent on the purpose of the paper and the available information.

The expansion of the paragraph "What Causes Alcoholism?" to the theme "Three Causes of Alcoholism" was accomplished in breadth by adding a third type of alcoholic. It was developed in depth by adding details to the first two types and to the introduction and conclusion. The theme could have been further expanded in depth by citing case histories and by providing further details about the research.

for discussion

How can you prove that the italicized sentence is the thesis statement? What's the difference between the topic sentence of the paragraph and the thesis statement of the theme? Have new facts and ideas been added to the theme, or have words been added just to make the theme longer? If the latter were true, what would be the effect on the theme? Compare the conclusions of the paragraph and theme. If you were to use just one sentence in the conclusion of the theme, which one would you use? Why?

Paragraph Outline 2 (Example)

Reading and Jobs

Reading plays a more important part in on-the-job success than many reluctant readers realize.
    I. Study of Army cooks
    II. Study of Army clerks
    III. Study of civilian repairmen
The need for reading is with us for life—if we expect to get and keep reasonably good jobs.

PARAGRAPH 2

Reading and Jobs

Reading plays a more important part in on-the-job success than many reluctant readers realize. A recent study shows that Army cooks, for example, must read recipes that are sometimes fairly complicated, and those with reading problems have trouble succeeding on the job. Another example from the same study shows that Army clerks must be able to read and fill in complicated forms, and reading problems inhibit success and advancement. In civilian life repairmen in almost every field are faced with constant changes in models. To keep up with the changes they must read complicated repair manuals. The need for reading is with us for life—if we expect to get and keep reasonably good jobs.

Theme Outline 2 (Example)

Schools and Jobs

Some students think that reading, math, and writing are a ''pain,'' and that they are required only because sadists run the schools. *All three subjects, however, play a more important part in on-the-job success than many reluctant students realize—and not only in top level jobs.*

    I. Study of Army cooks
      A. Reading recipes
      B. Reading other directions
      C. Problems with math
    II. Study of Army supply clerks
      A. Reading supply forms
      B. Following complicated directions
      C. Success related to reading and math ability
    III. Study of civilian repairmen
      A. Ever-changing models
      B. Need for reading, math skills
    IV. Importance of writing

Those who think of school as something separate from the "real world" are often unpleasantly surprised when they find the need for many school-taught skills on most jobs. The need for basic school subjects like reading, math, and writing is with us for life—if we expect to get and keep reasonably good jobs.

THEME 2

Schools and Jobs

Some students think that reading, math, and writing are a "pain," and that those subjects are required only because sadists run the schools. *All three subjects, however, play a more important part in on-the-job success than many reluctant students realize—and not only in top level jobs.*

Army cooks must know more about reading and math than many people realize. A recent study shows that Army cooks must read recipes that are sometimes fairly complicated. It was found, for example, that there are 40 separate tasks in the making of a jelly roll. It was also found that a cook must know about sanitation and food spoilage, or he can make an entire company of soldiers sick. Those with reading problems have trouble following complicated recipes and learning other information important to their jobs. Although math may enter into this job situation less than in many others, cooks have to be able to adapt recipes to different numbers of diners, and errors in their estimates can ruin whole batches of food. Mess sergeants usually have the responsibility for ordering large quantities of food, and mathematical errors can be costly. Thus, weaknesses in both reading and math can limit a cook's ability to do his job well and, certainly, to advance.

The same study shows that Army supply clerks, too, must have reading and math skills because they have many complicated forms to read and fill in. They are often responsible for ordering, storing, and issuing supplies worth many thousands of dollars, and they must be able to read and follow the many regulations controlling the distribution and recall of these supplies. Here again reading difficulties and inability to handle basic accounting problems may make it impossible to succeed on the job.

Repairmen, whether Army or civilian, must also have reading and math skills. Their problem lies in keeping up with constant model changes. Whether the repairman works with air conditioners, refrigerators, television sets, or automobiles, one "new and improved" version follows rapidly after another, and each creates new repair problems. Sometimes repairmen have to enroll in special refresher courses to keep up. The minimum requirement is that they be able to read and follow the technical repair manuals provided by the manufacturers. To understand most of these manuals, ability in both reading and math is usually necessary.

Writing is a skill that may or may not be helpful at the lower levels of various occupations, but as one proceeds up the employment ladder the need for written communication becomes increasingly great. At each level of advancement one must write more memos, letters, and reports, giving directions to subordinates and accounting for decisions to superiors.

Those who think of school as something separate from the "real world" are often unpleasantly surprised when they find the need for many school-taught skills on most jobs. The need for basic school subjects like reading, math, and writing is with us for life—if we expect to get and keep reasonably good jobs.

for discussion

Compare the thesis statement of the theme with the topic sentence of the paragraph. What influence does each of these have on the material that follows? In theme outline 2, a special category is made of writing (item IV). Why? Could the outline (and theme) have been organized more effectively in another way? Have new facts and ideas been added to the theme, or have words been added just to make the theme longer? Has the theme been expanded in breadth, in depth, or both? Suggest other ways in which it might have been expanded. Compare the conclusions of the paragraph and theme. If you were to use just one sentence in the conclusion of the theme, which one would you use? Why?

THE THESIS STATEMENT

The thesis statement is to the theme what the topic sentence is to the paragraph. Just as the topic sentence is the most important sentence in the paragraph from a writing point of view, so the thesis statement is important in stating the main idea of the theme and in setting its limits.

You have just finished analyzing two paragraph-to-theme expansions. In the process you have seen how important the topic sentences and thesis statements are.

In this section you will examine three outlines, each of which is followed by a series of thesis statements. Your problem is to decide which of these statements is best. You will then examine three additional outlines and write thesis statements for them.

PRACTICE 1

Study the following outlines in which the thesis statements have been omitted. After the outline you will find a choice of thesis statements. Select the one that most accurately reflects the main idea of each outline.

(1)   The Internationalization of Torture

     I. Testimony of Turkish woman
       A. Threatened with machine that pumps air into veins

B. Hung by wrists for hours
C. Beaten with truncheons
II. Testimony of Paraguayan man
A. Held for ten years without charges
B. Allegedly refused to lower prices on sugar cane
C. Suffers paralyzed leg and partial sight loss
III. Testimony of Indonesian woman
A. Detained without trial along with 55,000 others
B. Held because dead husband was Communist
C. Still in concentration camp

Leaders of Amnesty International believe that only pressure from other governments and an outcry from thousands of people throughout the world can halt this torture.

CHOICES:
a. Amnesty International, an organization devoted to the release of all political prisoners in the world, reports the torture of a Turkish woman.
b. Amnesty International, an organization devoted to the release of all political prisoners in the world, opposes Communism.
c. Amnesty International, an organization devoted to the release of all political prisoners in the world, shows that torture is still being used in many countries.
d. Amnesty International, an organization devoted to the release of all political prisoners in the world, asks for protests against the governments of Indonesia and Paraguay.

(2)   Science in the Twentieth Century

I. Increased knowledge of physical world
A. Theory of relativity
B. Splitting of atom
II. Much knowledge of medicine
A. Vitamins
B. Hormones
C. Sulfa drugs
III. New discoveries in astronomy
A. New galaxies
B. Black holes
C. Pulsars

In the above three fields alone, knowledge has been accumulating so rapidly that in the past 70 years more information has been gained than in all previous years of recorded history.

CHOICES:

a. In the past 70 years, great progress has been made in most fields of human endeavor but especially in the physical sciences, in medicine, and in astronomy.
b. Great progress has been made in most fields of human endeavor in the past 70 years, but most of it has been made in medicine.
c. So much progress has been made in medicine, the physical sciences, and astronomy in the past 70 years that it would be wise to cease research for awhile and digest the results.
d. Great progress has been made in the physical sciences, in medicine, and in astronomy in the past 70 years, and not enough progress has been made in the humanities.

(3)   The Cacique of the Taos Indians

    I. Spiritual leader
       A. Possesses knowledge of myths and rituals
       B. Leads tribal ceremonies
   II. Political leader
       A. Arbitrates conflicts within tribe
       B. Deals with local, state, and national governments
  III. Economic advisor
       A. Tells when to plant and harvest
       B. Counsels on buying and selling goods

Thus, the Cacique leads his tribe in almost all aspects of life.

CHOICES:

a. The Cacique of the Taos Indians of New Mexico is elected every ten years.
b. The Cacique of the Taos Indians of New Mexico is spiritual leader of the tribe.
c. The Cacique of the Taos Indians of New Mexico is the leader of the tribe.
d. The Taos Indians of New Mexico greatly respect their Cacique.

✔ CHECK YOUR ANSWERS.

METHODS OF DEVELOPMENT

In Chapter 12 you developed paragraphs by description, example, persuasion, classification, process, and comparison. You have seen the similarities in the organization of paragraphs and themes. You have already worked with themes developed by classification and example. Before progressing to full-scale theme writing, you will study themes developed by description, process, and comparison; then you will study a classification theme and a persuasion theme as they are developed to demonstrate the 7-step writing formula.

Remember that most paragraphs and themes are not "pure"; they are usually developed by a mixture of methods. Description, for example, is likely to be included in the writing of most types of theme development.

Development by Comparison/Contrast

Earlier we studied paragraphs developed by alternating comparison and block comparison, all within single paragraphs. Even in those relatively short paragraphs, you could see how complicated comparison writing can get. The comparison paragraphs on pp. 256–259 each compared only two subjects, but each of these (men-women, military versus civilian expenditures) had to be subdivided (male versus female traits, specific costs of military and civilian goods) for purposes of comparison. As your papers lengthen, comparisons become more complicated and careful outlining becomes more important.

Study the examples that follow. Consider the discussion questions carefully.

What Would You *Think of a Bearded Cop?*

British constable Malcolm Gair patrols his beat in London's Hyde Park wearing a full beard but no gun. Like all British policemen, Gair works unarmed except for a truncheon.

To use a gun to apprehend someone, he would first have to explain to his commanding officer in the London metropolitan police district that the criminal in question was not only armed but in the possible course of resisting arrest was likely to shoot a civilian. Only then would Gair be granted permission to check out a weapon from the precinct arsenal. In Great Britain, unarmed police are expected to subdue armed bandits and murderers.

Despite his lush and lovely beard, Constable Gair is not regarded by the Londoners he serves as a kook, a hippie, a weirdy, a queer, an artist, or an eccentric. They consider him as they do most policemen, a warm, decent, honest, brave, trustworthy friend whose job it is to help them. They do not regard him with fear, suspicion, or cynicism. They respect him and his position and the law he has sworn to enforce. Unlike many American policemen, he is not alienated from the community he serves. He is a part of it.

Over the years, most Englishmen have been reared to regard the cop on the beat as an ideal figure, someone to emulate, a man who stands for help, not punishment.

In the U.S., on the other hand, the police have rarely been con-

Reprinted from "What Would *You* Think of a Bearded Cop?" by Lloyd Shearer in *Parade* (October 27, 1968), p. 5, by permission of Parade Publications, Inc.

sidered ideal models. As unfair as it may seem, many citizens regard them as authoritarian, corruptible, cynical, resentful, aggressive, Fascistic, racist, misanthropic, a subculture of males who basically dislike and do not trust others outside their own fold, and are yet constantly on the alert for "a handout." The status accorded the police is low on the U.S. occupational list. In a 1961 survey it ranked 54th out of 90 occupations, just about on par with railroad conductors.

The average British policeman on the job does not smoke, loiter, drink, or accept free meals, samples, or other gratuities. He is not "on the take." He makes no distinction between "honest" and "dishonest graft." He accepts neither. Compared to the history of police department scandals in this country, the record of police honesty in Great Britain is a shining beacon of virtue.

Because the British police do not carry guns, neither do most professional British thieves. The British Firearms Act of 1937 calls for the registration of all guns. If an Englishman wants to buy a revolver, he applies to the local police and is given the necessary firearms certificate allowing purchase from the gun dealer who registers the sale.

In the U.S. more than 20 states require no license to own or sell guns and 31 have no laws against carrying concealed weapons. British police authorities regard this as the height of idiocy. Scotland Yard believes that police use of guns creates community resentment and leads to violence in kind. In 1967, in all of England and Wales, there were only 45 killings by shooting. In the U.S., a nation with four times the English and Welsh population, there were 7,617 such killings in 1967—170 times the British total.

It may well be, as many anthropologists suggest, that there is a fundamental flaw in the American character, or at least a fundamental contradiction. The people want law and order, yet they are, by nature and tradition, individualists who resent the authority necessary for the law enforcement they demand.

There are no basic standards for policemen throughout the U.S. They vary from town to town. The need for better police training, higher requirements, more pay, better working conditions—all of this has been advocated countless times. What we seem to forget, however, is that the police today are more representative of U.S. society than ever before.

If we do not respect them, the sad truth may well be that, deep down, many of us may not respect ourselves or our body of law.

for discussion

CONTENT: Does the British approach to policing seem to make sense? Would it work in the U.S.? Whom does the author blame for law and order problems in the U.S.? Why?

Development by Explaining a Process

How to Prevent Rape

There are two major considerations in dealing with the terrible crime of rape: learning to take precautions to avoid the rapist; dealing with the rapist if there is no other alternative.

Most precautions are fairly self-evident. Try to avoid going out alone at night. If you drive, park in lighted areas, always lock your car, and never enter it before looking inside first. When walking, stay away from shrubs, dark alleyways, and vacant lots. Never open the door to strangers. Be sure to have good locks installed. Demand identification of deliverymen unless you are expecting them. Have them slip the identification under the door. Call the company if there is any doubt.

If you are actually accosted by a rapist, you have two options: the first is to use physical resistance; the second is to use psychology. There is probably little use in reverting to physical combat unless you have had some training in karate or other self-defense methods. The use of weapons is also questionable unless you are willing and able to use them effectively. Either of these methods can be turned against you. There is some disagreement about whether you should scream and struggle. Some authorities believe that a rapist should not be antagonized. He is emotionally disturbed, and screaming and struggling will only make him more aggressive.

According to Frederic Storaska, director of the National Organization for the Prevention of Rape and Assault, "Women should resist intelligently." He says that they should appear to "go along" with the rapist until they find a way out. There is one case, for example, in which a woman confronted by a rapist told him that she would be glad to go with him but that she had to get her coat. She did go for her coat and also for the police.

Prevention is the best approach. Once confronted with a rapist, coolness is the key. No approach can be guaranteed because you are dealing with a mentally disturbed person.

for discussion

CONTENT: Does the advice in this article seem sound? Can you suggest other preventive or defensive approaches? Analyze the traditional male attitude toward rape. Does this attitude contribute to the problem? Are attitudes changing?

Development by Description

Clean Fun at Riverhead

The inspiration for the demolition derby came to Lawrence Mendelsohn one night in 1958 when he was nothing but a spare-ribbed twenty-eight-year-old stock-car driver halfway through his 10th lap around the Islip, L.I. Speedway and taking a curve too wide. A lubberly young man with a Chicago boxcar haircut came up on the inside in a 1949 Ford and caromed him 12 rows up into the grandstand, but Lawrence Mendelsohn and his entire car did not hit one spectator.

"That was what got me," he said. "I remember I was hanging upside down from my seat belt like a side of Jersey bacon and wondering why no one was sitting where I hit. 'Lousy promotion,' I said to myself.

"Not only that, but everybody who *was* in the stands forgot about the race and came running over to look at me gift-wrapped upside down in a fresh pile of junk."

At that moment occurred the transformation of Lawrence Mendelsohn, racing driver, into Lawrence Mendelsohn, promoter, and, a few transactions later, owner of the Islip Speedway, where he kept seeing more of this same underside of stock car racing that everyone in the industry avoids putting into words. Namely, that for every purist who comes to see the fine points of the race, such as who is going to win, there are probably five waiting for the wrecks to which stock car racing is so gloriously prone.

The pack will be going into a curve when suddenly two cars, three cars, four cars tangle, spinning and splattering all over each other and the retaining walls, upside down, right side up, inside out and in pieces, with the seams bursting open and discs, rods, wires and gasoline spewing out and yards of sheet metal shearing off like Reynolds Wrap and crumpling into the most baroque shapes, after which an ash-blue smoke starts seeping up from the ruins and a thrill begins to spread over the stands like Newburg sauce.

So why put up with the monotony between crashes?

Such, in brief, is the early history of what is culturally the most important sport ever originated in the United States, a sport that ranks with the gladiatorial games of Rome as a piece of national symbolism. Lawrence Mendelsohn had a vision of an automobile sport that would be all crashes. Not two cars, not three cars, not four cars, but 100 cars would be out in an arena doing nothing but smashing each other into shrapnel. The car that outrammed and outdodged all the rest, the last car that could still move amid the smoking heap, would take the prize money.

So at 8:15 at night at the Riverhead Raceway, just west of Riverhead, L.I., on Route 25, amid the quaint tranquility of the duck and turkey farm flatlands of eastern Long Island, Lawrence Mendelsohn stood up on the back of a flat truck in his red neon warm-up jacket and lectured his 100 drivers on the rules and niceties of the new game, the "demolition derby." And so at 8:30 the first 25 cars moved out onto the raceway's quarter-mile stock car track. There was not enough room for 100 cars to mangle each other. Lawrence Mendelsohn's dream would require four heats. Now the 25 cars were placed at intervals all about the circumference of the track, making flatulent revving noises, all headed not around the track but toward a point in the center of the infield.

Then the entire crowd, about 4,000, started chanting a count-down, "Ten, nine, eight, seven, six, five, four, three, two," but it was impossible to hear the rest, because right after "two" half the crowd went into a strange whinnying wail. The starter's flag went up, and the 25 cars took off, roaring into second gear with no mufflers, all headed toward that same point in the center of the infield, converging nose on nose.

The effect was exactly what one expects that many simultaneous crashes to produce: the unmistakable tympany of automobiles col-liding and cheap-gauge sheet metal buckling; front ends folding together at the same cockeyed angles police photographs of night-time wreck scenes capture so well on grainy paper; smoke pouring from under the hoods and hanging over the infield like a howitzer cloud; a few of the surviving cars lurching eccentrically on bent axles. At last, after four heats, there were only two cars moving through the junk, a 1953 Chrysler and a 1958 Cadillac. In the Chrysler a small fascia of muscles named Spider Ligon, who smoked a cigar while he drove, had the Cadillac cornered up against a guard rail in front of the main grandstand. He dispatched it by swinging around and back-ing full throttle through the left side of its grille and radiator.

By now the crowd was quite beside itself. Spectators broke through a gate in the retaining screen. Some rushed to Spider Ligon's car, hoisted him to their shoulders and marched off the field, howling. Others clambered over the stricken cars of the defeated, enjoying the details of their ruin, and howling. The good, full cry of triumph and annihilation rose from Riverhead Raceway, and the demolition derby was over. . . .

for discussion

CONTENT: Does this article somehow relate to "What Would *You* Think of a Bearded Cop?" Can you describe similar crowd reactions in other areas of U.S. life?

WRITING TECHNIQUE: This excerpt is organized chronologically. It tells how the idea for a demolition derby was spawned, discusses the "significance" and implementation of the idea, and then describes the big event. The author goes on to discuss the love of some Americans for violence. Here again, ordinary expository organization is not followed. The author uses a combination of narration and exposition. The article is used here primarily for its apt, exciting use of description. Note the use of image-producing words and phrases: "sheet metal shearing off like Reynolds Wrap," "gift-wrapped upside down in a fresh pile of junk," "a strange, whinnying wail." Find others. Humor is hard for some people to discern. What makes the article humorous?

PUT IT ALL TOGETHER

You have arrived at the point in theme writing that you earlier arrived at in paragraph writing. You have all the necessary information for writing a theme by yourself. You know about introductions, thesis statements, methods of development, and conclusions.

It's in-class writing time. The instructor tells you to write a 200 to 300-word theme in a 50-minute period. That's not much time in which to do a good job of writing unless you have a technique, a plan of operation.

It's eleven p.m. You're tired. You have a 500-word report to write. It must be turned in tomorrow morning. What do you do?

The next few pages will show you step-by-step what to do. Then you'll be on your own.

Pre-Preparation for In-Class Writing

Most in-class assignments are short (200 to 300 words) and based on common knowledge or assigned reading. After you have done the assigned reading, think through some of the ideas you might write about before you go to class. Better yet, bring a prepared outline if your instructor allows that. The outline would take you to step 5 of the formula below.

Writing Papers for Homework

Homework assignments are usually longer than class assignments, they are usually graded more strictly than in-class papers, and you are often expected to do some research. After you have done your research, follow the 7-step formula, remembering that you are expected to correct and polish your paper more carefully than you have time for in class. Take as much time as necessary to check the organization and development of your work, the diction (word choice), the grammar, spelling, and mechanics, and to recopy the paper neatly before submitting it.

7–STEP WRITING FORMULA

Once you have received an assignment in class, follow the 7-step formula described below and illustrated by the diagram.

STEP 1: **List Your Random Thoughts.** As soon as you know the subject of your assignment, zero in on it by making a list of every related idea that comes to mind in any order. Some of your thoughts may not even make sense, but writing them down helps you get started. It will help you avoid wasting time, sitting and wondering what to write about.

STEP 2: **Limit Your Subject.** Your random thoughts may take you in many different directions even if most of the ideas are related, but you must limit the subject so that your theme can be made unified and coherent and can be written in the allotted time and with the allotted number of words.

STEP 3: **Write Your Thesis Statement.** If you are like many other students, you will not immediately hit upon the exact subject that you want to develop. By the time you have finished limiting your subject, however, you should be prepared to write a thesis statement containing your main idea. It can serve as your complete introduction, or you may wish to embellish it with a few other sentences. In either case it serves as a guide for the organization and development of the balance of your paper. *Writing a good thesis statement is probably the most important single factor in the writing of a good paper.* When you write your thesis statement at the very beginning of the process, it means that you probably have gone through the first two steps mentally, and you are ready to start step 4.

STEP 4: **Plan the Body.** Write (in outline form) the major points you will use in explaining your main idea. Decide on the best order in which to present them. Now, consider how you are going to support those points. Each point must be explained, described, or proved as fully as possible. Just to say, for example, that the United Nations is a great organization does not mean any more than to say that it is a rotten organization. Your reasons, examples, and detailed descriptions are vital to the development of a good paper. (This step is explained more fully later.)

7-STEP WRITING FORMULA

ASSIGNMENT: Write a paper in which you classify your friends, neighbors, or instructors.

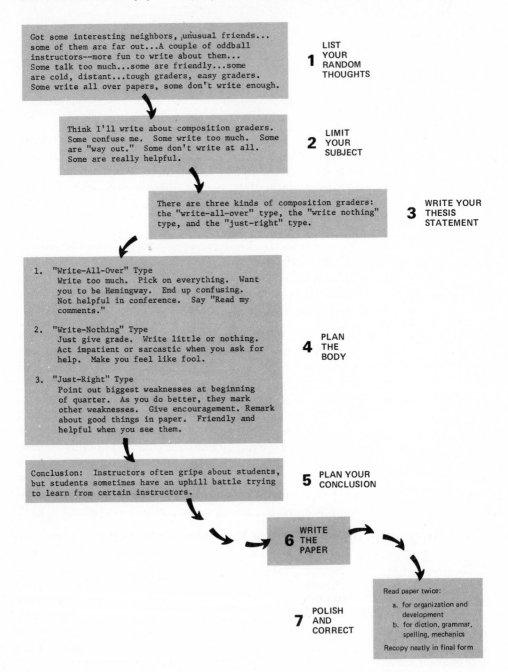

Got some interesting neighbors, unusual friends...
some of them are far out...A couple of oddball
instructors—more fun to write about them...
Some talk too much...some are friendly...some
are cold, distant...tough graders, easy graders.
Some write all over papers, some don't write enough.

1 LIST YOUR RANDOM THOUGHTS

Think I'll write about composition graders.
Some confuse me. Some write too much. Some
are "way out." Some don't write at all.
Some are really helpful.

2 LIMIT YOUR SUBJECT

There are three kinds of composition graders:
the "write-all-over" type, the "write nothing"
type, and the "just-right" type.

3 WRITE YOUR THESIS STATEMENT

1. "Write-All-Over" Type
   Write too much. Pick on everything. Want
   you to be Hemingway. End up confusing.
   Not helpful in conference. Say "Read my
   comments."

2. "Write-Nothing" Type
   Just give grade. Write little or nothing.
   Act impatient or sarcastic when you ask for
   help. Make you feel like fool.

3. "Just-Right" Type
   Point out biggest weaknesses at beginning
   of quarter. As you do better, they mark
   other weaknesses. Give encouragement. Remark
   about good things in paper. Friendly and
   helpful when you see them.

4 PLAN THE BODY

Conclusion: Instructors often gripe about students,
but students sometimes have an uphill battle trying
to learn from certain instructors.

5 PLAN YOUR CONCLUSION

6 WRITE THE PAPER

7 POLISH AND CORRECT

Read paper twice:

a. for organization and
   development
b. for diction, grammar,
   spelling, mechanics

Recopy neatly in final form

The finished essay is shown on the facing page.

Composition Graders I Have Known

Composition graders come in various sizes and shapes with all
kinds of personalities, but there are three major types: the Write-
All-Over Type, the Write-Nothing Type, and the Just-Right Type.

The Write-All-Over Type write almost as much as the student.
They are probably very sincere and dedicated teachers. Obviously,
they put in a lot of time, but they often confuse rather than help
the student. The student sees so many red marks that he doesn't know
where to start. When he tries to see the instructor, her attitude is
that she has already said all that is necessary. She is usually too
busy putting more red remarks on other students' papers, so she says,
"Read my comments."

The Write-Nothing Type thinks that the grade says everything.
To him the "C" is self-explanatory. Occasionally he will mark a few
punctuation or spelling errors, but more often he will write nothing
at all. When you ask for a conference, he'll look at you as if you ?
an invader from Mars, or as if you are not worth talking to. If he dou
say something, it's usually sarcastic, and you feel like a fool.

The Just-Right Type makes you feel good even when she's correcting
you. She always mentions the good parts of your work. She doesn't
throw all the red ink at you at once. Usually, she'll mark your biggest
weaknesses on your first papers, and as you improve she'll start zeroing
in on the minor ones. When you meet with her, she's always friendly
and encouraging.

Instructors often gripe about students, but students sometimes have
an uphill battle trying to learn from certain instructors. The Just-Right
Types are the writing instructors who make a difference.

STEP 5: **Plan Your Conclusion.**   Ideas for your conclusion should come easily at this juncture. Jot them down. Your conclusion should develop naturally, as an outgrowth of the introduction and body, not as something new and different. A good test is to read the conclusion and then the introduction. Do they complement each other? Do they seem to be part of the same package? They should.

STEP 6: **Write the Paper.**   This should be a relatively simple task if you have followed the formula to this point. You have already done the more difficult work. You have limited your subject and written your thesis statement. You have planned the organization and development of the body of your paper and jotted down ideas for your conclusion. If you have time, write a rough draft of the paper to quickly see how all the pieces fit together. If there isn't enough time, write the finished paper.

STEP 7: **Polish and Correct.**   Try to save as much time as possible for this chore. Read the paper twice, once to check organization and content, and a second time to correct the diction, spelling, grammar, and mechanics. Diction refers to your choice of words. You are asked to be aware of it at this point because, as students write longer papers, they tend to become wordy and repetitious. Use words carefully and economically. Do not repeat unnecessarily. If you have time, recopy the paper neatly. (At home, you should, of course, take more time for this step.)

As in outlining, the above steps are intended as an informal guide to writing, not as a rigid set of rules. Adapt them to meet your needs.

Applying the 7-Step Formula

Let's apply the formula to a typical assignment.

ASSIGNMENT: React to the picture and message that follow by taking a position for or against gun control in a theme of about 300 words.

Step 1: *Jot down your random thoughts.* Then, going back over the list, check those items that seem related and worthwhile.

✔ That picture is a strong way of dramatizing the need for gun control. Some people think that everyone should have the right to own a gun. Does that have something to do with democracy?
We've never had a gun in our house. People who want to keep guns must have murder in their hearts.
How are they going to get at all the millions of guns already in people's houses?
The government sticks its nose into too many things already.

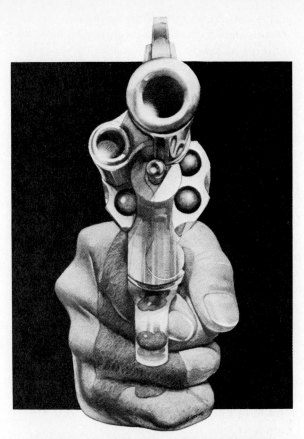

PORTRAIT OF A FELLOW AMERICAN
EXERCISING HIS "CONSTITUTIONAL RIGHTS"

✔ They say that if guns are outlawed only outlaws will have guns. But police will still have guns too.

✔ Will gun control really stop killing? Will it make people get along better?

✔ TV and movies make people think that violence is O.K.

✔ People usually kill when they're drunk or terribly frustrated. Hunters want to keep their guns. My cousin Carl almost shot his foot off once. He thought the gun wasn't loaded.

✔ Some police shoot too quickly. Sometimes they don't come when you call them, or they come too late.

✔ Some people are afraid of police.

How about women walking alone at night?

What do the Democrats think about it . . . and the Republicans?

✔ If guns aren't so handy, they won't be used easily.

Is there any proof that banning handguns will reduce killings?

This country has more killings than most other countries.

✔ There's too much violence in our society. What causes people to do so much killing?

Step 2: *Limit your subject.* Examining the items checked, you begin to see some general ideas emerging.

(a) Handguns should be outlawed.

(b) Handguns should not be outlawed.

(c) Outlawing handguns would not solve the problem of murder.

(d) People who oppose gun control support murder.

(e) Controlling handguns would lead to a police state.

You decide to choose (c). It is similar to (b), but you intend to look at some of the broader aspects of the problem. Statements (d) and (e) are unacceptable because they overgeneralize.

Step 3: *Write your thesis statement.*

"There are many good reasons for the control of handguns, but there are better reasons against it." (You will develop this idea more fully when you write the introduction.)

Step 4: *Organize and develop the body of the theme.* You list the major points with which you will support your thesis statement; then you jot down ideas under each point (an informal outline), which you will develop further as you write the paper.

1. Improve police protection before taking guns away. People don't always trust police. Sometimes they shoot too fast—and the wrong people. Police don't always respond on time. Confidence in police must be built up.

2. Change the atmosphere of violence. Cut down on TV and movie violence. Stop playing up violence in newspapers. Stop glorifying killing. Emphasize the positive.

3. Improve life so people won't want to kill: eliminate unemployment, alcoholism, drug addiction, terrible prisons and mental institutions. Better schools, recreation facilities, and job training are needed.

4. Play up the positive in society: work of scientists, doctors, teachers. Emphasize how people help each other. Tell good things people do. (Later, you decide to eliminate point 4 because it overlaps 2 and 3.)

5. Danger is that gun control would make a new set of criminals—people who keep guns because they're afraid to be without them.

Gun Control Won't Stop Killing

The gun points straight at you, menacingly. The message from the National Coalition to Ban Handguns says, "Portrait of a fellow American exercising his 'Constitutional Rights.'" The NCBH provides many good reasons for gun control, but there are stronger reasons against it, the strongest being that it won't stop the killing.

Before depriving people of guns, ~~it would seem that~~ local governments should ~~would~~ provide better police protection. Crime has been increasing ~~in this country~~ for many years, and many people, especially in poorer neighborhoods, complain that the police don't come when called or they come too late. Perhaps if the people had more faith in the police, they would be more willing to give up their guns. Many ~~of them~~ people are ~~not~~ convinced that the government isn't really trying to get the big criminals, those in organized crime, and this makes ~~the people~~ them distrust law enforcement in general.

Secondly, more should be done to reduce the atmosphere of violence. The media should be strongly encouraged to depict the positive aspects of life: the work of doctors, teachers, lawyers, scientists, and explorers. Programs that dramatize "justice" spewing from the barrel of a gun makes that kind of action seem normal. Violent death comes much, much too easily on TV, and ~~its~~ it's headline too much in the newspapers.

Finally, the social ills that cause people to murder should be dealt with. Unemployment must be cut. Vocational training and recreational facilities for young people must be improved. Ways to cure alcoholism and drug addiction have to be found. Prisons and mental institutions must be upgraded. Gun control by itself -- without the above-mentioned changes -- will create a new set of criminals, those who keep guns because ~~their~~ they're afraid to give them up.

The wide sale of handguns is an effect, not a cause. People buy and use the guns because they are afraid, frustrated, angry, and insecure. These are the problems that must be dealt with. Then people won't want or need guns. Gun control won't stop the killing!

NOTE: An opposing view is in Chapter 14.

Step 5: *Some ideas for a conclusion come to you at this point, so you jot them down.*

Gun control doesn't deal with real problem—why people kill each other. It's an illusion.

Step 6: *Write the theme, leaving ample space for corrections.*

Step 7: *Polish and correct the theme.* First you read the whole paper through to see if it makes sense, is logical, and does not contradict itself. (The paper is not likely to be contradictory if you did steps 1–4 carefully.) Then you correct for diction (choice of words), mechanics, spelling, and grammar. Notice especially how the sample paper is improved by changing inexact words and deleting unnecessary ones. It is now ready to be recopied neatly for handing in. There may not be time to recopy when themes are written in class, but themes should always be recopied when they are written at home.

HOW TO CREDIT YOUR SOURCES

Most ideas that students deal with come from their readings; therefore, when they write they use other people's ideas. This is acceptable as long as the students credit the sources of those ideas.

Credit can be given in three ways: in context, in footnotes, and in a bibliography.

In Context. Within the body of your paper you can indicate the source of your ideas or information either by direct or indirect quotation.

DIRECT QUOTATION

"We cannot know too much about the language we speak every day of our lives," says Simeon Potter, author of *Our Language.*

INDIRECT OR PARAPHRASED QUOTATION

Simeon Potter, author of *Our Language,* says *that* we should know as much as possible about the language we speak every day.

Patrick Henry said *that* he would rather die than give up his liberty.

Notice that the word *that* is used to introduce the paraphrased quotation.

In Footnotes. Examples of source footnotes appear in this chapter with the articles about the "Bearded Cop" and "Clean Fun at Riverhead." Other examples appear in Chapter 14.

In a Bibliography.   For longer papers or reports, the sources used are often listed at the end, as in a book's bibliography. In such a list you can give credit for both direct and indirect quotations and for works used as general background reading.

Using good sources intelligently and crediting them correctly adds much to the quality of your work.

Don't Lose Control

As you write longer sentences, keep control of the structure. When you add titles and authors and words or phrases to identify them (appositives), don't get confused. Continue to be aware of your subject-verb cores. Remember that prepositional phrases do *not* contain subjects or verbs. Study the examples below.

Incorrect:	In the July issue of *Scientific Citizen* <u>says</u>, ''Idaho potatoes don't always come from Idaho.'' (There is no subject for the verb *says*.)
Correct:	In the July issue of *Scientific Citizen,* Professor <u>Frank</u> <u>Zot</u> <u>says</u>, ''Idaho potatoes don't always come from Idaho.''
Incorrect:	According to an article by Seamon Xarbosh, Russian ambassador to Canada, <u>declares,</u> ''The U.S. and the Soviet Union should colonize Mars together.'' (There is no subject for the verb *declares.*)
Correct:	According to an article by Seamon Xarbosh, Russian ambassador to Canada, ''The U.S. and the Soviet Union should colonize Mars together.''

For a review of appositives, see pp. 165–166.

WRITING IS A TWO-WAY ROAD

As you develop your ideas with the 7-step formula, remember to keep checking back to your thesis statement to be sure that you are staying on the subject. When you write the final copy, you may get new ideas and want to add additional points or even change your basic idea. This means that you have to change your thesis statement. Any changes in your original plan, in fact, require you to recheck your whole paper to be sure that you aren't getting off the subject or contradicting yourself. Your finished product should be a unified whole with all parts working together.

STUDENT THEMES

Development by Example

Accepting Responsibility

There were a number of events in my early life that helped me develop responsibility.

When I was in elementary school, my mother started working second shift. This meant there was no adult available to prepare dinner. There would be weekend leftovers, meat for sandwiches, and the ingredients for a meal to be prepared from ''scratch'' in the icebox. Necessity, curiosity, or a combination of both enticed me to teach myself to cook. The mysterious lumps and strange scorched tastes are nostalgia now, but with a father who could overlook these defects and give praise, I forged ahead. By the time I was eleven I could prepare a variety of good meals as well as bake pies and cakes. It did not take long for me to realize that the responsibility for cooking meals carried with it an explicit responsibility for clean-up.

The supervision of my younger sister and responsibility for her safety also fell to me. We went to school, movies, and shopping together, though not by choice. Even at school, when my sister ''overlooked'' the need to do homework, I would be summoned to her first grade class and asked to explain and to help remedy this ''oversight.'' I can still vividly remember being called to a fifth grade classroom to be shown a table that my ''non-conformist'' ward had defaced with her pen. It was my duty to relay the details of this ''crime'' to our parents.

When I was twelve years old, my mother was placed in traction for seven weeks. While she was hospitalized, my father decided that I could handle paying the bills and doing the grocery shopping. Each of the pay days during that seven-week period I was given the household money. Just before my father died last year, I overheard him telling one of his nurses how I had managed his pay check at age twelve and had done as good a job as an adult could have done.

Our neighbors had a retarded son my age, and they would pay the cost of my sister and me to attend the Saturday afternoon movies in return for my taking their son with us and seeing to his safety.

There was a trade-off—some childhood experiences I never knew—for an early glimpse into the adult world.

Development by Classification

Those Men at the Bars

Many girls, at one time or another, go to a bar to have a good time and to meet a "nice guy." My many years of bar-hopping have taught me not only how to identify men at bars but how to escape from them.

The "Macho Man" is one you can't help but bump into. If you try to avoid him, he makes sure he bumps into you. He is the one with a very well-developed body and a one-track mind. He usually wears some type of gold chain and either a three-piece suit or very tight clothing to complement his physique. One Saturday, while dancing with my girlfriend, I was approached by a tall, muscular male dressed in a three-piece suit. He introduced himself as Rocky. We started dancing, and before I knew it I was being twirled around like a top, dipped like a yo-yo, and thrown around like a football. In the brief pauses between acrobatics, he pawed me and made suggestive remarks. As soon as my head stopped spinning, I politely excused myself and hid in the ladies' room to recuperate.

The second type, "The Urban Cowboy," is usually found sitting at the bar having a shot and a beer or at a mirror combing his hair and straightening his cowboy hat. His wardrobe includes jeans, a flannel shirt, and cowboy boots. This type looks and tries to act rough, tough, and rugged. He has an earthy smell. While I was sitting at a bar one evening with a friend, "Roy Rogers" himself sat down beside me and tried to strike up a conversation. This one smelled not only earthy but as if he had just finished cleaning a barn full of sick cows. After talking with him for about three minutes, I promptly excused myself and headed for the ladies' room, this time to apply a large dose of perfume.

No matter what bar you go to, you are sur to run into the third type, the "know-it-all." I call him "The Intel ct." This one is usually found by the electronic games. He is dres d c ervatively and wears a pair of thick glasses. He has a serious look n his face and a poor sense of humor. Several people seated near me were in a heated discussion about religion one night, when this intellect, who was seated on a stool next to me, said, "Who is God?"

I answered, "He's the big eye in the sky, and He's watching you right now."

He looked at me knowingly and whispered, "I think we should go out to my car and discuss this further." Needless to say, I went straight to the ladies' room until he returned to his electronic game.

Although I consider myself fairly good at judging men in bars, I guess that my real expertise lies in knowing how to escape to powder rooms.

Development by Comparison/Contrast

Two Modes of Travel

Should one drive his car or take the bus? Which mode is superior when traveling to, from, and about metropolitan areas, public or private transportation?

Both modes of travel have their advantages. With your own car you can be independent, going exactly when and where you want to go. You can play your radio as loudly as you please, whistle or sing to yourself, or hold a private conversation with your passenger. Private transportation is also a trifle safer than the public "human hauler." This is because there is a somewhat smaller chance of getting your head bashed in while walking to your car than when standing in one place waiting for the bus. One other advantage of private transport is the facility of carrying packages it provides: just throw them in the trunk or back seat.

The advantages of public transportation lie in not having to find parking spaces, feed hungry parking meters, or support parking lot owners and their attendants. The bus rider can be free of worry about accidents or stolen cars. He can read the paper or finish his college composition instead of paying attention to the road. He escapes much anxiety by leaving the driving to the paid professional—the ulcers too.

The drawbacks to driving one's own chariot to the rat race are the parking space problem, the "I-just-got-it-painted, he-just-scratched-it" blues, the danger of having it stolen, and the very real emotional problems that arise from the hostility toward other drivers, especially in traffic jams. You could carry this hostility into the office and unleash it on others, something that won't help your prospects for advancement, or, worse, unleash it on the wrong driver and get pummeled or shot.

Public transportation also has its drawbacks. Waiting for a bus in inclement weather is never a joy, but it is an especially negative experience when Old Man Winter is in a bad mood. Because it is a public service, there is a chance that the drivers or mechanics may call a strike at the last moment, and there you are left shivering at the bus stop. Buses sometimes get crowded, and your toe may get stepped on or your wallet might be liberated by a supple-fingered fellow traveler. Carrying boxes and packages onto a crowded bus is not a feat for the less than sturdy rider, nor is it wise for him to wait for his chariot at early or late hours, when he becomes a sitting pigeon.

The words above should help you to make a wise decision about your method of transportation, depending on whether you prefer private or public mayhem. Who was it that said, ''My kingdom for a horse!''?

Development by Comparison/Contrast

What the Rodeo Does to Wolf Point

Fifty-one weeks out of the year Wolf Point, Montana is a peaceful town, but during the week of the Wild Horse Stampede Rodeo it changes completely.

There is only one motel in Wolf Point, and a person can generally get a room there at a reasonable price. This is not true during the week of the rodeo. The rooms are filled to overflowing and the prices are doubled.

The stores in the community usually stock only items necessary for the population of an Indian reservation. These items are low priced so they can be purchased by the townspeople. The clerks in these stores are friendly and helpful. As soon as the rodeo comes to town, these stores do an about face. The inventories are expanded to include many souvenirs, the prices on everything are jacked up, and the clerks become pushy and are only out to make a buck.

The streets of Wolf Point are kept immaculately clean throughout most of the year. The inhabitants of the town take great pride in that fact. During the rodeo the streets become cluttered with trash. This trash comes from the tourists as well as from the people of the community.

The police force of Wolf Point is very small. It consists of a sheriff and about five deputies. Most of the year they tend to be very helpful and lenient. They won't put a person in jail unless he or she has committed a major crime. They have other ways of taking care of small crimes. During the Wild Horse Stampede Rodeo, however, the police force grows to about ten times its normal size. The officers then do not stand for any monkey business. They don't have time to deal patiently with problems a person may have. If you break any law, you can count on a trip to jail just to get you off the streets.

This should serve as a warning. If you come to Wolf Point during the Wild Horse Stampede Rodeo, come well heeled, well aware of sharp dealers, and well behaved.

Describing a Process

My First Tracheotomy Patient

The first time I did tracheotomy care is an experience I will never forget. I had studied the procedure thoroughly. My nursing instructor had reviewed it step-by-step in class, but I was still apprehensive about doing it on an actual patient.

My patient was a young lady who had recently gone through extensive surgery. She would have to live with an artificial airway for the rest of her life, and I didn't want to make any mistakes.

First, I thought to myself, "Pull yourself together. Stop being so nervous. First things first."

I assembled all of my equipment so that the procedure would go smoothly: the suction catheter kit, which included a sterile drape, tracheotomy ties, a suction catheter, a pipe cleaner, and a tracheotomy brush. It also included peroxide, sterile water, scissors, and a flat table surface to work from. My patient was in bed.

My hands showed that I was still a bit tense. They were wet from perspiration. They trembled a bit as I washed them and as I arranged my equipment in proper sequence on the table.

Now came the time to really pull myself together. I had to explain what I was going to do so my patient would know what to expect. I wanted her to view me as a confident nurse, so I smiled and said, "Hello, Susan. My name is Deborah. I'm the nurse who will be taking care of you today. The first thing I would like to do for you is to clean your tracheotomy tube. Please lie flat and relax as much as possible."

I removed her gown and put on sterile gloves. I covered her chest with a sterile towel and then began the "operation." First, I carefully removed her inner cannula. I placed it in the container of peroxide and cleaned it well with the small brush. There was a small mucous plug in the center of the tracheotomy tube, so I pushed it through with the pipe cleaner. Next, I rinsed the tube with sterile water and replaced it. I was careful not to contaminate the tube.

Now came the most dangerous step. I had to remove the ties that secured the tracheotomy tube to her neck. Safety was very important. If Susan coughed, and the ties were not secure, she could lose her artificial airway. As a result, she would not be able to breathe. I was careful to hold the outer part of her tracheotomy tube intact with one hand as I started to remove the ties. I removed them one side at a time, then replaced them one side at a time. I tied a secure knot, then tied it three times more.

Suddenly, I realized that it was all over. The smile on the face of my supervising nurse told me that I had done well. I was still a bit nervous, but now I was confident that I could perform tracheotomy care successfully.

what you have learned in chapter 13

In short expository themes, as in expository paragraphs, you attempt to express your ideas as clearly as possible. To achieve this you must first *limit* your subject so that it can be expressed well in the space and time allotted. When you have clearly stated the main idea of your work in your *thesis statement,* you must *organize* your paper so that it has a definite introduction, body, and conclusion; then you must *develop* the body so that it supports the main idea fully and effectively. This usually requires you to use description, examples, arguments, comparisons, classification, and other such developmental methods. The *conclusion* should tie the ideas together so as to add a sense of unity and completeness to the work.

P—Key 1

(1) c   (2) a   (3) c

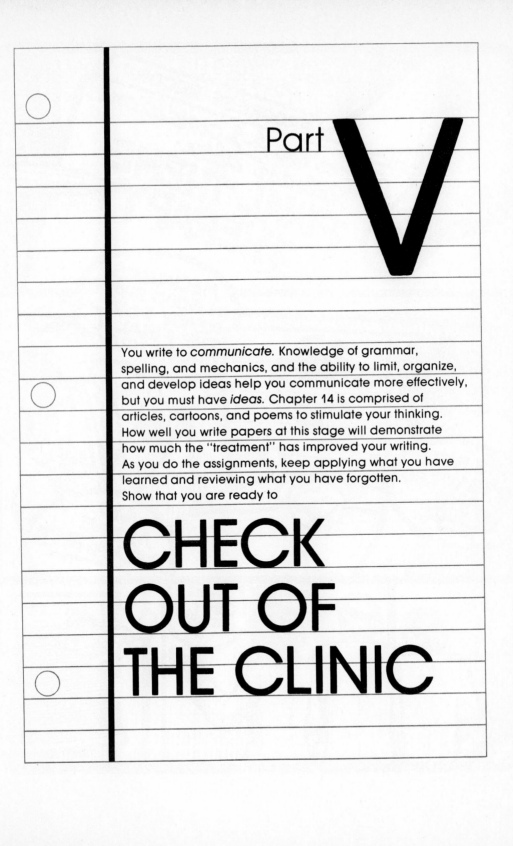

Part V

You write to *communicate*. Knowledge of grammar, spelling, and mechanics, and the ability to limit, organize, and develop ideas help you communicate more effectively, but you must have *ideas*. Chapter 14 is comprised of articles, cartoons, and poems to stimulate your thinking. How well you write papers at this stage will demonstrate how much the "treatment" has improved your writing. As you do the assignments, keep applying what you have learned and reviewing what you have forgotten. Show that you are ready to

CHECK OUT OF THE CLINIC

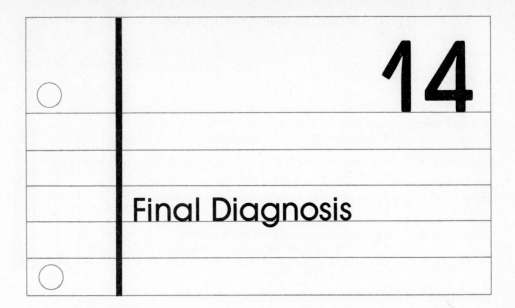

Final Diagnosis

In diagnosing your final papers, your instructor will look for the same qualities he sought in your first papers: the organization and development of your ideas and the accuracy of your grammar, spelling, and mechanics.

This chapter provides six challenging topics for you to write about: "Speak Out, America," "The Wonders of TV," "Women at Work," "Will the U.S. Drown in Trash?" "Handgun Control," and "The Art of Listening."

Each section contains discussion questions and writing suggestions for short papers on individual readings as well as suggestions for longer themes on the entire section. You may also want to refer back to pertinent materials in Chapter 1, elsewhere in this text, or to your previous reading and experience.

WRITING SUGGESTIONS

1. Read the directions for each assignment carefully.
2. Since all of the assignments provide choices, choose those which you know most about or feel most strongly about.
3. Use the 7-step formula (Chapter 13) to help you write the paper.

Check Points for Polishing Your Paper

When you get to step 7, check your paper against the key problem areas listed below. Pay special attention to those areas in which you know you are weak. Consult the following references where you need help.

FINAL DIAGNOSTIC RECORD

Record the strengths and weaknesses of your final papers on this chart. Then compare it with the Diagnostic Record you kept in Chapter 1. What progress have you made? Where do you need to work harder?

CONTENT AND ORGANIZATION:　Answer Yes or No in the proper box.

FINAL PAPERS

1　2　3

Reader Interest:　Does your composition have a message—an idea— that your reader will find interesting?

Thesis Statement:　Have you expressed your main idea in one clear sentence?

Unity:　Do the rest of your sentences stick to the same main idea?

Development:　Have you given reasons, facts, examples, or explanations that make your idea clear and convincing? (Have you avoided simply repeating the same idea in different words?)

MECHANICS:　Indicate G for Good, P for Problems, or N.E. for No Evidence (if, for example, you didn't use past tense, possession, or contractions).

Fragments, comma splices, run-ons

Present tense verbs (*has, have; does, do; is, are;* etc.)

Past tense and past participles of verbs (*walked; broke, broken;* etc.)

Singular and plural forms of nouns (*boy, boys; woman, women;* etc.)

Pronouns (*I, me, they, he,* etc.)

Apostrophes (*didn't, can't; girl's, girls';* etc.)

Easily confused words (*there, their, they're; to, two, too; its, it's; your, you're;* etc.)

Capitalization

Spelling

INSTRUCTOR'S COMMENTS:

Paper 1:_____

Paper 2:_____

Paper 3:_____

Sentence Structure: Is each group of words punctuated as a sentence *actually* a sentence? (Chapter 8)

Agreement of Subject and Verb (Chapter 5)

Agreement of Pronoun and Antecedent (Chapter 11)

Tenses: Are they consistent? Do you change them only for a definite reason? Do you add *ed* when necessary? (Chapter 10)

Number: Do you handle singularity and plurality correctly? Do you add *s* to plurals when necessary? (Chapter 5)

Spelling and Usage: Check the dictionary for definitions and spelling. Refer to "Word Traps" in the appendix of this book to check on words you tend to confuse (like *there* and *their, to* and *too*).

Possession and Contraction: Don't confuse one with the other. Place your apostrophes correctly. Do not use apostrophes in possessive words like *theirs, its, ours.* (Chapter 9)

Punctuation: Is your end punctuation correct? Does your internal punctuation help make the meaning of your sentences clearer? Are words grouped together or separated in a meaningful manner? (Chapter 9)

Capitalization: (Chapter 9)

THEME 1: Speak Out, America!

A banker, the president of the Chicago White Sox, two novelists, and a *chicano* poet speak about life in America in general and about their own lives in particular. Reading their comments may stir you to respond with your ideas about America and about yourself.

NOTE: The first three articles are interviews from *American Dreams: Lost and Found* by Studs Terkel. Because these views were expressed orally, they are not examples of polished writing.

Interview with
GAYLORD FREEMAN

He is chairman of the board of the First National Bank of Chicago. It is his last year; he has chosen his successor. His tie bears the bank's insignia: the name and the coin. "I got one of our boys to design it. I have never worn any other tie on a business day. I wear this as an indication to the troops that I'm thinkin' about the bank."

I came in in '34 and go out in '75. That's more than forty-one years. Do I feel withdrawal symptoms? (Chuckles softly.) A friend was telling me of her father, Edward Ryerson.[1] After his retirement,

---

[1] Chairman of the board of directors of Inland Steel Company during the thirties and forties, and a leading civic figure.

nobody invited him to lunch. He had to find somebody who didn't have a damn thing to do. I've already sensed it. As soon as we designated Bob as our successor, it was inevitable that people say: "Gale Freeman, he's a nice guy, but Bob's the fella we should be talking to."

I find now that every couple of weeks, I have a free luncheon engagement. It tickles me. I find it amusing. It doesn't upset me. I kind of laugh at myself because when I retire, where will I have lunch? I've had a magnificent dining room. I'll go to a club. I've belonged to the Midday Club for over thirty years, and I've never had lunch there. Now I'll have places to go to.

I won't be in demand. I'll be seeking company rather than being sought. If you're happy, that's all right. I'm very lucky. I've achieved everything I hoped to achieve. I'm not rich, but I'll be comfortable. I don't aspire to anything more. I don't feel short-circuited or let down. I'm graduating from business with a good report card. Already I feel less competitive. Let somebody else have the credit. I don't have to fight for that any more.

It can be very pleasing if it doesn't come too late. I remember a friend of mine who was a very tough man in business. When he was retiring, he said: "There's nobody in town that really likes me. From now on, I'm going to lead my life to be liked." It was too late. Attitudes were set, his habits were so ingrained, he couldn't make the change. He died an unhappy man, with great tension between himself and the children. The trick is (laughs) to put all that competitiveness into your life when it's necessary but to moderate it with a degree of love and modesty.

My good friend Milton Friedman[1] says the worst thing is for businessmen to feel responsible to society. He says that's a lot of baloney and it's contrary to the businessman's assignment. It's an arrogance he should not have. I don't accept that, though I greatly admire Milton.

Is this a Christian thought? No, we hope we'll be in business for years. There's nothing sacred about a profit-oriented society. There's no guarantee in the Bible or the Constitution that you can have private property. If we're going to continue to have these opportunities, it's only because this is acceptable to a high enough proportion of our people that they don't change the laws to prevent it.

At this point in my life, I feel deflated. I'm trying to earn enough money to pay for the things I like to do. I'd give anything for an exciting challenge, probably an arm. It's hard. A neighbor, an accountant for a large company, tried to interest them in my coming in and managing it. I was all excited. He called and said: "You're too old."

---

[1] Prominent University of Chicago economist.

Our profit system, the one we all live by, is presented as a fun game for young people training to be managers. If you can reduce the time it takes to do something, you increase the profit. Growth and investors' happiness are based on this. You can expand your facilities . . . that's why America is the land of the *plenty*. I'm so *proud* of the system. It's a wonderful thing that so much has been created, that we all have television sets and cars and pollution and everything. There's no place like it.

But what the hell is capitalism? Look what it's done to one of its greatest proponents. It's knocked me right on the head, and I'm crawling around on the street, trying to breathe.

There's a great line from the movie *Save the Tiger*. Jack Lemmon says to this highly skilled craftsman: "What are you really looking for? What's your objective in life?" The guy looks at him innocently and says: "Another season." Right now, I'm just looking for another season. I just wanna know things are gonna be all right for a little while ahead.

for discussion

What does Freeman mean when he says, "I'm just looking for another season"?

for writing

Take sides: A businessman does (does not) have a responsibility to society.

Interview with
BILL VEECK

He is president of the Chicago White Sox. He is sixty-four.

For the most part, we're losers. We're losers in a country where winning means you're great, you're beautiful, you're moral. If you don't make a lot of money, you're a loser. The bigness, the machines, the establishment, imbue us with the idea that unless you make a lot of money, you're nothing. Happiness has nothing to do with it. I'm challenging that, and I'm having fun doing it.

We have a lousy team out in the field right now, but they're singing in the stands. We have just about the worst ball club and the oldest park in the country. We have an exploding scoreboard in Comiskey Park. At first, they declared it illegal, immoral, fattening, terrible, too bush. (Laughs.) Funny how you pick things up. It came from reading Saroyan's play *The Time of Your Life*. All took place in a saloon. There's a pinball machine and the fella, he goes up to the bartender and he wants more nickels. He plays and plays, no luck;

and just before the final curtain, he hits a winner. The bells rang and the flag went up and it played "Dixie" and all sorts of extravagant things. That's what happens on our exploding scoreboard. Saroyan was sayin' something: You keep tryin' and tryin', and finally you do hit a winner. You hope, you dream, the guy's gonna hit a homer. Suddenly he hits it. The rockets go off, the bombs burst in air. (Laughs.) The loser has his day.

There is in all of us a competitive spirit, but winning has become life and death. We lose sight that it's only a *game*. It's a delightful game that is occasionally played by skillful men. Phil Wrigley once said that all you need is a winning club. It's a damning comment. We all like winners, but winning without joy isn't worth the candle. I hate to lose, but it's not the end of the world. Tomorrow may be better. (Laughs.) I'm the guy at that pinball machine waiting for all those rockets to explode.

I guess that's one of the reasons I was thrown out of organized baseball. I'd like to say I withdrew gracefully. They agreed to let the St. Louis Browns move to Baltimore if I withdrew. It was '53 when they terminated me. When I came back to the Sox thirteen years later, I was not welcomed with open arms. I didn't show proper respect.

I've reached the conclusion that I'm an anachronism. My wife and I have created a couple of other anachronisms: our sons. I'll settle for that.

for discussion

Explain: "I'm the guy at the pinball machine waiting for all those rockets to explode."

for writing

Take sides: Winning is (is not) the most important aspect of any game.

Interview with
JOHN HOWARD GRIFFIN

Novelist (The Devil Rides Outside), *anthropologist, theologian, he is best known for his memoir,* Black Like Me. *It is an account of his transformation from white to black, by means of chemicals; a response to a challenge: to wake up some morning in a black man's skin, to think human rather than white.*

My father is a man that I will never understand. He was from Georgia. He was brought up in that fundamentalist religion which said that anything remotely pleasurable was sin. He set aside Sundays as a particularly sober time. He was brought up in an incredibly racist atmosphere. But he never implanted any of these ideas in me. My dad was a kind of a miracle, a matter of pure grace. He was a wholly decent, uncorrupted human being.

It was a horrendous sacrifice on his part to send me to a French lycée at such a young age. In those days, we didn't even have air mail. It was the belief in the South that France was utterly immoral and Catholic. They didn't know which was worse.

I had what they used to call a photographic memory. I could memorize a whole school course in one week. I was bored out of my mind, so they sent me to France, because in French schools you could advance as fast as you could learn. Also, there was a medical scholarship, and I was utterly impassioned by the sciences.

I missed adolescence in this country and the revolt against my parents. This made me closer to them than most children. When I did *Black Like Me,* it was painful for him, though he never said a word. When the terrible public reaction came and I was constantly threatened, my dad became enormously protective. He sat there and kept watch with a gun. This is when he began to be radicalized. It was through the love of his child that his feelings altered.

It isn't my nature to be an activist. Your vocation doesn't necessarily conform to your nature. I was by nature a very quiet person. I love books, I love research, I love philosophy. But if you get calls, you can't say no.

It sprang from my horror. I had worked in France smuggling Jewish people out of Germany until France fell. I was twenty, a research assistant at the Asylum of Tours. When the war came, they conscripted all the doctors and medical students into the service. They couldn't conscript me because I was an American citizen. I was immediately ordered back to the U.S. I refused to go because France had formed me. How can I flee at this time of need?

I was put in charge of the asylum. Then I got involved with the French underground, smuggling Jews out of Germany, across France, into England. We would use asylum ambulances, put our refugees in straitjackets, and move them that way. They didn't have to speak. Many of them didn't speak French. They didn't have safe-conduct papers, of course. We didn't know how to steal, we didn't know how to forge. We were infants in this, but we did the best we could.

The Nazis were moving in. I will be haunted to my death by those scenes. We brought the people inside these rooms and kept them hidden. We had to tell the parents who had children under fifteen that we weren't going to make it. Suddenly, I experienced a double reality. The first: a parent said, "It's all over for us. Take our children." We would move anybody under fifteen without papers. You sat there and realized these parents were giving their children away to strangers. The second: I could go downstairs into the streets and find perfectly decent men who went right on rationalizing racism. I feel, unless we can view these things from inside such rooms, we are lost.

In this country, I've been sitting in those rooms for the past thirty years. I was in the same room with Clyde Kennard's mother after he was martyred.[1] He died of cancer because he was refused treatment when he was in Parchman Prison in Mississippi. Everyone knew it was a frame. They ordered him out of the hospital, back into prison, and into the toughest work gang. I've been sitting in rooms with countless mothers.

(Laughs.) I don't have a martyr complex. The most distressing thing about this year of helplessness has been the terrible willingness of people to rush me to eternity. (Laughs.) A young theologian wrote me: "After all your trouble, like St. Paul, you long to be dissolved in the arms of Jesus. *Vaya con Díos.* Go with God." I threw it in the wastebasket. (Laughs.) I was furious. I'm not anxious to get rushed on. (Laughs.) I want to live to the last moment.

When I was blind, I learned all the Brailles. I learned to type and wrote six books. They'd say: "You're extraordinary." I'd say I'm not. It's just that I refuse to let them put me into a cloistered workshop. I resent very deeply the underchallenging of the blind, the young, the blacks. The greatest crime you can commit against the young is to underchallenge them. In the early sixties, when we solicited the same "worthless" students to help us in Mississippi, you had extraordinary heroism.

God knows, nobody is more frustrated than people who reach maturity and are forced into retirement and a life of little significance. What a loss. This is a thing that murders us all. We aren't given a chance to have an early experience with heroism, with ideals. It withers into lovelessness. Every time you love, it's a risk.

Life is risk. What a horror if you don't feel these risks. You end up being totally paralyzed. You don't ever do anything.

I have the kind of heart condition where if they catch me in the first nine minutes, they have a chance of saving me. If they can't, why, they don't. It's really fascinating, because I've always lived in danger. I just naturally have a feeling that somehow I'm going to get through it.

Just before he died, J. Bronowski made one of the most electrifying remarks I ever heard: Justice has now become a biological necessity in man. It isn't a matter of choice, but a biological necessity. This is one of my great unfinished themes, because I don't know if I'll ever get to do that book. It absolutely possesses me.

---

[1] A black southern student who had sought admission to a state college.

Excerpts from
In Search of Our Mothers' Gardens
—ALICE WALKER

Black women are called, in the folklore that so aptly identifies one's status in society, "the *mule* of the world," because we have been handed the burdens that everyone else—*everyone* else—refused to carry. We have also been called "Matriarchs," "Superwomen," and "Mean and Evil Bitches." Not to mention "Castraters" and "Sapphire's Mama." When we have pleaded for understanding, our character has been distorted; when we have asked for simple caring, we have been handed empty inspirational appellations, then stuck in the farthest corner. When we have asked for love, we have been given children. In short, even our plainer gifts, our labors of fidelity and love, have been knocked down our throats. To be an Artist and a Black woman, even today, lowers our status in many respects, rather than raises it: and yet, Artists we will be.

In the late 1920s my mother ran away from home to marry my father. Marriage, if not running away, was expected of seventeen-year-old girls. By the time she was twenty, she had two children and was pregnant with a third. Five children later, I was born. And this is how I came to know my mother: she seemed a large, soft, loving-eyed woman who was rarely impatient in our home. Her quick, violent temper was on view only a few times a year, when she battled with the white landlord who had the misfortune to suggest to her that her children did not need to go to school.

She made all the clothes we wore, even my brothers' overalls. She made all the towels and sheets we used. She spent the summers canning vegetables and fruits. She spent the winter evenings making quilts enough to cover all our beds.

During the "working" day, she labored beside—not behind—my father in the fields. Her day began before sunup, and did not end until late at night. There was never a moment for her to sit down, undisturbed, to unravel her own private thoughts; never a time free from interruption—by work or the noisy inquiries of her many children. And yet, it is to my mother—and all our mothers who were not famous—that I went in search of the secret of what has fed that muzzled and often mutilated, but vibrant, creative spirit that the Black woman has inherited, and that pops out in wild and unlikely places to this day.

But when, you will ask, did my overworked mother have time to know or care about feeding the creative spirit?

The answer is so simple that many of us have spent years discovering it. We have constantly looked high, when we should have looked high—and low.

For example: in the Smithsonian Institution in Washington, D.C., there hangs a quilt unlike any other in the world. In fanciful, inspired, and yet simple and identifiable figures, it portrays the story of the Crucifixion. It is considered rare, beyond price. Though it follows no known pattern of quiltmaking, and though it is made of bits and pieces of worthless rags, it is obviously the work of a person of powerful imagination and deep spiritual feeling. Below this quilt I saw a note that says it was made by "an anonymous Black woman in Alabama, a hundred years ago."

If we could locate this "anonymous" Black woman from Alabama, she would turn out to be one of our grandmothers—an artist who left her mark in the only materials she could afford, and in the only medium her position in society allowed her to use.

And so our mothers and grandmothers have, more often than not anonymously, handed on the creative spark, the seed of the flower they themselves never hoped to see: or like a sealed letter they could not plainly read.

And so it is, certainly, with my own mother. Unlike Ma Rainey's songs, which retained their creator's name even while blasting forth from Bessie Smith's mouth, no song or poem will bear my mother's name. Yet so many of the stories that I write, that we all write, are my mother's stories. Only recently did I fully realize this: that through years of listening to my mother's stories of her life, I have absorbed not only the stories themselves, but something of the manner in which she spoke, something of the urgency that involves the knowledge that her stories—like her life—must be recorded. It is probably for this reason that so much of what I have written is about characters whose counterparts in real life are so much older than I am.

But the telling of these stories, which came from my mother's lips as naturally as breathing, was not the only way my mother showed herself as an artist. For stories, too, were subject to being distracted, to dying without conclusion. Dinners must be started, and cotton must be gathered before the big rains. The artist that was and is my mother showed itself to me only after many years. This is what I finally noticed:

Like Mem, a character in *The Third Life of Grange Copeland*, my mother adorned with flowers whatever shabby house we were forced to live in. And not just your typical straggly country stand of zinnias, either. She planted ambitious gardens—and still does—with over fifty different varieties of plants that bloom profusely from early March until late November. Before she left home for the fields, she watered her flowers, chopped up the grass, and laid out new beds. When she returned from the fields she might divide clumps of bulbs, dig a cold pit, uproot and replant roses, or prune branches from her taller bushes or trees—until night came and it was too dark to see.

Whatever she planted grew as if by magic, and her fame as a grower of flowers spread over three counties. Because of her creativity with her flowers, even my memories of poverty are seen through a screen of blooms—sunflowers, petunias, roses, dahlias, forsythia, spirea, delphiniums, verbena . . . and on and on.

And I remember people coming to my mother's yard to be given cuttings from her flowers; I hear again the praise showered on her because whatever rocky soil she landed on, she turned into a garden. A garden so brilliant with colors, so original in its design, so magnificent with life and creativity, that to this day people drive by our house in Georgia—perfect strangers and imperfect strangers—and ask to stand or walk among my mother's art.

I notice that it is only when my mother is working in her flowers that she is radiant, almost to the point of being invisible—except as Creator: hand and eye. She is involved in work her soul must have. Ordering the universe in the image of her personal conception of Beauty.

Her face, as she prepares the Art that is her gift, is a legacy of respect she leaves to me, for all that illuminates and cherishes life. She had handed down respect for the possibilities—and the will to grasp them.

For her, so hindered and intruded upon in so many ways, being an artist has still been a daily part of her life. This ability to hold on, even in very simple ways, is work Black women have done for a very long time.

This poem is not enough, but it is something, for the woman who literally covered the holes in our walls with sunflowers:

They were women then
My mama's generation
Husky of voice—Stout of
Step

With fists as well as
Hands
How they battered down
Doors
And ironed
Starched white
Shirts
How they led
Armies
Headragged Generals
Across mined
Fields
Booby-trapped
Ditches
To discover books
Desks
A place for us
How they knew what we
Must know
Without knowing a page
Of it
Themselves.

Guided by my heritage of a love of beauty and a respect for strength—in search of my mother's garden, I found my own.

for discussion

What is the meaning of the title? What is the role of the black mother in America?

for writing

Write about your own mother or about someone else who deeply influenced your life.

stupid america

—ABELARDO DELGADO

stupid america, see that chicano
with a big knife
in his steady hand

From *Chicano: 25 Pieces of a Chicano Mind* by Abelardo Delgado, © Barrio Publications, 1972. Reprinted by permission of the author.

he doesn't want to knife you
he wants to sit on a bench
and carve christ figures
but you won't let him.
stupid america, hear that chicano
shouting curses on the street
he is a poet
without paper and pencil
and since he cannot write
he will explode.
stupid america, remember that chicanito
flunking math and english
he is the picasso
of your western states
but he will die
with one thousand masterpieces
hanging only from his mind.

for discussion

According to Delgado, what is America wasting? Can such waste be remedied? How?

for writing

(1) If you agree with Delgado, write a paper which states his thesis. Support that thesis with examples. (2) If you disagree, give examples of the advantages of living in the United States.

THEME 2: The Wonders of TV

In the following article, columnist Pete Hamill tells of his friend Maguire's losing struggle against television's hold on his family. Refer also to the picture of TV violence in Chapter 1.

Rotting Mind Means Tube Syndrome

—PETE HAMILL

The year his son turned 14, Maguire noticed that the boy was getting dumber. This was a kid who had learned to talk at 14 months, could read when he was 4, was an A student for his first six years in school. The boy was bright, active and imaginative. And then, slowly, the boy's brain began to deteriorate.

"He started to slur words," Maguire told me. "He couldn't finish sentences. He usually didn't hear me when I talked to him and couldn't answer me clearly when he did. In school, the As became Bs, and the Bs became Cs. I thought maybe it was something physical, and I had a doctor check him out. He was perfectly normal. Then the Cs started to become Ds. Finally, he started failing everything. Worse, the two younger kids were repeating the pattern. From bright to dumb in a few short years."

Maguire was then an account executive in a major advertising agency; his hours were erratic, the pace of his business life often frantic. But when he would get home at night, and talk to his wife about the kids, she would shake her head in a baffled way and explain that she was doing her best. Hustling from the office of one account to another, Maguire pondered the creeping stupidity of his children. Then he took an afternoon off from work and visited his oldest boy's school.

"They told me he just wasn't doing much work," Maguire said. "He owed them four book reports. He never said a word in social studies. His mind wandered, he was distracted, he asked to leave the room a lot. But the teacher told me he wasn't much different from all of the other kids. In some ways, he was better. He at least did some work. Most of them, she told me, didn't do any work at all."

Maguire asked the teacher if she had any theories about why the kids behaved this way.

"Of course," she said. "Television."

Television? Maguire was staggered. He made his living off television. Often he would sit with the kids in the TV room and point out the commercials he had helped to create. Television had paid for his house in the suburbs, for his two cars, his clothes, his food, the pictures on the walls. It even paid for the kids' schools.

"What do you mean, television?" he said.

"Television rots minds," the teacher said flatly. "But most of us figure there's nothing to be done about it anymore."

At work the next day, Maguire told his secretary to do some special research for him. Within a week, he had some scary numbers on his desk. The Scholastic Aptitude Tests (SATs) showed that the reading scores of all American high school students had fallen in every year since 1950, the year of television's great national triumph. The math scores were even worse. The average American kid spent four to six hours a day watching television, and by age 16 had witnessed 11,000 homicides on the tube.

"I came home that night, and the kids were watching television with my wife," he said. "I looked at them, glued to the set. They nodded hello to me. And suddenly I got scared. I imagined these four people, their brains rotted out, suddenly adding me to the evening's homicide count because I wanted them to talk to me. I went to the bedroom and for the first time since college, I took down 'Moby Dick' and started to read."

In the following week, Maguire accumulated more and more ideas about the impact of television on the lives of Americans. All classes and colors had been affected intellectually; reading requires the decoding of symbols, the transforming of a word like "cat" into a cat that lives in the imagination. Television shows the cat. No active thought is required. Television even supplies a laugh track and music to trigger the emotions the imagination will not create or release.

"I read somewhere that the worst danger to kids who become TV addicts is that while they are watching TV, they're not doing anything else," Maguire said. "They're not down in the schoolyard, playing ball, or falling in love, or getting in fights, or learning to compromise. They're alone, with a box that doesn't hear them if they want to talk back. They don't have to think, because everything is done for them. They don't have to question, because what's the point if you can't challenge the guy on the set?"

Television had also changed politics; Maguire's kids had political opinions based on the way candidates looked, and how they projected themselves theatrically. Politics, which should be based on the structure of analysis and thought, had become dominated by the structures of drama; that is to say, by conflict.

"I knew Reagan would win in a landslide," Maguire said. "As an actor, he fit right into the mass culture formed by 30 years of television."

Maguire tried to do something. He called a family conference after dinner one night, explained his discoveries, suggested a voluntary limiting of television watching, or its complete elimination for three months.

"I said we could start a reading program together," he told me. "All read the same book and discuss it at night. I told them we'd come closer together, that I'd even change my job so I could be home more, and not work on television commercials any more."

After 10 minutes the kids began to squirm and yawn, as if expecting a commercial. Maguire's wife dazed out, her disconsolate face an unblinking mask. He gave up. Now, when he goes home, Maguire says hello, eats dinner and retreats to his bedroom. He is reading his way through Balzac.

Lost in the 19th century, his mind teeming with unfaithful women, reckless nihilists, secret passages, voracious businessmen, Maguire is sometimes happy.

Beyond the bedroom door, bathed in the cold light of the television set, are the real people of his life. Their dumbness grows, filling up the room, moving out into the quiet suburban town, joining the great gray fog that has enveloped America.

for discussion

How much exaggeration and how much truth is there in Hamill's article? Evaluate Maguire's "solution" to the problem.

for writing

(1) Tell about your own battle against TV. (2) Suggest what role TV should play in the home. (3) Tell how TV is making the world smaller.

THEME 3: Women at Work

Sylvia Porter, a veteran syndicated newspaper columnist and financial expert, attacks a "male chauvinist" columnist for his views on working women. Three women who made it to the top discuss their journey.

Porter Pulverizes Comments on Working Women

—SYLVIA PORTER

A theory rapidly gaining circulation is that our unemployment figures are gross exaggerations because the swollen totals count so many millions of women workers. A columnist who usually restricts his observations to politics put this point in print recently with the following:

"The work force, as never before, includes large numbers of women . . . whose unemployment would only mean loss of an extra job, not a catastrophe." And then he went boldly on to pontificate that, because of this, it would be "wise policy" if we "would take a little more unemployment over a little longer period" if by so doing, we could help break the inflationary spiral.

The ignorance, expressed and implied, in these comments would make me speechless were I not so enraged. But since it's probable many of you male chauvinists out there may feel the same way about women-and-jobs, I'll submit instead the statistics that by themselves pulverize the theory.

• Approximately 35 million American women are now in the labor

Reprinted from syndicated column *Your Money's Worth* by Sylvia Porter, by permission of Field Newspaper Syndicate.

force. We, according to the U.S. Department of Labor's Employment Standards Division, "work for the same reasons men do."

• To dramatize this, 7 million of the total are single women workers, most of them working "to support themselves or others." Another 6.3 million are widowed, divorced or separated from their husbands, and these millions—particularly the women who also are rearing children—also are working for what the Labor Department calls "compelling economic reasons."

• There are 3.7 million married women workers with husbands who had incomes below $5,000 at latest reporting date, and an additional 3 million with husbands who had incomes between $5,000 and $7,000. These women, says the Labor Department, are "almost certainly working because of economic need."

• On top of these millions are 1 million wives with husbands not in the labor force and more than 500,000 wives with unemployed husbands—women working or seeking work because many are their family's sole support.

• To pulverize the theory even more—if it needs it—among all wives working, the average contribution is more than one-fourth of the total family income. Among all wives who work year-round fulltime, the average contribution is nearly two-fifths of the family's income. About 2.6 million wives contribute half or more of the family's income.

Now, having crushed the theory coolly and competently, I trust, let me blow off a bit.

First, if any woman is happy to be outside the job market and wants to concentrate on making a happy home for her husband and children—and if she can afford it—then good for her. But millions of American women who live this life are not happy with it. They neither create happy homes nor do they make happy mothers nor do they fulfill themselves. For this woman, a job outside the home is essential to her well-being.

Julius Shiskin, nationally respected economist and currently Commissioner of Labor Statistics, conceded the validity of this point when asked a few weeks ago about whether there should be greater emphasis in measuring the effect of unemployment on the breadwinner who is the family's sole support.

"It is a value judgment," answered Shiskin, "to say that one type of unemployment is worse than another." Then Shiskin told of his own two daughters who are married, have children and hold jobs. "It would be very hard for them to make an adjustment if they lost their jobs," he said. "They're living at a standard set not by their husbands' incomes, but by that of both parents."

Second, the theory disgracefully downgrades the crucial role women play in our economy—and all but ignores the fact that if many women quit working in industry and the services, our economy would grind to a halt in a matter of hours.

And a third, deeply personal view: by what standard does any man determine that his right to work (or privilege of working) is greater than a woman's? By what yardstick does that columnist judge that his loss of a job would be "a catastrophe" but mine would merely be "loss of an extra job"?

for discussion

Before reading the foregoing article, did you know how many women are employed? Had you realized that most of them *need* to work? Had you considered their *right* to work? Why do women of your acquaintance work?

for writing

Take sides: (1) Women should (should not) get equal pay for equal work. (2) A woman's right (or privilege) to work is (is not) equal to that of a man's. (3) A woman's place is (is not) in the home. (4) A man's place is (is not) in the home.

Three Who Made It to the Top

When Betty McFadden got married in the mid-1940s, she decided that she wanted to devote full time to raising a family. But while she was waiting for the babies to arrive, she took a job at Jewel Companies, Inc., in Barrington, Ill., because, she says, "it looked like an interesting building." At first she worked in the accounting office for $35 a week, but by the late 1950s she had worked her way up to fashion coordinator for the big retailer, and in 1967, at the age of 45, she became the company's first woman officer. One year later, McFadden finally got pregnant.

"I had been at Jewel 23 years, so I thought I would retire and have a new life," she recalls. But after a few weeks at home, McFadden realized that she had to return: "I knew I'd drive myself and the child crazy." Before long she was back at her old job, at a much higher salary, and in 1976 she was named president of Jewel's direct-marketing division. Three months ago, when Jewel spun off the division to form a separate corporation, IHSS Inc., McFadden became its chairman and chief executive officer.

It has been lonely at the top. In the course of her career, McFadden made few personal friends and developed few outside interests. Eventually her marriage disintegrated. Although she thinks the new generation of women executives is better prepared and better qualified than she was, she thinks all two-career marriages are vulnerable. "I'm sure there are successful relationships, but not too many,"she says. "Somebody suffers." But even so, says McFadden, if she had it to do over again, she would not give up her serendipitous success.

Paula Hughes never went to college, but it seems to have made little difference. Today she is a first vice president, director and top producer at Thomson McKinnon Securities, Inc., managing nearly $600 million in customer accounts—and last year she grossed more than $1 million in broker commissions. Under the Carter Administration, Hughes was named the first woman governor of the U.S. Postal Service. She was the first woman member of Pittsburgh's blue-chip Duquesne Club, and, despite her lack of a college degree, she now sits on the board of trustees at Carnegie-Mellon University.

Hughes, 49, became a broker after eight years in advertising, when the breakup of her first marriage left her with a daughter to support. In her first job as a broker, she was paid $200 a week less than her male peers. Frozen out of the professional organizations patronized by men, Hughes turned to The Women's Forum, a group organized to give women the same kind of contacts provided by the "old boys' network," for what she sees as essential support. "The higher up you go, male or female, the lonelier you get," she explains. "You tend to think your problems are unique, and you find you have to reach out to others." Success also took a toll on her personal life. Her second marriage broke up after twenty years, and she says candidly that it is difficult to find "eligible men who can preserve their self-esteem and still tolerate" a woman earning about $1 million a year.

A decade ago physicist Betsy Ancker-Johnson shocked her bosses at Boeing Co. by asking for a change of career: she wanted to drop her highly successful work in electronics research in favor of a management job. "I was just getting restless," explains Ancker-Johnson, now 52. "I guess I wanted a bigger playpen."

She got it. After surviving three tough years in Boeing management during the company's massive retrenchment, Ancker-Johnson served four years as the first female Assistant Secretary of Commerce, then moved on to become an associate lab director at Argonne National Laboratory. Today she heads the environmental-activities staff at mighty General Motors—the first woman vice president in GM history.

Looking back, Ancker-Johnson says her Boeing years were the most difficult. Unlike most of her male colleagues, she never had a top-management mentor to guide her. On the contrary, her employers viewed her ground-breaking success with passive astonishment. "Ye gods, this woman is handling this thing!" she mimics.

Ancker-Johnson and her husband, Harold, chairman of the mathematics department at Trinity College near Chicago, have kept their marriage intact through what she calls a "weird arrangement." When she was first hired by GM, she commuted from Chicago. Now Harold and their four children, 17 to 21, have moved to suburban Detroit—and Harold commutes. "We're both doing exactly what we want to do," says Ancker-Johnson. And, she adds, she hopes the majority of other women will soon be able to say the same. "I can hardly wait until the day when this article you're doing would just be utterly boring," she says with a smile.

for discussion

Discuss the last quotation in the Ancker-Johnson story.

for writing

MEN: I would (would not) agree to my wife becoming a full-time career woman. I would (would not) resent it if she made more money than I did.
WOMEN: I would (would not) marry a man who refuses to share the burdens of a two career family.

THEME 4: Will the U.S. Drown in Trash?

In Chapter 1 Chief Luther Standing Bear discusses the love that the Lakotas had for the earth. In this section Lynwood Mark Rhodes describes the "Trash Explosion," the cartoonist Interlandi illustrates it, and Art Buchwald satirizes it.

Trash Explosion

—LYNWOOD MARK RHODES

Whatever happened to America the Beautiful?

Well, it still exists—covered and cluttered with millions of tons of what ecologists, experts who study the relationship between life forms and their environment, call solid wastes.

Every day, each of us throws out about 5½ pounds of waste, a figure that collectively adds up to a mind-rattling 400-plus billion pounds a year. In 1968, for example, Americans tossed away 55 billion cans, 26 billion bottles, 60 billion metal and plastic bottle caps,

Reprinted from *TWA Ambassador* Magazine by permission of the author and publisher. © 1970, Trans World Airlines, Inc.

30 million tons of paper. We also, unbelievably, junked 7 million automobile carcasses and 100 million rubber tires weighing a million tons. Put another way, currently we produce enough trash annually to fill the Panama Canal four times over. That amount will triple in 10 years.

On one day alone—Memorial Day—says an independent conservation organization called Keep America Beautiful, Inc., picnickers disposed of enough litter to "create a 3,000-mile memorial wreath two feet wide and four inches high covering an area the size of Minnesota, Ohio, Wyoming, and Texas." The Quinault Indians in Washington State were so peeved by such callousness that they went on the warpath. They've barred campers from 25 miles of scenic oceanfront. The white man, it seems, was leaving too much litter on the Indians' reservation.

Litter Means Money. "These figures are . . . meaningless until we bracket them with dollar signs," concedes Charles A. Schweighauser of Williams College Center of Environmental Studies in Massachusetts. For, he points out, the country's annual trash bill "is estimated at $4.5 billion a year, a sum that for public services is exceeded only by schools and roads."

Modern Packaging. The statistics are frightening, "a national disgrace," according to Health, Education and Welfare's Bureau of Solid Waste Management. What makes them all the more stomach-churning is the steady production of conveniently packaged consumer items, things that are used once, then pitched away. Trouble is, notes a special report by the National Academy of Sciences, "as the earth becomes more crowded, there is no longer an 'away.' One person's trash goes into another's living space."

Complicating the problem further, many of today's newer products don't deteriorate quickly or at all. The tin can used to rust away, but the immortal aluminum can may outlast the Pyramids. Nonreturnable bottles and plastics are the biggest headaches of all, say sanitary engineers. "Plastics are completely immune to biological decomposition," a study by the Karman Center of Aero-Jet General Corporation of California states with a shudder. "If we burn them, they contribute hydrocarbons and oxides of nitrogen—both dangerous air pollutants—to our atmosphere." If we bury them, we add trash-for-posterity to our soil. And that may be just the beginning. On his recent reed-boat crossing of the Atlantic, Thor Heyerdahl encountered floating containers and plastic bottles. "Man," he wrote disgustedly, "is starting to pollute the open ocean."

Old Ways Won't Work. What's happening is that many of our old ways of trash disposal simply won't work in the 20th century. A recent HEW survey found 94 percent of the 12,000 existing dumping sites around the country "unacceptable."

Burying the stuff is not much better, primarily because we're running out of burial space. New York City pours 4.5 million tons of refuse into its nearby marshes each year; at this rate, available space will be used up within four to nine years. Chicago expects to reach its crisis in three to eight years.

San Francisco dumps so much trash into its Bay that conservationists fear the famous body of water will one day simply cease to exist. Already, the Bay has lost some 250 square miles of its original 700. "If we put another layer out there," predicts Leonard Steffanelli of the Sunset Scavenger Company, "it's going to look like a mountain."

Fortunately, technology is beginning to come down off the shelf and come up with some possible solutions. Industrial designer Jerome Gould is working on a glass bottle that melts when broken. Dr. Samuel F. Hulbert of South Carolina's Clemson University is investigating an "evaporating" glass bottle, one that becomes soft and greasy and eventually disappears entirely. Reynolds Metal Company is making a dent by offering a half-cent bounty for each aluminum beer can turned in at its Los Angeles and Miami collecting depots. Other scientists are exploring formulas that will cause paper cartons to dissolve in water, while specialists at Firestone Tire and Rubber Company seek to boil down old tires for the chemical gas and tar in the casings.

These are stopgaps, at best. The bigger problem is disposing of the heavier stuff. Some cities, Philadelphia and Washington among them, are thinking of hauling wastes by railway to abandoned mine shafts or dumps far beyond their borders. But their neighbors naturally disapprove, claiming not unwisely that they have quite enough trash of their own to worry about. For a time, San Francisco considered hauling its refuse by train into the desert—until conservationists pointed out that this was merely moving pollution from one pile to another.

Incineration. Incineration, provided the resulting smoke can be controlled, still promises the best solution. European countries are far ahead of the United States in getting the most out of this method. At its Issy-les-Moulineaux plant near Paris, French technicians use the heat generated by trash incinerator plants to produce steam for electricity, feeding it into a national grid network. In Italy, Milan will run its streetcars and subways on power produced the same way. Montreal already has such a plant, and New York officials are considering building one.

The incineration method might have more merit than meets the eye—or the nose. Engineers have retrieved iron and aluminum, plus small amounts of gold and silver (mostly from costume jewelry, old coins, electronic scrap, the sparkle dust used on Christmas and birthday cards) from the fly-ash.

"It all adds up," grins Carl Rampacek of the Bureau of Mines. "With the amount of refuse we burn every year, a half-million tons of fly-ash are produced"—which could yield 150,000 pounds of silver alone. This burner bonanza might not make a municipality rich, but it could help pay for its garbage collection.

Turning wastes back into usable materials is another technique under study, especially the method invented by Japanese scientist Dr. Kunitoshi Tezuka. His machine compresses refuse into cubes, disinfects them to overcome the bacterial hazard, then coats the product with asphalt or concrete to produce a rock-like building block that's immune to decomposition.

Meanwhile, the favorite way of disposing of solid wastes remains the sanitary landfill method. Better than a dump, it covers a layer of waste with a layer of earth, another waste layer, and so on. The end result topped with earth could be a green area planted with trees and called a park. Eventually, however, the question is where to start the new landfill once the old one is completed.

Whatever the answer, one thing is certain—trash continues to accumulate. To help out, Congress has appropriated $4.3 million to create a research and development program to solve the ever-growing problem—and why Americans persist in adding to it.

Public Apathy. A New York sanitary specialist agrees. "People are up to their knees in garbage, but they don't really care," he says. "When they're up to their waists in it, they'll start screaming."

Perhaps that is an overly bitter indictment, but there's no denying that the only perfect, nonpolluting container we've ever invented was the ice cream cone. Put bluntly, man—at least in the polluting sense—is the world's dirtiest animal.

Still, the smell of success may be longer in coming than we hope. "It's so difficult to make people understand the seriousness of the threat," admits ecologist David M. Gates, director of the Missouri Botanical Gardens at St. Louis. "They don't realize how much we've lost already. It's very likely we won't be able to stem the momentum, but we have to try. We have to learn to care about what kind of environment we're going to live in. The question is, will we learn in time?"

Drawing by INTERLANDI. © 1970, Los Angeles Times.

**"Yes, sir, we enjoy the highest standard of living
known to the world!"**

for discussion

What else besides material things should be considered as part of a nation's
standard of living? Do Americans seem to be concerned with these other considerations?

for writing

Tie the cartoon by Interlandi to the article "Trash Explosion" and to the essay on
the Lakotas by Chief Luther Standing Bear in Chapter 1.

Is There Life on Earth?

—ART BUCHWALD

There was great excitement on the planet of Venus this week. For the first time Venusian scientists managed to land a satellite on the planet Earth, and it has been sending back signals as well as photographs ever since.

The satellite was directed into an area known as Manhattan (named after the great Venusian astronomer Prof. Manhattan, who first discovered it with his telescope 200,000 light years ago).

Because of excellent weather conditions and extremely strong signals, Venusian scientists were able to get valuable information as to the feasibility of a manned flying saucer landing on Earth. A press conference was held at the Venus Institute of Technology.

"We have come to the conclusion, based on last week's satellite landing," Prof. Zog said, "that there is no life on Earth."

"How do you know this?" the science reporter of the *Venus Evening Star* asked.

"For one thing Earth's surface in the area of Manhattan is composed of solid concrete and nothing can grow there. For another, the atmosphere is filled with carbon monoxide and other deadly gases and nobody could possibly breathe this air and survive."

"What does this mean as far as our flying saucer program is concerned?"

"We shall have to take our own oxygen with us, which means a much heavier flying saucer than we originally planned."

"Over here you will notice what seems to be a river, but the satellite findings indicate it is polluted and the water is unfit to drink. This means we shall have to carry our own water which will add even greater weight to the saucer."

"Sir, what are all those tiny black spots on the photographs?"

"We're not certain. They seem to be metal particles that move along certain paths. They emit gases, make noise and keep crashing into each other. There are so many of these paths and so many metal particles that it is impossible to land a flying saucer without being smashed by one."

"What are those stalagmite projections sticking up?"

"Prof. Zog, why are we spending billions and billions of zilches to land a flying saucer on Earth when there is no life there?"

"Because if we Venusians can learn to breathe in an Earth atmosphere, then we can live anywhere."

Buchwald makes his point by helping us see ourselves through the eyes of other creatures. Why is this an effective method? What value do you see in humor of this kind? Is it merely entertaining?

for writing

(1) Consider some of your own experiences with pollution and what effect they have had on you. (2) Compare a place you have seen before and after it was polluted. (3) Classify the kinds of pollution you see in your daily life. (4) Examine your own life style. How much do you contribute to pollution? (5) Try a humorous approach to convince your reader of the importance of the pollution problem.

THEME 5: Handgun Control

In Chapter 13 you read an argument against handgun control. Here are the views of those who are in favor of controlling these weapons.

Myths and Facts about Handgun Control

MYTH 1: Guns don't kill people. People kill people.

FACT: Over half of all murders and suicides are committed with handguns, which are five times more likely to cause death than knives, the next most popular murder weapon.

Most murders are spontaneous acts, committed during the heat of violent passions. Without a handgun available, many murders would be turned into non-fatal assaults if the attacker were forced to use some less potent weapon. The 3,000 who die in gun accidents every year would live if no gun were around.

The South's murder rate is double the rate in the Northeast, where only half as many households have guns. Handguns make murder and suicide quick, convenient and sure.

Even granting for a moment that guns don't kill people, it is painfully clear that people with guns do kill people.

MYTH 2: Handguns are needed for self-protection.

FACT: A handgun in the home is much more likely to result in death or injury to family members than it is to burglars.

A mere 2% of burglars are shot every year on the average, and for every burglar who is stopped, six family members are shot in accidents. One fourth of those accidentally killed are less than 14 years of age.

Reprinted by permission of the National Coalition to Ban Handguns.

Few intruders kill their victims. Nearly three-fourths of all murders occur between family members, friends or lovers, a situation which is encouraged by the easy access to handguns in the home.

Instead of protecting family members from intruders, a handgun in the home is like a firebomb.

MYTH 3: The Constitution guarantees the personal right to bear arms.

FACT: The Second Amendment to the U.S. Constitution states that ''A well regulated militia being necessary to the security of a free State, the right of the people to keep and bear arms, shall not be infringed.''

The United States Supreme Court has ruled four times that this does not guarantee the right to personal gun ownership. Instead, it establishes the right of the State Militias—now the National Guard—to bear arms. The Constitution protects the collective right to bear arms for military purposes in maintaining the security of the state. The right of an individual to possess handguns exists only in myth, not in the Constitution.

MYTH 4: Saturday Night Specials are used in most handgun crimes.

FACT: The Saturday Night Special is generally described as a cheap, short-barreled, low caliber handgun.

The myth that Specials are used in most handgun crimes has encouraged the false belief that only these cheap handguns need be eliminated to reduce crime. Most proposed anti-Special laws would only stop their manufacture and have no provisions for taking care of the millions of Specials already in circulation.

The New York City Police Department has reported that only 30% of the handguns it confiscates are Saturday Night Specials. Both attempts on President Ford's life were with regular, standard-sized pistols.

Most of the 40 million handguns in this country are quality weapons, and elimination of the Saturday Night Special alone would have little effect on reducing handgun crimes, suicides or accidents.

MYTH 5: Handgun control won't work.

FACT: In Great Britain, where handguns are strictly controlled, there are less than 500 handguns per 100,000 people. In the U.S., there are 12,000 handguns per 100,000 people. In 1974, Houston, Texas, alone had over four times as many handgun murders as all of England and Wales, with over 50 million people.

The gun murder rate in the U.S. is 200 times higher than in Japan, where private handgun ownership is totally prohibited. New York City, which has the toughest gun control law in the country, has the second lowest murder rate of the nation's ten largest cities.

Proper gun control laws do work and could save thousands of lives in America every year.

MYTH 6: The National Rifle Association can block any attempt at handgun control.

FACT: Many people who favor handgun control have given up because they believe the N.R.A. is all-powerful.

While the N.R.A. does have the power to mount massive letter-writing campaigns which have frightened some legislators, its ability to sway elections on the issue of gun control is highly questionable. The N.R.A. has taken credit for defeating a few pro-control Senators and Congressmen, but these men actually lost for reasons other than gun control.

In the January 1975 issue of the *American Rifleman* even the N.R.A. admits that 27 Congressmen who opposed gun control lost in the previous elections—while not one Congressman who favored control was defeated.

Obviously the N.R.A. is not all-powerful, and the more people learn that, the more they will decide to take a positive stand for handgun control.

for discussion

After reading the "myths and facts" above, review the sample theme on p. 285, then consider the strong and weak points of each argument. Which reasons seem strongest? Why? Has either article changed your original position? Explain. Is the style of presentation used above more or less convincing than a theme which uses basically the same information?

for writing

(1) Using three of the above arguments that you feel are strongest, write a theme. (2) Write a theme in which you counter any three of the arguments in the "myths and facts" sheet above or in the theme on p. 285. (3) Write an argument of your own on handgun control. It can be pro or con. (4) Describe a tragedy which you would blame on the ownership of a handgun.

THEME 6: The Art of Listening

Listening is, in a sense, reading with your ears. In Chapter 2 you were advised of the importance of following directions, paying attention to detail, and reading widely. Equally important is the art of listening. It is *not just hearing* but a more complicated skill that takes time and effort to develop. It is worth the time and effort because an improvement in your ability to listen can profoundly affect your life.

Ten Keys to Effective Listening

Of the 80% of our waking hours we spend communicating, about half of that time is spent listening. Yet, looking at our school experiences, education concentrates on reading, writing, speaking, but neglects listening.

We are beginning to appreciate what a costly oversight this is, not only for students who may not listen well to instructors, but also in our personal lives and in our businesses, where listening errors cost time and money. Both on and off the job, good listening is necessary for our individual success. Fortunately, listening is something we can **learn** how to do better.

You will soon see that there is much to learn about listening—far more than can be contained in this brief statement. But the basics of good listening are contained in the ten keys to effective listening outlined here.

1. Listen for ideas, not facts.

Good historians are contemptuous of history books which merely pile detail upon detail—names of kings, dates of battles—without working these into an intelligent framework. There is a name for this formless, fact-filled history—the "one-damned-thing-after-another-school-of-history."

Don't be a "one-damned-thing-after-another" listener. Do not allow yourself to be a mere collector of facts. Listen for ideas and themes. Ideas are the framework of any talk. Ideas may not be easy to find, but they are there. Facts are only included to prove the validity of the ideas. While listening, ask yourself: "Why am I being told that fact?" "What does it lead to?" "If that is true what does it show?" And if it truly does demonstrate an idea—"what does that idea lead to?" Listen for ideas, not facts.

From *Your Personal Listening Profile* by Dr. Lyman K. Steil, Department of Rhetoric, University of Minnesota and Communication Development, Inc., and Sperry Corporation, Copyright 1980. Reprinted by permission of Dr. Steil and Sperry Corporation.

2. Judge content, not delivery.

One of the great plays of this century is George Bernard Shaw's "Pygmalion." Both in its original form and as the musical "My Fair Lady," it was an artistic and financial triumph.

Professor Henry Higgins, one of the show's main characters, can, by listening to a single sentence, tell the speaker's place of birth, social status, occupation and numerous other facts. However, although he pays attention to the *way* something is said, he often fails to hear *what* is being said. Eliza Doolittle tells Higgins over and over that she wants to be accepted as a human being, who has feelings and emotions. But Higgins hears only her delivery, never the content of her message, and consequently loses her forever.

The story underscores an important point about listening. **Content** is the essence of any message. **Delivery** is secondary. As listeners we must train ourselves to look for and lock in on the content.

The person who speaks with charm and style may really be saying nothing, although he says it agreeably. A person who speaks with an air of authority may still be dead wrong. The unpolished speaker may really have something important to say. Overcome your prejudices and listen to him. You may be glad you took the trouble.

Listen carefully to what people say. Judge their words, not their delivery.

3. Listen optimistically.

No matter how dry a subject seems at first glance, there are hundreds of persons, perhaps thousands, who have made that subject the consuming interest of their lives. It may appear to be dry, detail-packed and dull at the beginning but, when you make the effort to try to interest yourself, you may be surprised at what you can get out of it.

Everyone has had the experience of taking an instant dislike to someone only to have that person later become a close and valued friend. The same thing is true of subjects—some that we may find boring at the beginning can later become our favorite.

But why waste the time waiting to be attracted to a person or a subject? There is a better way. Make the conscious effort to be interested from the beginning.

If we meet new material with an optimistic attitude, we may find an exciting thing happening. The new subject will be easy to assimilate, enjoyable. And who knows—we may even grow to love it and to pass that knowledge along to others. Listen optimistically.

4. Don't jump to conclusions.

Sometimes we hear the beginning of what someone is saying to us and we immediately figure we can fill in the rest—that we know just what is going to be said. At that point we tune out.

Later, we are convinced that the speaker has really said what we thought he was going to say. But the speaker says he was misunderstood. The speaker is right.

Jumping to conclusions—it's a common fault among listeners. By assuming we know what is coming next we can seriously damage our understanding of what is being said right at that very moment. And from there on out, it's downhill. We lose the speaker's flow and become hopelessly mired in our self-made mental quicksand. Wait. Keep listening. Pay attention. Clear your head of your own ideas and listen to the speaker's. Don't jump to conclusions.

5. Adjust your note-taking to the speaker.

Successful listeners are flexible listeners. They know that the beginning of good listening is the recognition that each speaker is unique and each should be listened to in an individual way. For one speaker a lot of notes are appropriate. For another, few notes are best. The style of note-taking should reflect the style of the speaker—not of the listener!

Try to figure out as soon as you can how the speaker is organizing his ideas, and suit your note-taking to his style of organization.

Sometimes long passages can be summarized in a single sentence. The illustrations are not important to remember. They are only there to help you understand the point.

Sometimes the facts and details are vital: they *are* the point. You must make a note of them. If your boss is giving you instructions, or if a customer is giving you specifications for the job you are doing for him, the details are the message. The same can be true with a public speaker.

Some speakers are very compact; most of what they are saying is important. Some need lots of time to make each point. Some have a long, slow, windup, full of stage setting, and then suddenly compress a lot of content within a short span when they reach their main ideas.

Watch for the different style of each speaker.

And listen for the speaker's attitude, as well as his words. Is he telling something in order to make fun of it? Then it is probably an illustration. Can you tell by his attitude that he is telling a joke? Or that what he is saying is deeply important to him? These are signals for the note-taker and for the listener. Be alert to them.

The better your notes, the better you have listened. Take note: notes make good listeners.

6. Concentrate.

The good listener avoids distractions either by removing the distraction itself or by resisting the impulse to give in to it when it cannot be totally removed. The poor listener is easily distracted. In fact, the poor listener at times appears both to invite and incite distractions.

You do not concentrate by holding yourself stiffly, jaw clenched, eyes burning, knuckles white with tension. That is the type of pseudo concentration which makes it impossible to do anything—hit a tennis ball, learn to dance, enjoy a lecture.

With true concentration you are relaxed but attentive. You have an open and interested mind. You arrive at a meeting (or a lecture, film, play, or speech) early in order to get a seat up front where you can hear. And where the distractions in the audience are behind you and not between you and the speaker.

Don't wait for the speaker to capture you. Focus on him. Give him your attention and thought. Look at listening as an opportunity. Look for the value in what he says. And don't turn off after that: there may be more.

Listen the way you would want someone else to listen to you, and you and the speaker will both get the most out of the exchange. When you are concentrating, it shows, and the speaker will know.

Become aware of what interferes with your concentration, and fight it.

When you concentrate correctly, you are not working at concentrating, you are concentrating.

7. Use your thought/speech advantage.

You can think four times as fast as any speaker can talk. That means your thoughts can race ahead of the speaker and you can quickly become detached from what is being said. Later, when you try to catch up with the speaker's train of thought, it often becomes an impossible task. Even with a slow-paced delivery, the speaker has passed you by. You then give up hope of finding out where he has been and where he is going . . . and fall into day-dreaming.

The good listener uses fast-thought-versus-slow-speech to advantage. Good listeners use the extra time to summarize the speaker's ideas, to interpret the speaker's choice of words, to evaluate the strength and logic of the speaker's arguments, and to respond . . . with facial expressions, body movements, shakes or nods of the head.

The good listener asks, "Is this actually a fact?" "How does this assertion jibe with another assertion by the same speaker?" "How does it square with my own experience?"

Make productive use of your thought/speech advantage.

8. Work at listening.

Dr. Sigmund Freud was one of the most intense listeners who ever fastened a gaze on a speaker. Indeed, all of psychoanalysis is founded on listening.

Freud understood the healing value we all find in speaking to a good and understanding listener. And he also knew that we reveal things in the deepest recesses of our thoughts and feelings through our choice of words, manner of speaking (and of not speaking), hand movements, facial expressions. Freud trained himself to pay close attention to all of these, and colleagues who watched him at work recalled later that he was extraordinarily intent, alert, *alive* as he listened.

The good listener works at listening—and he lets the speaker know it. He gives the speaker feedback. Whenever possible, he repeats what the speaker has told him in his own words, so that he can check whether he has really understood him properly. He asks questions when he doesn't understand something. He nods to indicate when he has understood. He thinks about the consequences of what is being said and asks questions that show he is doing this. This gives the speaker a chance to correct misunderstandings and to fill in gaps, so that he can really make his message clear.

Listening is hard work, but it is rewarding. Work at listening.

9. Keep your mind open . . . hold emotions in check.

Beware of emotion-laden words. Words that trigger our thoughts, feelings, and memories. For poor listeners, easily distracted by anything, the list of emotion-laden words is virtually endless. Many poor listeners are emotional tinderboxes awaiting only the wrong word to lose track of the conversation or be distracted from the central ideas of the speech or meeting.

You won't be able to ignore some emotion-laden words, but you can defuse them. Remember what words arouse strong feelings in you as a listener. Then, when you hear any of these words in a speech or conversation, simply note the appearance of the word and go on,

By permission of Johnny Hart and Field Enterprises, Inc.

concentrating your attention on the central ideas of what is being said. By doing this you can check the potentially powerful distracting effect of "color" words.

Keep an open mind . . . hold your emotions in check.

10. Exercise your mind.

As we all know from physical exercise, you only grow, strengthen yourself, increase your power, improve your performance, through the expenditure of effort. The same is true of mental effort. Only by handling difficult material do we gain confidence in our mental capacities. And stretch those capacities.

The listener who responds to complex material by "tuning out" can be missing a great opportunity to learn, to discover, to broaden himself. We have all had the experience of mastering a body of information, and then—when the material has become entirely familiar—using it as a foundation for understanding additional, even more complex information. It is a heady feeling—one of the joys of learning. And it can only be felt if we as listeners greet the arrival of complex information with anticipation. Not with anxiety.

Good and bad listeners show no discernible differences in intelligence levels. But the good and the bad listener develop markedly different attitudes toward "difficult" material to expand their minds and increase their powers of concentration.

Exercise your mind.

for discussion

Explain the "one-damned-thing-after-another" listener and the references to *Pygmalion* and Freud in "Ten Keys to Effective Listening."

for writing

Relate the suggestions in this article to your own listening experience in school, on the job, and/or in family relationships.

Now that you are acquainted with this "clinic,"
use its facilities whenever you are unsure of yourself
or have forgotten something. Refer to it about grammar
and mechanical problems in the same way that you refer
to a dictionary for spelling problems. So, good writing,
and be sure to use the Appendix and Index

FOR
REFERENCE

Appendix:
Word Traps

Listed below are words that are often confused and misused because they are similar in sound or meaning. Don't fall into these word traps. With a little effort, you can learn to make the proper distinctions.

a and **an**

A precedes all words that begin with a consonant, with two exceptions:

1. When *h* begins a word and it is not sounded, *an* is used: *an* honorable agreement, *an* honest error, *an* heirloom.
2. When certain consonants that start with vowel sounds are used as letters of the alphabet, *an* is used: *an* FHA loan, *an* MIT scholar **but** *a* BBC broadcast, *a* PBQ station.

Examples

> *a* cat, *a* buffalo, *a* bingo game, *a* purple onion, *a* rotten apricot, *a* hair, *a* horrible movie, *a* hermit, *a* hornet

An precedes all words that begin with vowels, with one exception: When *u* makes the same sound as the *y* in *you,* *a* is used.

Examples

> *an* eagle, *an* idiot, *an* intelligent man, *an* uncle, *an* umbilical cord, *an* uprising, *an* orgy, *an* eggplant, *an* artichoke, *an* opera, *an* up stairway, *a* union, *a* united front, *a* unicorn, *a* U.S. Flagship

accept (*verb*) = to take something that has been offered
I *accept* the money with gratitude.
except (*preposition*) = leaving out, excluding, other than, but
Everyone *except* Hudmilla was invited.

advice (*noun*) = suggestion
advise (*verb*) = to give advice
If you *advise* him not to go, he will heed your *advice*.

affect (*verb*) = to influence or produce a change
His views *affected* my decision.
The cloud-seeding *affected* the weather.
effect (*verb*) = to bring about, cause, accomplish, produce as a result
The doctor *effected* a complete cure.
The economist *effected* a change in his country's economy.
effect (*noun*) = result, consequence, influence
The *effect* of the alcohol was immediate.
He showed no ill *effects* from the harsh treatment.
His discovery will have a lasting *effect*.

all ready = completely prepared
I am *all ready* now.
We are *all ready* to go.
already = previously, beforehand
The meal had *already* been cooked.

all-right (*adj.*) considered slang
He's an *all-right* guy.
all right = satisfactory, safe condition
Everything is *all right*.
alright considered nonstandard or misspelling of *all right*

all together refers to being in a group or acting in unison
We arrived *all together*.
Try singing *all together*.
altogether = wholly, entirely
You are *altogether* despicable.

altar (*noun*) = a raised table-like structure in a church
They stood before the *altar*.
alter (*verb*) = to change
The company will *alter* its plan.

among (is used with more than two persons or things)
We danced *among* the tombstones.
between (is used for two persons or things)
They planted watermelon seeds *between* the two fig trees.

angel = heavenly being
　　You are a perfect *angel*.
angle = mathematical term
　　He drew a right *angle*.

angry = infuriated
　　She was very *angry* with her husband.
mad = insane (*Mad* means angry only in informal speech.)
　　He was found to be quite *mad*.

cite (*verb*) = to quote, commend, or summon
　　He *cited* long passages from the Bible.
　　Letitia was *cited* for bravery.
　　The defendant was *cited* for contempt of court.
site (*noun*) = place or location
　　They found a beautiful *site* for their home.
sight (*noun*) = view, the capacity to see; (*verb*) = to catch sight of
　　It was a beautiful *sight*.
　　The operation returned his *sight*.
　　They *sighted* the planes on radar.

conscience = sense of right and wrong
　　He had a guilty *conscience*.
conscious = aware
　　The child was *conscious* during the operation.

council (*noun*) = a deliberative body
　　The city *council* passed many bills.
counsel (*noun*) = advice; attorney
　　He sought *counsel* from the lawyer.
　　He is my legal *counsel*.
counsel (*verb*) = to give advice to
　　He *counseled* me wisely.

few (used for number)
　　There were relatively *few* dropouts this year.
less (used for amount)
　　Is there *less* nicotine in cigars than in cigarettes?

formal(ly) = following accepted rules and regulations
　　They were *formally* presented to the president.
former(ly) = previously
　　The convict had *formerly* been with the FBI.

its (used only as a possessive pronoun)
　　The cat licked *its* paws.
it's = contraction for *it is*
　　It's a melancholy song.

lead (rhymes with *creed*) present tense of the verb *to lead;* (*noun*) = leadership, forefront

We *lead* a quiet life.

He took an early *lead*.

lead (rhymes with *bed*); (*noun*) = a metal substance

He was hit with a *lead* pipe.

led = past tense and past participle of the verb *to lead*.

We have *led* a quiet life.

The Pied Piper *led* the children into the cave.

learn = to acquire knowledge, get instruction

He *learned* his lesson well.

teach = to give knowledge or instruction.

She *taught* the class how to swim.

let = to permit or allow someone *to do* something

We *let* them leave early.

Please *let* me come in.

leave = to cause or allow someone or something *to remain* (behind)

Don't *leave* me here alone!

He always *left* food on his plate.

loose (*adjective*) = free, unfettered, not bound or restrained

They set the dog *loose*.

I use a *loose*-leaf book.

lose (*verb*) = to mislay; become unable to find

I hope they don't *lose* the diamond.

past (*adjective*) = not current, gone by, ended

They are *past* presidents of the club.

The *past* week has been a busy one.

passed = past tense and past participle of the verb *to pass*

The parade *passed* our house.

The day has *passed* slowly.

principal (*adjective*) = chief; highest in rank, worth, or degree; main; (*noun*) = the amount due on a loan; the director of a school

You are the *principal* character in this play.

You paid the interest, but you still owe the *principal*.

The *principal* spoke to the students.

principle (*noun*) = basic truth, fundamental rule

He stuck by his *principles*.

The *principle* of self-determination is at stake.

quite (*adverb*) = indicates indefinite quantity depending on context
She is *quite* (rather) small.
He is *quite* (very) pleasant.
Are you *quite* (entirely) finished?
We are *quite* (completely) alone.

quiet (*adjective*) = silent
The birds are *quiet* today.

their (used only as a possessive)
That is *their* rhinoceros.

there (used as an adverb of place and as an expletive)
Put it over *there*.
There are many ants here.

they're = contraction for *they are*
They're very snobbish people.

then = at that time, in that case, therefore
They listened to his warning; *then* they left quietly.
They overheard the conversation; *then* they decided not to go in.

than (used for comparison)
He is fatter *than* she.
They have more money *than* we have.

to (*preposition*) sign of infinitive
He went *to* the store *to* buy supplies.

two (*number*)
They have *two* pickles.

too (*adverb*) = very, also
You are *too* kind.
The dress is *too* tight.
Glendon wants to go *too*.

Index

Complex sentences (*continued*)
  noun clause in, 110–11
  patterns, 108–15, 128–30
  review, 128–29
  subordinate clause in, 103–15,
      117–19
  subordinate conjunctions in, 103–19
  without conjunctions, 115
Compound sentences, 92–100, 127–28,
      129
  and–but pattern, 93, 127
  commas in, 93–95, 127–28
  coordinate conjunction–semicolon pat-
      tern, 94–95, 96, 127
  either . . . or pattern, 94, 128
  main clause in, 92
  patterns, 93–95, 127–28, 129
  review of, 127–28, 129
  "semicolon alone" pattern, 95, 127
  "semicolon-*however*" pattern, 94–96,
      127
  semicolon in, 94–96, 127
Conclusions, in paragraph and theme
      writing, 239, 240, 241, 244, 265.
      See also Expository writing
Conjunctions:
  and or *but* to start a sentence, 121
  coordinate conjunctions, 92–94, 96
  subordinate conjunctions, 103–19. *See
      also* Subordinate conjunctions
Connectives. *See* Conjunctions
Conscience / conscious, 337
Consequently as a coordinate conjunction,
      94, 96
Contractions, 170
Coordinate conjunctions, 92–94, 96
Council / counsel, 337
CULLEN, COUNTEE, 17

D

-d or *-ed:*
  errors of omitting, 195
  with past and perfect tenses of verbs,
      182–84, 186
Dash, 169
Dates, commas with, 168
Declarative sentences, 156
DELGADO, ABELARDO, 308
Dependent clause. *See* Subordinate
      clauses
Description, development by, 237, 242,
      260–61, 276–78
Development methods, 250–62, 272–78

classification, 250–53, 261, 265–67,
      280–81, 289
comparison/contrast, 256–59, 261–62,
      273–74, 290–91
description, 237, 242, 260–61,
      276–77
examples, 238, 242, 259–60, 268–69,
      288
persuasion, 238, 243, 282–86
process explanation, 253–55, 262, 275,
      292–93
DE VITO, E. B., 17
Diagnostic record, 4, 298
Dialogue, 118–19, 158
Direct object, 51, 52, 111
Direct quotations, 118–19, 158, 286
Do / does / did as auxiliaries, 49

E

Either . . . or pattern in compound
      sentences, 94, 128, 129
"El Hoyo" (Suarez), 20–21
Ellipses, 159
Everyone, everybody:
  as singular pronouns, 216
  with singular verb, 216
"Everyone Suffers Slipped Disciplines"
      (Rooney), 23
Examples, development by, 238, 242,
      259–60, 268–69, 288
"Ex-Basketball Player" (Updike), 16
Exclamation point, 157
Exclamatory sentences, 157
Existence (state of being) verbs, 46.
      See also Be verbs
Expletive *there,* 65
Expository writing, 237–93. *See also*
      Paragraph; Theme
  body, 240, 241, 250, 264
  conclusion, 239, 240, 241, 244, 265
  defined, 240
  development, methods of, 250–62,
      272–78
  introduction, 240, 241, 242, 244
  ordering of ideas, methods, 249–50
  polishing and correcting, 239–40,
      252–53, 255, 259, 282, 287,
      297–99
  seven-step writing formula,
      279–86
  thesis statement, 264–72
  topic sentence, 241–42, 244–49,
      265–70

F

Feeling (sensory reactions), verbs of, 47, 225n
Few / less, 337
Fish / fishes, 75n
Footnotes, to show sources, 286
Formal(ly) / former(ly), 337
Fragments of sentences, 116–21, 133–36, 196, 199–200
FREEMAN, GAYLORD, interview with, 299–300
Furthermore as a coordinate conjunction, 94, 96
Fused sentences. *See* Run-on sentences
Future tenses, 179–80, 184–85, 186, 187, 190–92

G

Gender of nouns and pronouns, 217–18
Geographical sections, capitalization of, 175
Gerund, 190
GOETHE, 7
Good / well, 227–28
GRIFFIN, JOHN HOWARD, interview with, 302–4

H

Habitual present tense, 182, 202
Had, to form past perfect tense, 180, 182, 183, 186, 187, 190
Had been, to form past perfect progressive tense, 180, 184, 186, 190, 191, 192
HAMILL, PETE, 309–12
"Handgun Control, Myths and Facts about," 322–24
Have / has / has been, to form present perfect tenses, 180, 182, 186, 187, 189, 190
Have / has / had as auxiliaries, 49
Helping verbs. *See* Auxiliary verbs
Hence as a coordinate conjunction, 94, 96
Historic present tense, 202
However as a coordinate conjunction, 94, 96

I

I / me, 220
Imperative mood, 194
"Incident" (Cullen), 17

Independent clause. *See* Main clause
Indicative mood, 194
Infinitives, 51, 181
ing forms:
    effect on action verbs, 52, 182
    as nouns or adjectives, 52
"In Search of Our Mothers' Gardens" (Walker), 305–8
Interjections:
    commas with, 164
    exclamation points with, 157
Interrogative sentences, 63–65, 157. *See also* Questions
Introduction, 240, 241, 242, 244. *See also* Expository writing
Introductory adverbial phrases, 65–66
Inverted sentences, 63–66
    with expletive *there,* 65
    with introductory adverbial phrases, 65–66
    in questions, 64–65
Irregular verbs, 186–92
"Is There Life on Earth?" (Buchwald), 321
Italics in titles, 175
Its / it's, 337

L

"Lakotas, The" (Chief Standing Bear), 22
Lead / led, 338
Learn / teach, 338
Let / leave, 338
Lie / lay, 198
"Listening, Ten Keys to Effective" (Steil), 325–31
Logical order in themes and paragraphs, 249
Loose / lose, 338

M

Main (independent) clause:
    in complex sentences, 103–5, 107–11
    in compound sentences, 92–95
May / might as auxiliaries, 49
Mechanics, 3
Moods, 194–95
More / most in comparisons, 231
Moreover as a coordinate conjunction, 94, 96
Multiple subject-single verb, 62
Must / ought to as auxiliaries, 49

N

Neither . . . nor as coordinate conjunctions, 94
Neuter pronouns, 218
Nevertheless as a coordinate conjunction, 94, 96
Not only . . . but also as coordinate conjunctions, 94
Noun clause, 110–11
Nouns:
    of address, 42–43, 164
    characteristics of, 209
    collective nouns, 216–17
    common nouns, 174–75
    formed from verbs, 52, 53
    as infinitives, 51
    plurals, 74–76, 210
    possessive forms, 210
    proper nouns, 75, 174–75
    singular only, 76
    singular or plural, 76
Nouns of address, not subjects of sentences, 42–43
Number:
    of collective nouns, 216
    of nouns, 74–77, 215–16
    of pronouns, 76, 215–16
    of verbs, 78–84
Numbers in series, parentheses with, 169

O

Object of the preposition, 84–86, 110
Object pronouns, 219–22
Order of ideas:
    chronological, 249
    emphatic and dramatic, 250
    logical, 249
    spatial, 249
Otherwise as a coordinate conjunction, 94, 96
Ought to as an auxiliary, 49
Outlining, 241–44
    examples of, 241–42, 244, 250–54, 256–59, 265–66, 268, 270–72

P

Paragraph, expository, 237–62
    expansion to theme, 265–70
Parentheses, 169–70
Parenthetical expressions:
    commas with, 164
    dash with, 169
Participles, 52, 53, 182, 187–89, 190–91, 230–31. *See also* Past participles; Present participles
Passive voice, 193–94
Past participles:
    as adjectives, 53, 230–31
    confusing terminology, 190
    effect of *ed, en,* 53
    functions, 190–91
    identical with past tense, 182
    of irregular verbs, 187–89
    in present perfect, 190
    in regular verbs, 182, 190
Past / passed, 338
Past perfect progressive tense, 184
Past perfect tense, 183
Past progressive tense, 183
Past tense. *See also* Tenses of verbs
    of *be,* 81
    irregular verbs, 186–90
    regular verbs, 181–86
Period, 156–57
Person: first, second, third, 74, 77–79, 81, 213–14
Persuasion, development by, 238, 243, 282–86
Phrases:
    distinguished from clauses, 106
    introductory adverbial phrases, 65–66
    prepositional phrases, 84–87, 287
    in series, commas with, 162
Plurals. *See also* Nouns; Number
    of collective nouns, 216–17
    formed by internal change, 76
    of nouns, 74–77, 215–16
    possessive forms, 172
    of pronouns, 215–16
    of proper nouns, 75–76
PORTER, SYLVIA, 312–14
''Porter Pulverizes Comments on Working Women,'' (Porter), 312–14
Possessives:
    apostrophe in, 171–73
    forms of, without ownership, 173
    nouns, 171–73, 210
    pronouns, 171, 219
    verbs, 46
Prepositional phrases, 84–87, 287
Present ''future'' tense, 203
Present participles:
    as adjectives, 52

Present participles (*continued*)
  as direct objects, 52
  effect of *ing,* 52, 182
  functions, 190
  of irregular verbs, 187–89
  in progressive tenses, 190
  as subjects, 52
Present perfect progressive tense, 180
Present perfect tense, 180
Present progressive tense, 180
Present tense. *See also* Tenses of Verbs
  of *be,* 81
  habitual present, 202
  historic present, 202
  of irregular verbs, 186–92
  present "future" tense, 203
  of regular verbs, 181-83, 185–90, 192
  universal present, 202
Principal parts of irregular verbs, 187–89
Principal / principle, 338
Process, development by, 253–55, 262,
      275, 292–93
  check points, 255
Progressive tenses, 182–86, 189–92
Pronouns:
  agreement with antecedents, 215–16
  case of, 219–23
  for collective nouns, 216–17
  gender of, 217–18
  neuter pronouns, 218
  number of, 215–17
  object pronouns, 219–22
  person of, 213–14
  personal pronouns, 211–13
  possessive pronouns, 171, 219
  relative pronouns, 108
  subject pronouns, 41, 219–22
  as subordinate conjunctions and sub-
      jects, 108–10
  unclear reference of, 223–24
Proper nouns, 75, 174–75
Punctuation, 155-77. *See also* Comma;
      Semicolon
  of appositives, 165–66
  colon, 160
  comma, 162–68
  dash, 169
  ellipses, 159
  exclamation point, 157
  of non-restrictive clauses, 166
  parentheses, 169–70
  of parenthetical remarks, 164, 169–70
  period, 156–57
  purpose of, 155

  question mark, 157
  quotation marks, 118, 158, 175
  semicolon, 94–96, 160-61
  and sentence structure, 156
  of series, 160, 161, 162–63, 169

Q

Question mark, 157
Questions, 63–65, 157
  sentence patterns of, 64–65
Quite / quiet, 339
Quotation marks:
  setting off direct quotations, 158
  setting off special words, 158
  in titles, 158, 175
Quotations:
  colon preceding, 160
  commas in, 158
  in dialogue, 118–19
  direct, 158, 286
  paraphrased, 286
  quotations within quotations, 158

R

Real / really, 228
Reasons, development by. *See* Persuasion
Regular verbs, 181–86. *See also* Tenses of
      verbs
Relative pronouns, 108
  as subordinate conjunctions and sub-
      jects, 108–10
Restrictive appositives, 166
RHODES, LYNWOOD MARK, 316–19
Rise / raise, 197
ROONEY, ANDY, 23
"Rotting Mind Means Tube
      Syndrome" (Hamill), 309–12
Run-on sentences, 97–100, 131-32

S

Salutations:
  colon after, 160
  commas in, 168
"School Should Be a Place for Praise
      and Laughter" (Eppley), 24–25
Semicolon, 160–61
  in compound sentences, 94–96, 161
  with coordinate conjunctions, 94, 96,
      161
  in series, 161, 162
Sensory (feeling) verbs, 47, 225n

Subordinate conjunctions, 103–19
  absent in phrases, 106
  as connectors and subjects, 108–11
  omitted in complex sentences, 115
  relative pronouns, 108
  in sentence fragments, 116–19
  to start a sentence, 109
  as subject of subordinate clause,
    108–11
Superlative degree, 231

T

Tenses of verbs, 179–206. *See also* Past
    tense; Present tense
  comparison of regular and irregular
    verbs, 192
  future tenses, 179–80, 184–85, 186,
    187, 190–92
  irregular verbs, 186–92
  past tenses, 179–84, 185–90, 192
  present tenses, 182–83, 185–90, 192
  problem areas, 195–200
  regular verbs, formation, 181–86
  shifts in writing, 201–202, 204–305
TERKEL, STUDS, 299–304
Than / as, with subject pronouns, 220
That:
  to introduce a subjunctive clause, 195
  to introduce a paraphrased quotation,
    286
The, capitalization of, in titles, 176
Their / there / they're, 339
Theme, expository, 264–93. *See also*
    Development methods; Exposi-
    tory writing
  defined, 264–65
  development, 272–78
  organization of, 264–65
Then as a coordinate conjunction, 94, 96
Then / than, 339
There as an expletive, 65
Therefore as a coordinate conjunction, 94,
    96
Thesis statement, 264–72
Thus as a coordinate conjunction, 94, 96
Time words, 179
Titles of articles or books:
  capitalization, 175
  quotation marks with, 158, 175
  when italicized, 158, 175
  when underlined, 158, 175
Titles of persons, capitalization of, 174

To:
  dropped, to form present tense, 181,
    185
  effect of, on action verbs, 51
To / two / too, 339
Topic sentence, 241–42, 244–49, 265–70
  formulation of, 245–46
"Trash Explosion" (Rhodes), 316–19
TWAIN, MARK, 18

U

Unclear pronoun reference, 223–24
Universal present tense, 202
UPDIKE, JOHN, 16

V

VEECK, BILL, interview with, 301–302
Verbs, 39–54, 58–71. *See also* Auxiliary
    verbs; Tenses of verbs
  action verbs, 56
  as adjectives, 52–53
  agreement of, with subject, 74–89
  auxiliaries, 49–50, 196–97, 199–200
  be, tenses of, 49, 81–82
  characteristics of, 45–46
  confusing verbs, 197–98
  contracted forms of, 170
  deactivating or "freezing," 50–53
  defined, 39
  ed, en, effect of, 53
  existence (state of being) verbs, 46
  of feeling or sensory reactions, 47,
    225n
  function of, 50–53
  infinitives, 51
  ing, effect of, 52, 182
  in inverted sentences, 63–66
  irregular verbs, 186–92
  main verbs, 49
  participles 52, 53, 182, 187–89,
    190–91, 230–31
  person, 74, 77–79, 81, 213–14
  phrases, verb, 49–50
  possessive, verbs, 46
  principal parts of irregular verbs,
    187–89
  regular verbs, tenses of, 181–86
  sensory verbs, 47
  simple verbs, 49
  in subjunctive mood, 194–95
  tenses, 179–206
  to, effect of, 51

Verbs (*continued*)
    types, 46–47
    voice, 193–94
    with "*you* understood" as subject, 42,
       59, 66
VIORST, JUDITH, 14–15

W

WALKER, ALICE, 305–308
Was / were, 49, 183–84
Were, in the subjunctive, 194–95
We / us, 221
"What Would *You* Think of a Bearded
    Cop?" (Shearer), 273
Who, what, which test, for subject, 39–40
Who / whose / whom, 222
Will / would, 49
Wishes, subjunctive with, 194

WOLFE, TOM, 276
"Women's Liberation Movement
    Woman, A" (Viorst), 14–15
"Words," (deVito), 17
Word traps, 335–39
Writing, check points for, 239–40,
    252–53, 255, 259, 282, 297–99.
    See also Expository writing; Seven-
    step writing formula

Y

y changing to *i* to form past tense, 186*n,*
    196
Yet, as a coordinate conjunction, 93
You:
    meaning *I,* 213–14
    or *one,* as impersonal pronoun, 214
"*You* understood," as subject, 42, 59, 66